J

A

C

r

Country
Houses

Fine Homebuilding
GREAT HOUSES
Country Houses

The Taunton Press

Cover photo: Jefferson Kolle
Back-cover photos: top left, Rich Ziegner; top right, Charles Miller;
middle left, Scott Gibson; bottom left, Jefferson Kolle

Taunton
BOOKS & VIDEOS
for fellow enthusiasts

First printing: 1996
Printed in the United States of America

A FINE HOMEBUILDING Book

FINE HOMEBUILDING® is a trademark of The Taunton Press, Inc., registered in the
U.S. Patent and Trademark Office.

The Taunton Press, 63 South Main Street, PO Box 5506,
Newtown, CT 06470-5506

Library of Congress Cataloging-in-Publication Data
Country houses.
         p.   cm. — (Great houses)
     At head of title: Fine homebuilding.
     "A Fine homebuilding book"— T.p. verso.
     Includes index.
     ISBN 1-56158-140-2
     1. Country Homes — United States — Design and construction.
     2. Country homes — United States — Designs and plans.
I. Taunton Press.
II. Fine homebuilding.
III. Series.
TH4850.C69   1996   96-11746
728.7´2 — dc20   CIP

Contents

Introduction   **7**

Three Buildings, One House   **8**   Separating the parts of a home into different buildings connects the owners to their environment

A Cost-Conscious House in North Carolina   **12**   On an old infill lot, this house nestles into a small forest of pines without disturbing the trees or the well-rooted neighborhood

Country House and Studio   **16**   Restraint, economy and a sense of proportion create a spare but comfortable home

Eurostyle Rustic   **22**   Danish design and American tradition are joined by restrained detailing and fine wood craftsmanship

Cozy in Any Weather   **29**   Creating comfortable spaces in a home that faces New England's harsh winters and hot summers

A Cascade of Roofs   **34**   Multiple gables, long overhangs and metal roofing dominate the design of this house in Georgia

Louisiana Country House   **39**   Behind the traditional facade is an uncommon tribute to the sun, the river and the site's first inhabitants

Simplicity with Style   **44**   A hillside house and a realistic budget combine visual drama with a basic floor plan

Natural Selections   **49**   A house in North Carolina borrows shapes, colors and details from the landscape

A House Among the Oaks   **54**   A carpenter turned designer plans a house with simplified construction details in mind

A Contemporary Farmhouse   **60**   Complex shapes, unusual materials and a surprising color scheme enliven this house in the Sierra Nevada foothills

At Home in the Redwoods   **66**   Open, vertical spaces inside make this single-story house feel as tall as the trees around it

Japanese Influence on a Western House   **72**   A courtyard garden and an exposed timber frame are among the inspirations from another culture

Live Large, Look Small   **78**   Bungalow details bring a big house down to earth on a spectacular site

Living by the Lake   **84**   A separate bunkhouse, connected by a porch, affords privacy for three generations

House on the River   **88**   Concrete piers, cantilevered steel and prefab framing support a rustic hideaway

Minnesota Lake Cabins   **93**   Midwestern architect Edwin Lundie borrowed
Norwegian themes for his Lake Superior retreats

Rustic Retreat   **96**   Inspired by East Coast lodges, this
stick-framed California house is dressed
with hand-hewn log siding

A House that Fits its Site   **102**   The right design starts with a careful survey of the land
and conversations with the owners

Superinsulated in Idaho   **108**   Lessons learned from an energy-efficient house

A Mountain Retreat   **113**   A designer/builder blends curved walls
and windows with traditional New England
shapes and materials

Home in the Hills   **118**   An open floor plan organized around a central corridor
takes advantage of the site and the view

Roadside Mountain Retreat   **122**   Squeezed onto a narrow lot, this house lets in the sound
of the river and shuts out the noise of the nearby road

The House on the Trestle   **126**   On a mountainous site, an arched truss carries
the weight of a rustic vacation house

A Romantic House   **132**   In this hectic, high-tech age, playful
detailing and asymmetrical plans
make a more comfortable home

The House Steps Down the Hill   **136**   Creating intimacy and grandeur on a
slightly sloping site

Index   **141**

Introduction

Country houses are deeply rooted in the American frontier tradition. Today's country houses are no longer rugged homesteads; instead, they are retreats from the bustle of modern city life. Whether they are tiny secluded retreats or large homes designed for year-round living, these houses reconnect people to the landscape while providing shelter against the elements.

In this collection of 26 houses, originally published in *Fine Homebuilding* magazine, are some of the best examples of custom country houses built in recent times in all regions of the country. What unifies this collection is a strong respect for the building site and the comfort of the inhabitants. Builders, designers and owners took their first cues from the surroundings; a house on a mountaintop soars, while a house among the trees blends into the forest.

The well-built homes shown here are far from the drafty cottages of the past. These energy- and resource-efficient homes shelter their inhabitants from (often extreme) elements while still offering a view of the scenery beyond. Because country living is simple, these houses offer uncomplicated details and casual style that celebrate fine craftsmanship, even in the most modest homes. This book is an excellent source of ideas and inspiration for anyone planning a house in the country.

Julie M. Trelstad
Editor, Fine Homebuilding *Books*

Fitting into the landscape. At the end of a winding footpath, the three-building compound emerges in a clearing: the studio to the left, the central main house and the bedroom cabin at the right. Photo taken from A on site plan.

Three Buildings, One House

Separating the parts of a home into different buildings
connects the owners to their environment

by Jeffrey Prentiss

Dave and Carole Grumney live and work in Los Angeles—most of the time. Their second home is on Orcas Island, which is about as unlike Los Angeles as two places can be unlike. Orcas Island is the largest of the San Juan Islands, an archipelago in the middle of Puget Sound on the U. S.-Canadian border. The Grumneys bought their property, a small meadow gently sloping to a tiny beach and cove, backed by a steep forested hillside, because it offered a remarkable site upon which to build a peaceful retreat, a place to escape the frenzy of Los Angeles.

Given the beauty of the site, the last thing the Grumneys wanted to do was to stomp on local aesthetic toes. They wanted a house that weaved well into the natural site and altered it as little as possible. Having heard that I am a native of the islands and an architect who works well with site, the Grumneys asked me to design their island retreat.

A footpath instead of a driveway—The Grumneys wanted to avoid the type of situation in which, for convenience, one could jump directly out of the car into a protected building,

A transition from indoors to out. The main house's front porch, with its long steps, fieldstone fireplace and several doors, encourages outdoor living. Log supports add a rustic flavor reminiscent of the area's first settlements. The office is in the background, and having to walk outdoors to get to it from the other dwellings reinforces a sense of departure. Photo taken from B on site plan.

experiencing neither sun nor rain nor air movement nor shadows in trees nor whir of insects. So in Dave and Carole's case we left the cars at the property's edge and created a footpath that winds through the woods into the dwelling site (top drawing, right), enhancing the sense of discovery and arrival as you meander in. Yes, the footpath means that luggage and groceries have to be carried in, but in return some elemental quality of the site is preserved. This sets a tone for the ambiance of the spot. By the use of the winding footpath, we slowly disclose the destination, keeping the construction site relatively hidden until the path opens up to it.

You have to go outside—In formal neighborhoods, lawns, shrubs and fences demarcate property lines. The inhabited landscape is distinct from one house to another. At the Grumneys', we wanted to fit the structure into the landscape, blurring the distinction between the natural surroundings and the building.

Here, I first began to consider that the house might actually be a cluster of buildings, just as plants cluster in nurturing soils. By having space between structures, there would be more sense of integration of buildings and landscape (photos facing page). Separate buildings allow the landscape to wrap around them, which seemed an ideal way to minimize the impact of construction on the site.

The Grumneys wanted their home to address certain functions, and I separated the functions into the three strongest parts: public (cooking, laundry, guests, living room), work (the studio) and private (the bedroom). In the compound, the public space is centered between the studio and the bedroom (floor plan, right).

This separation of functions and structures places the Grumneys in continual contact with the environment. They need to leave the bedroom cabin each morning to get to the coffeepot and leave the coffeepot to go to work. As the day progresses, they must leave the work space to return for meals and socializing with their houseguests, then leave the social rooms to go to bed.

The property has a natural bowl-like contour, which is mirrored by the siting and massing of the buildings. Sited in a semicircle with the largest building in the middle, each building has a different view toward the channel, and the semicircular siting creates a sense of protection just like an original settlers' compound.

Simple shapes, simple materials—Architecturally, the buildings owe a lot to the old Hudson Bay Co. structures that dot the Pacific Northwest. These simple gable-roof structures were built from materials at hand: logs for walls, cedar shakes on the roof. I didn't want to replicate the Hudson Bay buildings, just work with the basic ideas: simple gable structures with lean-tos and porches attached.

To match the simplicity of the building forms, I specified materials that are simple, straightforward, strong and tactile. There is also a similarity of materials between interior and exterior, and all the structures are similar but not identical in use of materials and design elements. Maintain-

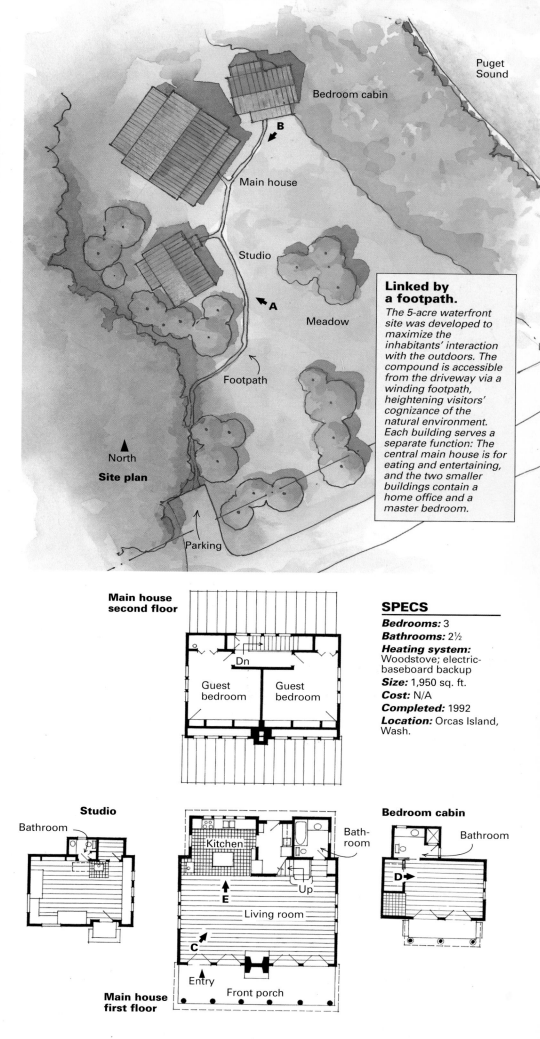

Linked by a footpath.
The 5-acre waterfront site was developed to maximize the inhabitants' interaction with the outdoors. The compound is accessible from the driveway via a winding footpath, heightening visitors' cognizance of the natural environment. Each building serves a separate function: The central main house is for eating and entertaining, and the two smaller buildings contain a home office and a master bedroom.

SPECS

Bedrooms: 3
Bathrooms: 2½
Heating system: Woodstove; electric-baseboard backup
Size: 1,950 sq. ft.
Cost: N/A
Completed: 1992
Location: Orcas Island, Wash.

Drawings: Malcolm Wells

In the main house. The center building is designed as a public area for entertaining family and friends. The living room has a pine floor and a cedar ceiling with 10x10 fir beams running into a clerestory light well, seen here in the upper right corner. Even though the windows are large, the covered porch and abundant trees darken the room. The clerestory windows over the porch roof brighten the living room. Photo taken from C on floor plan.

ing similarities among the buildings and between interior and exterior is another way in which the compound eases into the natural setting.

The colors and materials blend with the colors of the woodlands, not totally camouflaged but not glaringly contrasting either. For the exterior, horizontal shiplap siding was prestained in a natural weathered wood tone similar to the color of the aged bark of the surrounding trees.

At the porches, raw logs were used for the posts and the main-porch beam. The logs keep the house from appearing too finished and add the Hudson Bay-shelter character we were seeking. Unlike those old structures, these buildings have metal roofing instead of roof shakes, which were

too expensive and would create a fire hazard and need to be replaced too soon. Metal roofing fit the bill, and its dark green Kynar finish, the premium paint grade for metal roofing, fit into the natural surroundings.

To strengthen the sense of the roofs' mass, the cedar fascias are stained green, slightly lighter than the roofing. The green fascias add a layer of interest to the buildings, too.

For the chimney, Dave wanted a stone fireplace, and he chose local stone picked from the fields. The mason, Vern Landon, did a great job of packing two fireplaces—one facing the porch, the other facing the living room—back to back in a tight area. He also provided a couple of

shelves built into the chimney for use when cooking on the outdoor grill.

Viewing the outdoors—One of the most important aspects of these buildings is their large and plentiful windows. The compound worked well because all the rooms have light and views from several directions. To have as much interaction between inside and outside as possible, one should always be able to look out in several directions from a given spot, with each orientation of the windows giving a different view.

To this end, in the main house, there are four sets of French doors opening to the front porch. The front porch is like a long gallery operating as a transitional layer between indoors and out. Long steps spanning the entire front of the porch and the series of doors encourage people to move in or out anywhere along the south facade.

This long covered porch is also a place to inhabit: The roof provides cover for sitting outside during the Northwest drizzle; the fireplace allows outdoor living in the cool maritime climate. Combined, these two elements—the porch roof and the fireplace—yield the opportunity to experience outdoor sounds and movements without freezing to death from cold and wet.

In the main rooms of each building, light enters from every direction. The Pacific Northwest is often overcast, and the Grumneys' decision to keep almost all of their trees around and in the middle of the compound meant we could be into the dark and gloomies if we were not careful. Putting the porch all across the south facade of the main structure was not going to help either.

To offset the porch shadows, I designed clerestory light wells, framed at the second-floor level, that draw light into the lower floor (photo facing page). The ceiling beams run into the lightwells, which accents the massive 10x10 fir timbers.

These lightwells were created by narrowing the upstairs guest bedrooms, building interior knee-walls 3 ft. in from the exterior wall. The resulting taller kneewalls improved the bedrooms' proportions, and built-in bookcases in the kneewalls occupy what would have been lost space.

In the guest bedrooms and in the bedroom cabin (top photo, right), tall gable-end windows reach up to the cathedral ceilings. There are no collar ties. In the main house contractor Rick Delgarno used a structural ridge bearing on 6x8 window headers. In the bedroom cabin, a structural ridge bears on a 4x6 header high in the gable wall. The gable window is so tall that the header, which is horizontal, extends above the plane of the ceiling.

The windows we selected (Northwest Windows, 3227 164th Ave. S.W., Lynnwood, Wash. 98037; 206-743-4446) have Douglas-fir frames and sashes. The fir is sealed with oil to show off its golden glow, brightening the buildings while remaining in our natural-color palette.

Inside, natural wood was also the desired selection, but not so much that the interior became too dark. Wood floors, wood ceiling and wood trim on the natural-finish windows were enough. As an accent the stairwell is paneled in cedar with a fir railing and fir treads.

For the ceiling 10x10 fir beams cross at 5 ft. on center with T&G fir and hemlock car decking as the finished surface for both ceiling and floor. The large beams, although kiln-dried, checked far more than expected, but we found this an appealing look and kept them.

In the kitchen, painted cabinets of a traditional design brighten the house (bottom photo, right). A long low window above the counter brightens work areas and gives a view of the outdoors from the kitchen, another reminder to the Grumneys that the compound of buildings on the shore of Orcas Island is a long way from Los Angeles. □

Jeffrey Prentiss is an architect in the San Juan Islands and Seattle, Wash. Photos by Rich Ziegner.

In the bedroom cabin. This bedroom, a large closet and a small bathroom make up the bedroom cabin. The gable window's trimmer studs support a large header that supports a structural ridge, allowing for the open cathedral ceiling. The atrium door is one of a pair that open onto a small front porch. Photo taken from D on floor plan.

Kitchen located in main house. For the sake of economy, kitchen cabinets made primarily of medium-density overlay plywood (MDO) were selected. The door frames, while constructed of solid wood, were painted in a light color to brighten the kitchen. Photo taken from E on floor plan.

A Cost-Conscious House in North Carolina

On an infill lot, this home nestles into a small forest of pines without disturbing the trees or the well-rooted neighborhood

by Scott Neeley

Neighbors tend to take neighborhood trees seriously. Several years ago, a woman next door threatened to chain herself to the trunk of a large hackberry tree I planned to take down. The tree was centered in the only place on the narrow infill lot where the new house would fit. The woman and I later became friends, but it took her months to get over the loss of the tree.

You occasionally find similar undeveloped infill lots in old, well-rooted neighborhoods where trees form a canopy over streets. These sites are scarce, and neighbors hold them in great es-

teem. When such a lot came on the market in Durham, North Carolina, I jumped.

The site was full of towering loblolly-pine trees (photo facing page), and it was one of the larger green areas in this established neighborhood and had become something of a postage-stamp park. Because of the lot's place in the neighborhood, I approached the design with trepidation.

Could a new house be built within existing trees?—All of the neighbors I met on my preliminary site visits expressed concern about the

A small house in the tall pines. Although its gable rises fairly high for such a small house, the building is dwarfed by a towering stand of 90-ft. loblolly pines. Fortunately, only one tree came down to make room for the house. Photo taken at A on floor plan.

Mixing light and privacy. A high window on the east side of the house provides overhead light throughout the day. A privacy fence around the deck outside the lower windows protects the privacy of the dining room and creates a private outdoor area. Photo taken at B on floor plan.

High ceilings for the master bedroom. A western exposure and a rectangular pattern of windows in the gable wall give the master bedroom strong light, which bounces off the faceted ceiling. Photo taken at C on floor plan.

trees. Topping their list was a large 150-year-old shrub referred to variously as a grandfather's beard, a feather tree and a thunder bush. The official name is fringe tree, I learned. For a few short weeks in April and May, the tree is a stunning ball of feathery, fragrant white blossoms.

The loblolly pines, 16 in. dia. to 24 in. dia., rose to heights of about 90 ft. These trees are tall and slender with most of the branches and needles concentrated near the top. The county botanist told me that these trees have a shallow root system, and he predicted I had a 25% chance of losing a tree from construction within 6 ft.

A tall, thin house fits nicely in the pines— The 1,352-sq. ft. house I designed would be formed of two shapes: a tall, thin, two-story volume with a steeply pitched roof enclosing the bedrooms, the bathrooms and the kitchen. Adjacent to this tall gabled form hangs a shed-roofed saddlebag for the dining room (photo p. 12) and the living room (photo facing page). Positioning the living and dining rooms to the south side provided an opportunity for passive-solar strategies and allowed a framed view of the fringe tree. The tall character of the house also would reflect the visual character of the lofty pines. And fortunately, only one tree would have to come down. The footprint encompasses two offset rectangles, 12 ft. by 40 ft. and 14 ft. by 28 ft.,

running east-west (floor plan below). I calculated that a 4-ft. overhang along the south side would block high summer sun but let in low winter sun. At the front of the house, I added a porch. At the rear, a secluded deck provides an outside space.

The simplest way to create maximum volume within this small envelope was to finish the rafter bottoms, which would be simple for the large downstairs room. The ceilings follow the slope of the roof and impart a lofty feeling to a house that might feel claustrophobic with standard-height ceilings. On the second floor of the house, the bottoms of the collar ties were finished in the bedrooms to give a 12-ft. ceiling height (photo left).

Careful use of stock materials gives the house custom appeal—For an exterior skin, I chose ⅝-in. resawn-fir plywood siding with 1x2 battens at 8 in. o. c. I centered all openings with respect to the battens to produce a crisp look.

I held the eave and the rake tight to the side of the house with just enough of a projection for a strong shadowline. Along the eaves, a 2¼-in. rafter projection allowed for the continuous soffit vent and a 1x3 frieze board. T-111 siding grooved 4 in. o. c. sheathes the overhang and the front porch, where 4x4 finger-jointed fir columns support 4x6 yellow-pine beams.

SPECS

Bedrooms: 3
Bathrooms: 2
Heating system: Electric heat pump
Size: 1,352 sq. ft.
Cost: $66 per sq. ft.
Completed: 1995
Location: Durham, North Carolina

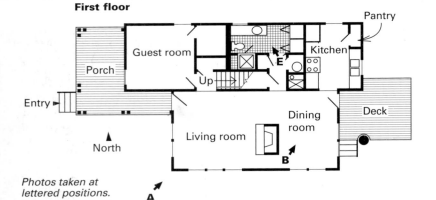

First floor

Pantry
Guest room
Kitchen
Porch
Up
E
Entry ▶
North
Living room
Dining room
Deck
B
A
Photos taken at lettered positions.
0 2 4   8 ft.

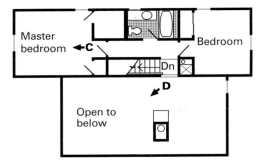

Second floor

Master bedroom ◀ C
Bedroom
Dn
D
Open to below

A small house that feels big. *A large, open area under a shed roof comprises the living area and is punctuated only by a fireplace wall that soars to the 18-ft. ceiling. Elsewhere, rooms and ceilings are of a more modest scale, although ceilings in the master bedroom and study rise to the level of the collar ties.*

Drawings: Mark Hannon

I selected white paint for the exterior of the house, but I added a small amount of gray to decrease glare. I used matte-gray spray paint to unify the chimney's base flashing, the exposed metal of a skylight and the store-bought lighting fixtures and mailbox.

Simple detailing carries over inside—I kept the inside of the house clean and simple. The tub and shower surrounds in the two bathrooms began with stock 4¼-in. square glazed ceramic tile. I chose five closely valued colors for each surround and arranged the inexpensive tile at random (bottom photo). The ¼-in. wide gray joints set off the tiles nicely.

I used the same moldings for baseboards and window and door casings. They are milled from 1x3s with a slightly stepped profile to add another shadowline to the trim. The fireplace hearth is concrete. I used a packaged-concrete mix that I reinforced with galvanized wire lath. After I stripped the forms and set the hearth in place, I mixed up a strong concentration of yellow fabric dye and brushed it onto the concrete. I then belt-sanded the concrete and applied two coats of clear paste wax to get a mottled green-gray color. ☐

Scott Neeley is an architect in Durham, North Carolina. Photos by Steve Culpepper.

Tall views of the living area. The stairway is walled off from this shed-roofed living area, except for the second-floor landing, where a frameless window opens onto the first floor. Windows on the south side of the living room frame a 150-year-old fringe tree, one of the oldest in Durham. Photo taken at D on floor plan.

Blending inexpensive tiles gives a rich look. Stock fixtures and components look lavish against the reflected image of rich ceramic tile. The ¼-in. grout lines of gray set off the five randomly mixed colors of ceramic tile in the shower surround reflected in the mirror. Photo taken at E on floor plan.

Country House and Studio

Restraint, economy and a sense of proportion create a spare but comfortable home

by Victor Lazzaro

In 1961 we took all the money we had and bought a five-acre parcel of gently sloping land in West Redding, Conn. I was a young architect anxious to leave New York City and to build a home that would be a good place to live and work and bring up children.

William Ryder, a recently retired building contractor, sold us the property and also found us a rental apartment very near our newly acquired land. The apartment was part of a complex of three buildings on a large estate—a barn with two other units around a gravel courtyard. The configuration was so pleasing that my wife Maria and I decided to incorporate some of those elements in our own house. The barn, unused at the time but with the large doors open on both sides, provided an unparalleled view to the fields beyond. Its large and simple shape, with few openings to break up its surface, gave a satisfying sense of volume and weight.

Ryder had been a neighbor of the composer Charles Ives, and he still looked after the Ives estate for the heirs. One day he took me to see the house, a simple structure on a beautiful site. Ives shunned luxury, and his house was unpretentious indeed. I liked what I saw and the philosophy it represented.

Two years went by before I hired Ryder's two former carpenters and started building my house. I used to go over and sit on the site, trying to decide where the house should be located and what it ought to be like. There were so many possibilities. We had always lived in apartments, and it was hard to know what we really needed.

The property had frontage on two roads. Coming in from the high side offered a view, but with it came northern exposure. It also meant putting the house below the road, which did not please me. Using the other approach, although it would need a longer driveway and wouldn't give the same long view, did site the house in the most open part of the property. It had been a cornfield at one time and now was high grass, cedars, small pines and some second growth, with much larger trees along the old stone perimeter walls. This location, with the opportunity for a good southern exposure, was my choice.

Taking shape—There wasn't much talk about energy conservation in 1963. Oil was only 15¢ a gallon, and I didn't give it a lot of thought. At the same time I did want to take advantage of the sun as much as possible. I decided to open the house to the south and keep it closed on the north. This served an aesthetic purpose as well,

giving a severe look to the house as it was approached from the north.

I also liked the idea of long roof overhangs. With a 9-in-12 pitch and 5 ft. of overhang on the eave ends, I could block out the high summer sun but let in the winter light. One of the young deciduous trees was directly south of my proposed site, and I knew we would appreciate its shade as it grew larger (photo facing page, bottom right). On the west side, I left many of the second-growth trees to screen out the setting summer sun.

In front of the house, I planned to build a studio with a garage under it as a separate structure (photo above), taking advantage of the grade that sloped down to the north. The main house would loom up from behind the studio as if it were part of it (photo facing page, bottom left). Only as you walked up the front path would you be aware that the house and the studio were in fact two separate structures.

A courtyard at the basement/garage level between the house and the studio would allow an interesting play of decks and walkways, easing the transition to the grounds and providing a bridge from the house to the studio (photo facing page, top). I also liked the idea of giving varied access to the outdoors by building decks off each of the major rooms.

The plan of the house as it finally took shape is decidedly barn-like. The central section of the 24x50 rectangle is open to the roof peak. On the second floor, an open gallery links the two ends. The foundation and basement that underlie the rectangular structure are cruciform in plan, as shown in the drawing on p. 18. On the

two ends of the house, the floor joists cantilever 3 ft. out over the side foundation walls. I was trying to achieve a feeling that the house was hovering or floating by building the block foundation walls 2 ft. above natural grade and cantilevering the ends this way.

I also was able to get a 24-ft. wide house using 2x10s with an 18-ft. span. The weight of the exterior wall on the end of the cantilever gave me a more rigid first floor. And since the floor joists could clear-span the foundation walls, the basement space could be free of supporting posts and load-bearing partitions except in the central area, which was necessarily broken by the stairwell. The open area of the basement on the west end is now a workspace with lots of daylight possible when I open the redwood batten doors onto the courtyard to expose full-length glass panels.

Economy vs. simplicity—Economy was a big factor influencing my choices. I like a restrained, spare look, with surfaces and junctures uncluttered by built-up moldings, and I wanted to keep the house that way, thinking it would help keep costs down. Simplicity can be deceptive though. Sometimes it costs more in time and effort. With no forgiving moldings to hide a bad joint or fit, the workmanship has to be first rate. And when structural elements become a part of the texture of the finished building, there might be a temptation to use more refined or costly framing materials. I was willing, in the interests of economy, to settle for a rough finish and to sacrifice some practical considerations as well, as I'll explain later.

Fortunately, carpenters Hawley Silkman and Bob Pattison were sympathetic to my approach. They were not tedious workers but had pride in their craft, and in their ability to do a careful job. In fact, when I once remarked about their neatness in rough framing the house, I was told, "Well, if the house was ever to be dismantled, some other mechanic would see our work." It

From the north (facing page, bottom left), the main house and studio present a severe facade. A stepped path leads to the entry deck, where one can look down into the courtyard or back toward the studio. The studio (above) looks a bit like an old sugar shack. Clerestory windows give northern light. Access is from the entry deck and bridge. On the south (facing page, right), the house opens to the backyard. The house has ample overhangs, symmetrical glazing and inviting decks (facing page, top).

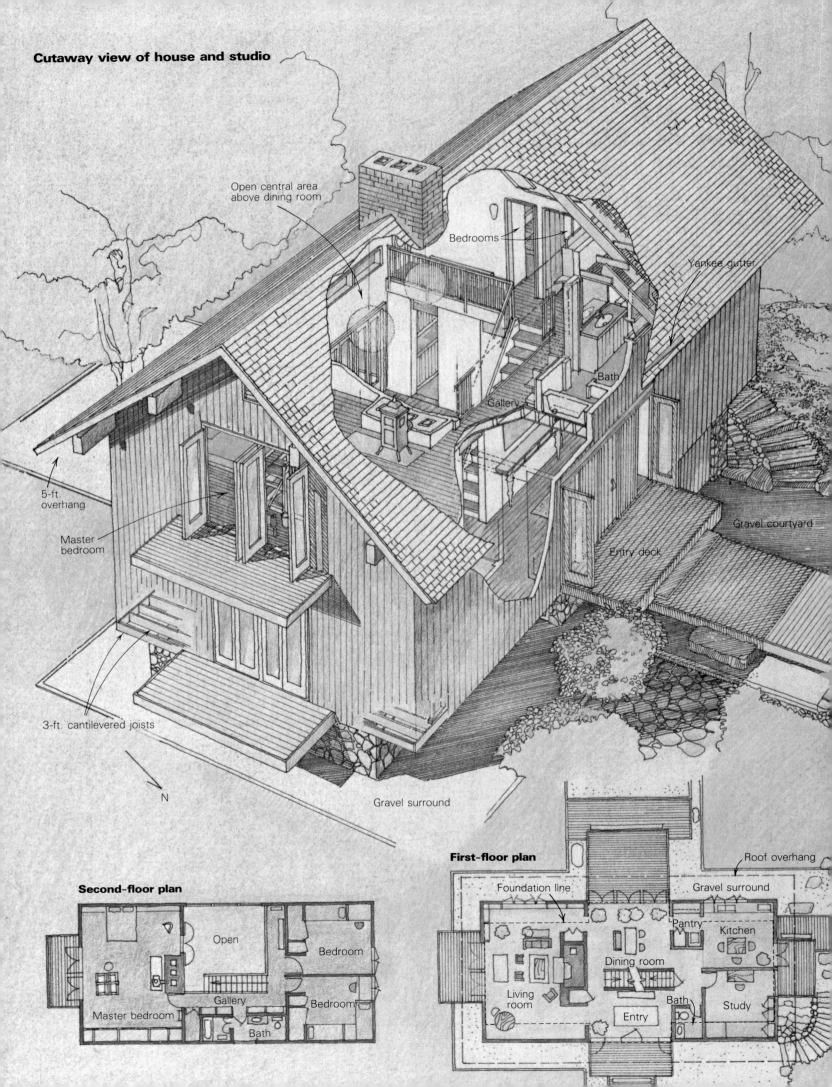

Cutaway view of house and studio

Open central area
above dining room

Bedrooms

Yankee gutter

Bath

Gallery

5-ft.
overhang

Entry deck

Gravel courtyard

Master
bedroom

3-ft. cantilevered joists

N

Gravel surround

Second-floor plan

Open

Bedroom

Bedroom

Master bedroom

Gallery

Bath

First-floor plan

Roof overhang

Foundation line

Gravel surround

Pantry

Kitchen

Dining room

Living
room

Bath

Study

Entry

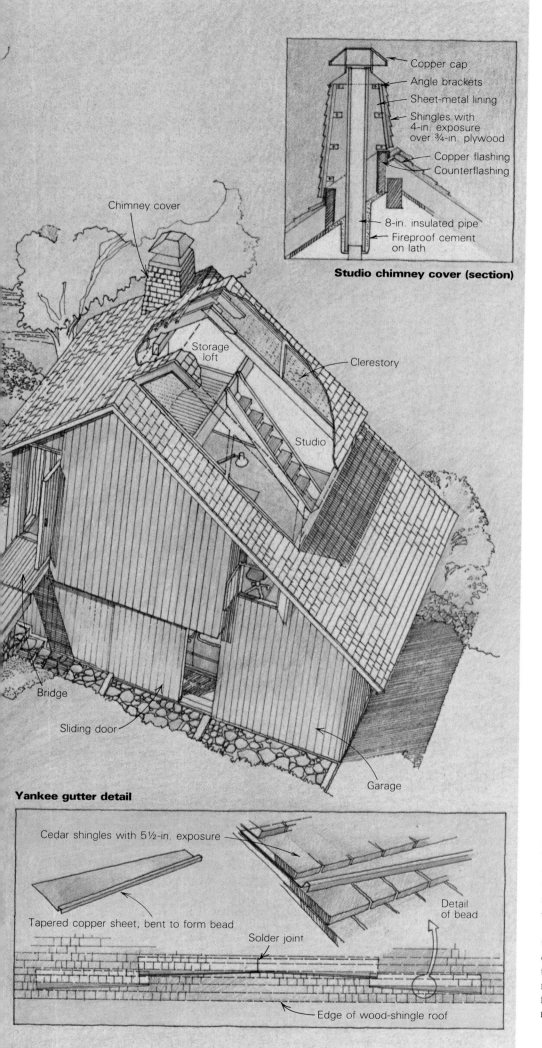

Studio chimney cover (section)

- Copper cap
- Angle brackets
- Sheet-metal lining
- Shingles with 4-in. exposure over ¾-in. plywood
- Copper flashing
- Counterflashing
- 8-in. insulated pipe
- Fireproof cement on lath

Chimney cover

Storage loft

Clerestory

Studio

Bridge

Sliding door

Garage

Yankee gutter detail

- Cedar shingles with 5½-in. exposure
- Tapered copper sheet, bent to form bead
- Solder joint
- Detail of bead
- Edge of wood-shingle roof

made me think of Phidias perfecting the unseen parts of his sculpture for Zeus' eyes.

Before we actually started construction, we decided to set aside all the clear framing lumber to use for doors, windows and their trim. In 1963 it was still all kiln-dried fir and of good quality, so we were able to find more than enough pieces that were knot-free, straight and perfect for our needs. All the jambs were made from rough 2x8 stock that was cut, planed, sanded and routed to receive drywall or exterior siding. We used no additional casings.

The 24-ft. width of the house is the standard length of a 2x10, and therefore no cutting was required for the joists. The walls are 2x4s. The roof rafters are standard 2x6s placed 2 ft. o. c. They are 20 ft. long, and at 9-in-12 pitch extend 5 ft. beyond the house. The tails are not enclosed by soffits. I wanted to be able to look up and see the structure of the roof overhang. An uncomplicated solution, but one that entailed a lot of careful cutting and fitting of the vertical redwood T&G siding where it butted up to the underside of the cedar-shingle roof and around each rafter.

To get around the problem of applied gutters with their added-on look, their tendency to ice up and their need to be cleaned, we surrounded the house with a bed of gravel, as shown in the drawing, to catch the runoff from the roof. It has worked well, even in the worst rainstorms. On the south side, two subsurface drains connect with the footing drains. At other points the grade slope alone is enough to disperse any water. Over the front door there is a Yankee gutter (drawing, bottom right) made of four pieces of copper bent lengthwise to form a right-angled bead and worked under the shingles like flashing. The copper strips are positioned to divert the worst of the roof runoff from the entry deck.

I finished the exterior siding with a good soaking of Woodlife (Roberts Consolidated Industries, Inc., 600 N. Baldwin Park Blvd., City of Industry, Calif. 91749), and have left it alone ever since.

Glazing is modular. I looked at some of the prehung and stock windows on the market, and although I might have gotten better thermal qualities for my money, I didn't like their clumsy look. I prefer the unembellished single-glazed windows that Silkman and Pattison made in three sizes. Two 2-ft. by 7-ft. casements flank the front door, and a small 20-in. by 4-ft. 6-in. horizontal bathroom window under the eaves are the north-side openings. On the south, three pairs of 4-ft. by 7-ft. French doors are centrally grouped with three pairs of 20-in. by 4-ft. windows aligned above them, forming a horizontal band. Symmetrically placed to both sides are two more pairs of 3-ft. by 4-ft. casements. On the east elevation, two pairs of French doors, one above the other, open onto small decks; the west end is similar, but without the upper deck.

The upper deck is supported by extensions of the east-west running second-floor joists. The deck framing is covered with 1x12 redwood trim, which is separated from the framing by furring strips and brought flush with the top of the fir decking. The bridge to the studio is just a series of 2x4s and spacers spiked together. The

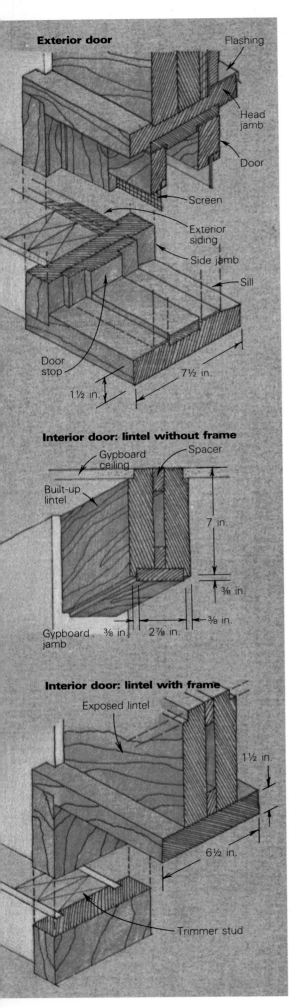

Exterior door

Flashing

Head jamb

Door

Screen

Exterior siding

Side jamb

Sill

Door stop

1½ in.

7½ in.

Interior door: lintel without frame

Gypboard ceiling

Spacer

Built-up lintel

7 in.

⅜ in.

⅜ in.

Gypboard jamb

⅜ in.

2⅞ in.

Interior door: lintel with frame

Exposed lintel

1½ in.

6½ in.

Trimmer stud

whole unit is bolted on 8-in. centers to the rim joist of the deck and to a ledger on the studio end. I treat it once a year with Woodlife.

Interior finish—I was working for a feeling of spaciousness and clean lines. I wanted one space to flow into another both on the main level and up through the high central area. I made an interior window with a pair of shutters that can be opened during the day so that the master bedroom, which is also Maria's studio, can overlook this central portion (photo facing page, right). A variety of views results both from room to room and to the outdoors. I always admired that quality of seeing through and through again to a space beyond in the Dutch interior paintings of Vermeer and DeHooch. I had also experienced it in that rental space with its barn and courtyard by being able to look through both sets of barn doors into the fields beyond.

Our carpenters were used to working in the traditional manner, but they didn't object to trying something different. My method of leaving them little three-dimensional sketches of how a detail should be handled, rather than complete working drawings, seemed to work out fine. They turned our lumber into finished woodwork, frames and doors on site with limited equipment: mostly a hand plane, a hammer, a table saw and a skillsaw. Fitting and cutting the long pieces of cedar for the bedroom ceiling had to be done with precision because I wanted no extra trim where ceilings and walls met.

The finished exterior door and window frames began as ordinary 2x8s, and were surfaced to 1½ in. thick by 7½ in. wide. Jambs were routed in one 5½-in. wide groove to accept the drywall, trimmer studs, sheathing and siding (drawing, left). Interior doors were routed with two ½-in. deep grooves for the drywall. All door and window frames stand about 1 in. proud on the inside and out. Lintels, which are really exposed headers over all the doorways and windows, are built up from two spaced 2x8s on edge, routed to accept a flat trimmed-down 2x4. All the lintels and frames have been stained with a mix of Benjamin Moore walnut and ebony stains and waxed with beeswax (rubbed on). They contrast sharply with the white gypboard walls. This simple detail is used repeatedly throughout the house. Some lintels span a single opening. Others span two adjacent doorways. Where there is an opening without a door frame, the wood lintel is still used and is recessed back from the face of the drywall (photo facing page, top left).

A small pantry between the dining room and kitchen eliminated the need for overhead cabinets in the kitchen, thereby making it feel more spacious. The cabinet doors in the kitchen and pantry were made from T&G fir porch decking and battened horizontally on the inside.

Bookcases are an important feature in this intentionally spare house. There are high ones on the upper gallery that become a focal point and help to unify the space by continuing the color of the cedar ceiling back down to the gallery floor. The bookcases in the living room form an ell and frame a window—a more intimate effect.

Above the living-room fireplace is a recom-

bination of decorative wood pieces from a Brooklyn brownstone that was about to be demolished (photo facing page, bottom left). I bought several mantelpieces, but none was right for our fireplace. Their elaborate machine carving was too ornate. Finally my wife and I quite literally dismantled all of them. After a great deal of struggle we came up with an arrangement that pleased us for its decorativeness and the way it created visual interest in the room.

At first I worried about using more than one wood but it didn't seem to matter. By using similar pieces from several mantels, we created a rhythmic effect that worked well. Silkman cut up some of the pieces and made a lintel. Below that we alternated flat and raised carvings. Finally, around the fire opening we used parts from a kitchen hutch. It all worked together with a minimum of cutting required to make it all fit, and the pieces were nailed in place.

William Ryder, our good friend by now, provided us our front door. It is an old battened ash door, rough on the outside, which had once graced some New England farm long since gone. The original forged latch opens and closes as efficiently now as it must have for its previous owners. For us it is the perfect entrance solution.

From the front deck, the bridge gives direct access to the second-story studio. Once inside, you can see back to the house and down into the little, sheltered gravel court. The building (photo p. 16) is reminiscent of a sugar shed, a New England outbuilding where maple sap is boiled down into syrup or sugar. The eave is higher on the house side. The rafters continue past the main ridge beam for about 3 ft. to form the clerestory that provides lighting for the studio. It also adds height, making it possible to have a storage loft accessible by a ship's ladder. A woodburning stove is supplemented by electric heat, and on the roof the insulated metal flue is covered with a shingled coat topped by a copper hat (detail drawing, previous page).

Twenty years have passed since we built the house, but the process of finishing and adjusting goes on even today. The foundation has a stone veneer that I completed myself. Well, almost. I often wish now I had done this or that differently, finished it all when building was so much less costly, and bought more adjoining property.

Yet, for all that, it has been a good house, not large but certainly adequate for my family. As our trees grow bigger, the character of the land changes. But the house only mellows. It reveals characteristics that never cease to charm and delight us.

I don't think I was aware at the time of all the influences I was subjected to as I set out to design our house. I certainly wasn't thinking in terms of designing a traditional house. Yet when I was through, in 1965, it didn't turn out to be what might have been called contemporary. It ended up looking as if it had always been there. Soon after it was done, a delivery man asked me what it had been before I converted it.   □

Victor Lazzaro is an illustrator and erstwhile architect in West Redding, Conn. Drawings by the author.

Clean lines, simple detailing. The floor-to-roof dining area (above) with its generous southern light is the central space to which everything else in the house relates. Clean lines and simple detailing are apparent, especially in the window and door treatments. The quality of looking through and beyond openings and the rhythm set up by the repetition of the exposed lintels reveal themselves in the photo top left, in the view from the kitchen through the pantry, into and beyond the dining area to the living room. The mantelpiece in the living room (left) is an assemblage of salvaged mantels and interior woodwork from a brownstone in Brooklyn. Bookcases are a welcome contrast to an otherwise deliberately spare interior.

Eurostyle Rustic

Danish design and American tradition are joined by restrained detailing and fine wood craftsmanship

by Graeme Means

The site near Carbondale, Colo., is a Rocky Mountain study in contrast. During the winter, cold windy snows alternate with bright sunny skies, while the dark and frigid Crystal River slides silently by on its bed of icy rocks. In spring, the dry branches of cottonwood and brush oak begin to bud, the willows and grasses green and by summer the vegetation threatens to engulf all. Still later, hot gusts soothed by the Crystal provide a welcome dose of cooling air during the hot mountain summer. On this narrow spread of land between cliffs and river, the tall cottonwoods filter the summer sun, and the ground is bathed in ever-changing light until fall.

As an architect—and sometimes a builder—I find life particularly satisfying when I get the chance to resolve an interesting and demanding program, and to work with the ideas of thoughtful, patient clients. On this site, that opportunity arose. It was important that a home here reflect its powerful setting, yet stand proudly to add its own identity and character. It had to encourage its owners to enjoy the outdoors in good weather, but provide them with a warm, sheltered retreat from the elements.

Design by three, then four—I was casually acquainted with David and Nanna, the young couple who came to me, and they had never been through the process of designing a house before. But both of them had strong ideas about it and were insistent on understanding most aspects of the project well enough to make intelligent and imaginative decisions. This led to lengthy design sessions and to solutions which we all had to agree on—usually. From the personalities and experiences of its designers, the character of the house emerged.

David's first vision of the house was of a traditional American log cabin, something with a basic, honest, rooted-to-the-land nature. We thoroughly explored this possibility, but eventually decided to build a frame house over a radiant-slab floor. But we wanted to keep the rusticity and structural honesty of a log home. To achieve this we relied heavily on wood, and worked it with a high degree of craftsmanship.

Nanna brought a different point of view to our discussions. She grew up in Denmark, and had a

Graeme Means is an architect in Aspen, Colo.

Graeme Means

Lodged bedween the river and a cliff (above), this Colorado house employs an exposed roof-truss sytem held together with wooden dowels, nuts and washers (facing page). The owners used many European products in the house, from lighting fixtures to cabinet hardware.

refined sense of modern Scandinavian aesthetics. Danish design has long been characterized by strong shapes, clean proportions, meticulous joinery and a spare use of materials. Nanna's quiet insistence on maintaining this standard deeply affected the design of the house, particularly the interior. We accumulated mountains of catalogs, both European and American, from which we got design and product ideas for light fixtures, plumbing, hardware and furniture (see the sidebar on p. 28).

As the third member of the design team, my task was to harmonize the elements of backwoods Americana with modern European style. My contribution to the design itself comes from a strong love of wood and woodworking. I guess I developed it in furniture-design courses with

Tage Frid during my architecture studies. Frid is particularly well known for his mastery of wood joinery. My goal was to consider and design each detail of the house with the same care I would give if it were a piece of furniture.

Midway through the design process there arrived a fourth member of the design team, although he was not totally unexpected. Newly born Andreas couldn't tell us about his desires, but he had considerable influence anyway. We would often consider what his needs and reactions to the house would be at different times of his life. By encouraging us to examine family interactions more closely, he led us to a higher standard than we would otherwise have reached.

A plan, and a program—I've acted as general contractor on some of my projects, and on projects like this I find the additional role to be a big advantage. It makes for more direct communication between designer and craftsmen, which reduces mistakes and makes it easier to make quick on-site decisions. The designer also gets more feedback from the craftsmen, so the project is more likely to benefit from the craftsmen's technical knowledge and experience. Furthermore, it means that the clients have only one person to deal with, which simplifies their involvement in a complicated process.

The program we settled on called for two bedrooms, two baths, a den (which could also serve as a guest bedroom) and open living/dining areas. In addition to the 2,100 sq. ft. of enclosed space, the clients wanted outdoor areas that in summer would feel like extensions of the interior. The house would also have to deal with the large swings in Colorado temperature. Since southern sun in winter is scarce on this site, the strategy was to build a tight house capped with a well-insulated roof. At the heart of the house would be a massive masonry chimney that would vent a woodstove and a Rumford fireplace.

Birch dowels and maple nuts—One of the things David liked about log construction is that its structural system is expressive and visible. So in this house we used exposed roof trusses to accomplish the same thing. If we had built with logs, we would have used spruce, so we decided on spruce for the trusses.

The mountains surrounding this area are full

From the carport to the front door. The carport (top left) provides storage for yard tools, as well as sheltered parking for one car. Just visible in the lower roof are simple Exolite skylights. To lower the grade between the garage and the house, retaining walls of Colorado rose sandstone (middle left) support flagstone walks. On the house's east side (bottom left), the ventilating light well is visible behind the chimney. It draws sunshine into the rear of the house and exhausts warm air in the summer.

of old mining structures built out of this wood, and the expressive structural nature of trestles and tipples, towers and tunnels has always fascinated me. There are large stands of spruce in the mountains not far from here, but many of them were killed by a beetle infestation some 40 years ago. They've been curing on the stump in the dry Colorado air ever since—you can probe them with a moisture meter and get consistent readings in the 12% to 14% range. The logs are laced with cracks and knots, but we were able to pick out the best material right at the mill. The rest makes good firewood.

An additional advantage in having the old spruce trees milled to our specifications was that I could give local sawyer Bill Bullard a list of exact sizes and lengths to cut from his mountain of logs. When I was designing the trusses, it was great to know that I could get the material sawn to virtually any dimension that I specified, give or take ⅛ in. As a bonus, the boards came off the 4-ft. dia. sawblade with just the rough-sawn texture we wanted.

Spruce is a very soft and light wood. It's easy to work and has a light color that rapidly turns to amber with exposure to the sun. Spruce does have its share of shortcomings, however. It isn't very strong, and the knots and cracks encourage points and planes of weakness within each board or timber. So I decided to build up the trusses and some beams with layers of smaller pieces, each one no thicker than 3 in.

By using repetitive members instead of larger single ones, the weakness in each individual board is reduced. Much as in a gluelam beam, a knot or crack would never go entirely through the cross section of a truss. Another very important advantage of this system is that the built-up members never generate enough twisting or cupping force to distort end blocking. All too frequently I've seen thick, exposed beams with unsightly twists that have cracked drywall where they enter the wall, and I reasoned that with a built-up structural system we would be able to avoid this pitfall.

With engineer Bob Pattillo looking over my shoulder, I began to design the house's trusses and rafter system, and soon realized that joinery would be a crucial consideration. Three, four or in some cases eight pieces of wood would pass through a single joint in the truss, and because these members would usually be subjected to tension or bending stresses, they would have to maintain their structural integrity right through the joint. Also, instead of relying on any kind of wood or metal gusset plates, I wanted the members to transmit their forces directly to each other even when in tension. The intricate notching that would be necessary called to

Top photo: Graeme Means

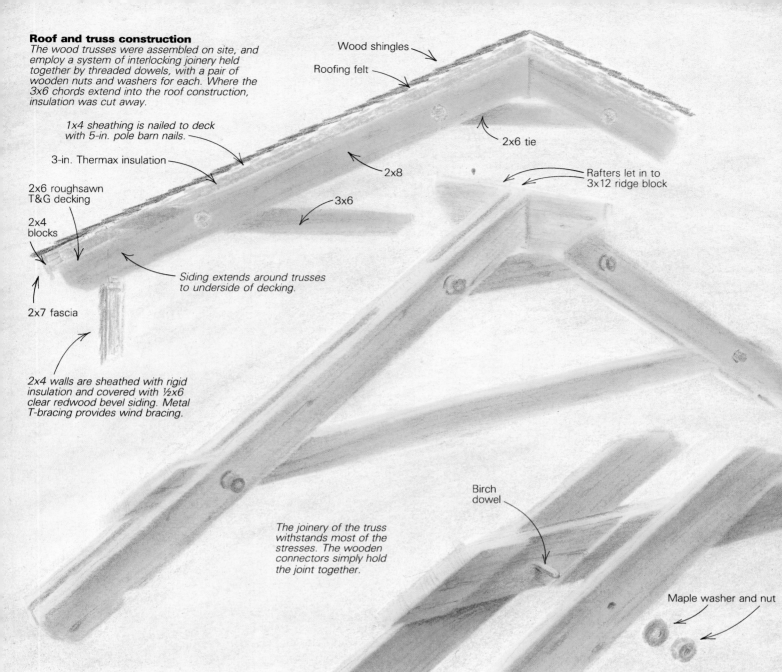

Roof and truss construction
The wood trusses were assembled on site, and employ a system of interlocking joinery held together by threaded dowels, with a pair of wooden nuts and washers for each. Where the 3x6 chords extend into the roof construction, insulation was cut away.

Wood shingles

Roofing felt

1x4 sheathing is nailed to deck with 5-in. pole barn nails.

3-in. Thermax insulation

2x6 roughsawn T&G decking

2x4 blocks

2x7 fascia

2x4 walls are sheathed with rigid insulation and covered with ½x6 clear redwood bevel siding. Metal T-bracing provides wind bracing.

2x8

3x6

2x6 tie

Rafters let in to 3x12 ridge block

Siding extends around trusses to underside of decking.

The joinery of the truss withstands most of the stresses. The wooden connectors simply hold the joint together.

Birch dowel

Maple washer and nut

mind the wonderful wooden joints used in the roof structure of Japanese temples and homes. Japanese craftsmen use notched members to form a sandwich of interlocking parts to make up a rigid truss.

But I needed some sort of fastener to hold the "sandwich" together and prevent the individual parts from slipping out of alignment with each other. The obvious solution was to bolt the joints together, but I really didn't want to use any metal in the trusses. Instead, I devised a system of oversized wooden nuts, dowels and washers that would hold the trusses together (drawing, above).

Bolting the structure together seemed an ideal solution to the problem—the wooden dowels could easily be cut to fit the various thicknesses of the joints, and the oversize wooden washers (3½ in. in dia., as they turned out) would spread out the compressive forces of the nuts to prevent crushing the soft wood fibers of the spruce. I also thought it might be an advantage to be able to tighten up the connections and tune up

the structure if the wood happened to shrink any further over the years.

I chose maple for the nuts and washers because of its hardness and durability, and because its coloring is similar to spruce. Since all the connectors would be visible in the living areas, a contrasting color would have overemphasized them—I wanted them to show, but not too much. Birch dowels, ⅞ in. in dia., were used because they're strong, straight grained and take threads well.

But I soon found that designing the wooden connectors was only half of the problem—it sure wasn't easy to find someone to make them. Plenty of woodworkers were intrigued by the idea, but when I mentioned that I needed 500 of them, with washers, enthusiasm quickly evaporated. Finally, when I was on vacation in Pawtucket, R. I., I walked into Robert's Woodworking and found the kind of expertise I needed. The old mill building was packed full of the most marvelous collection of old woodworking machinery. As I walked from machine to ma-

chine with one of the workers there, he demonstrated the operations needed to complete the parts just the way I wanted. The price was very reasonable, and it was exciting, months later in Colorado, to receive boxes of parts completed exactly as I had envisioned them.

I realized that I would need a special wrench to tighten the nuts, and it seemed appropriate to have a couple made out of laminated maple. But they split about halfway through the job so head carpenter Jamie Arnold fashioned a new pair out of plywood and duct tape, and those finished the job.

Assembling the trusses was really not too difficult. We snapped chalklines on the floor slab and laid out the trusses full size, and this allowed us to lay out all the notches exactly as they would be cut. One advantage of this approach was that we could easily compensate for slight differences in the dimensions of the lumber, thereby increasing the accuracy of the joinery. When all the pieces were cut, they were brushed with a clear wood finish, lifted into

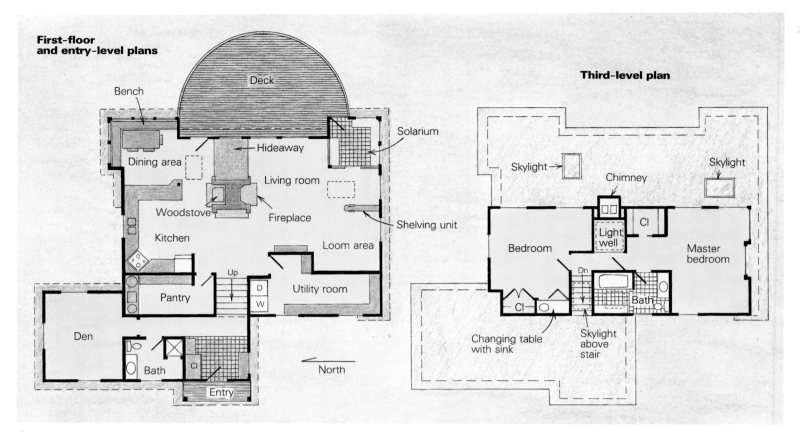

First-floor and entry-level plans

Bench

Deck

Dining area

Hideaway

Solarium

Living room

Woodstove

Fireplace

Shelving unit

Kitchen

Loom area

Up

D W

Utility room

Pantry

Den

Bath

Cl

Entry

North

Third-level plan

Skylight

Chimney

Skylight

Light well

Bedroom

Cl

Master bedroom

Dn

Cl

Bath

Changing table with sink

Skylight above stair

---

place and tacked together with 16d finish nails until we could hold things together with the wooden connectors. The nuts, dowels and washers had been soaking in Watco oil for about a week before we installed them.

A walk through the interior—The house is a split-level design, with a large, open living area and kitchen on the first level and bedrooms on the third level (drawing, above). Joining the upper and lower levels is a small second level that contains a tiled entry, a bath and the den.

The entry to the house was designed with Colorado's winter climate in mind. Its location midway between the living areas below and the bedrooms above keeps drafts well away from either area. A built-in wooden bench provides convenient seating for prying off snowy boots, and a ceramic-tile floor makes it easy to clean up afterwards.

The entry contains an armoire and a bureau. The bottom panel of the armoire (bottom left photo, facing page) is covered with ceramic tile to match the floor, so one need not hesitate to load it with dirty wet boots. The bureau top is a handy place to toss keys and gloves, while drawers store fresh mittens, gloves and hats for outbound travelers. The den, also on this level, has a lovely view upriver. Isolated from the rest of the house, it offers temporary refuge from family life, and the adjacent bathroom helps it serve as a guest bedroom.

The living area of the house is down a half-flight of stairs from the entry level. With its network of exposed trusses shouldering the roof loads, the living area has some of the best views of the wooden connectors that hold the truss joinery together (photo p. 23). This area was laid out as one continuous space but includes

enough nooks and variety to give individual areas within it a distinct identity.

Near the center of the house stands a large masonry core, around which the different living areas are grouped. A Rumford fireplace, by mason Chip Chilson, faces toward the living room (top photo, facing page). At one edge of the core is a 25-sq. ft. light well that rises two stories to the roof, where it is capped by an operable skylight. The well helps to brighten up the center of the house, and accents the rugged face of the adjacent masonry. It also helps to ventilate the house.

At the corner of the living room is a tiled solarium surrounded on the living-room side with counter-height walls. Though it gets plenty of sun, it was designed more as a low-maintenance, easy-cleanup area for working with and growing plants. A tile floor and matching tile counters, abundant light, a door to the outside and a small water spigot provide the necessary features for potting and watering house plants. I was concerned about cumulative damage to the countertop edges, so I devised what should be a durable alternative to wood or tile edging. Lengths of 1½-in. dia. copper water pipe were cut lengthwise to fit over the edges, and backed up with mortar.

On the opposite side of the chimney mass is a large open kitchen, located to help the cook keep in touch with things. In the kitchen, a large pantry keeps unsightly supplies hidden. All of the cabinet drawers were lined with sheet cork to reduce the clatter of kitchen utensils, a noise that can be distracting in an open-plan house. Across a wide maple countertop, the dining area juts out from a corner of the building (bottom right photo, facing page). By keeping this area small and supplying it with lots of windows,

the views toward the river and the nearby cottonwood trees are emphasized and shared with the kitchen.

In order to make such a small space work, we built a trestle table (derived from Quaker designs) with continuous bench seating along two sides. I was skeptical when David and Nanna requested that the bench be built entirely of wood, with no cushions, because I was convinced that it would be nearly impossible to make it comfortable for any length of time. But they insisted. So we made a mockup of the seat and took turns sitting on it, making adjustments until everyone found it comfortable.

The final benches were built almost like an inverted boat hull, with ribs of ¾-in. particleboard to give them their basic shape. The finished seating surface was coopered together using 3½-in. by 1½-in. fir boards with the edges beveled to allow them to butt tightly over the changing contours of the framework. The fir was then sculpted slightly and sanded to refine the shape. The benches have proven to be very comfortable and easily maintained—there are no cushions to stain or fray, and it's almost fun to slide down the bench into the corner.

Between the dining area and the living room, adjacent to the chimney, is a small "house" within the house (top photo, facing page). Equipped with its own gable roof, privacy curtains and plenty of cushions, this multi-purpose area is about the size of a king-size bed. Andreas and his parents can curl up in it together and read a book, or lie back and gaze through the large round window toward the river. A small footstool stored beneath one side allows Andreas and his friends to climb into the space without help—they all love a space that's scaled to their size. The space can even accommodate

A double-sided masonry chimney faced in sandstone serves as the focal point for the first level of the house (above). Facing the kitchen is a deep niche for a woodstove, and a Rumford fireplace faces the living room. To the right is a cozy sitting area, open to the living room and the dining area. Depending on need, it can be a reading hideaway, a children's play area or a guest bed for two. The dining area (below) was kept small so that views to the river just 20 ft. away would be easily visible from the kitchen. Beneath the windows, contoured fir benches provide plenty of seating.

Ceramic tile in the main entry (and on the floor of the armoire as well) takes the punishment of winter's snow-caked boots. Small, routed basins in the bureau top catch keys and coins; drawers hold gloves and scarves. A doorstop protects the armoire from the main entry door.

a couple of overnight guests. Underneath, there's room for firewood.

Upstairs, a half-flight of stairs from the entry, are two bedrooms and a bath connected by a short hallway. Because this hallway opens out into the light well, it feels quite spacious. The master bedroom, at the south end of the house, has views both upriver and of the clifftops above.

Special care with wood—In addition to custom-made cabinets and passage doors, we furnished many spaces with built-ins and custom-designed furniture. It was important that we choose our woods carefully since there was so much woodwork. Most hardwoods would have seemed too slick and precious alongside our rough-cut spruce. Douglas fir is homey and unpretentious, but a beautiful wood which served well as our dominant finish material. Its coloring is warm, and the wood is wonderful to touch.

Fir isn't always easy to work, however. The growth rings can be wide, and the difference in hardness between earlywood and latewood is great, making it difficult to thickness-plane smoothly—the wood will sometimes chip out along the soft summer rings. To minimize these effects, we used quartersawn stock, which also reduced the amount of distracting figure in the wood—we didn't want the wood to overwhelm the architecture. Fir is more prone than some other woods to scratches and dents, but we felt these signs of wear would enhance the sense of passing time in much the same way as would the softly worn treads of an old stair.

Where we thought the fir would wear excessively, inlays of purpleheart were positioned to bear the brunt of hard use. Purpleheart, sometimes called amaranth, is a very durable South American hardwood with a fine close grain. Though bright purple when first cut, the wood

can dull to almost purple-brown on exposure to sunlight. Around the nosing of the dining table, there is a ½-in. wide purpleheart inlay protecting the soft end grain of the fir from chair-back bruises and other hard knocks. The purpleheart looks so elegant next to fir that we sometimes used the combination purely for looks. On the stair handrail (photo below), a recessed purpleheart inlay provides a highly polished surface for fingertips to glide along.

Exterior materials—Roof forms are derived from traditional gable and hip styles, but the massing of the house comes more from such factors as topography, sun, access and interior layout. From the centrally located light shaft, roofs fall away to low, protecting eaves. The tall stone chimney adjacent to the light shaft serves visually as a giant stickpin holding down the leaves of the roof. Since the cliffs behind the house block the southern sun in winter, and the southern sun in summer can be plenty hot, the house opens up mostly to the east.

Exterior materials are simple and natural, chosen for their ability to age with dignity and character. Cedar roofs, redwood siding, locally cut spruce rafters, and Colorado rose sandstone were chosen for their proven durability in the intense Colorado sun. In choosing windows, we debated between the low maintenance of clad windows and the natural feel of wood. We achieved both of these aims by using windows with an exterior cladding of teak (Duratherm Window Corp., Rte. #32, North Vassalboro, Maine 04962). Untreated teak will weather to a soft grey and should withstand many seasons of Colorado weather.

A matching garage—Instead of building a garage at the same elevation as the house, we de-

cided (after getting the necessary variances) to build a small entry building at road level, 10 ft. above grade (top photo, p. 24). It provides sheltered parking for one vehicle, along with some storage, an enclosed trash area and a little bench on which to rest groceries or pass a meditative moment or two. We designed it with the same care accorded to the house—its roof trusses were assembled with wood connectors as well.

Low, curving retaining walls of drystacked sandstone, laid up by mason John Isaacs, gently lower the grade to house level, and shield a flagstone stair and walkway (middle photo, p. 24). Flanking the porch are two simple wooden benches. They provide one last parking place for groceries while you fumble for the door key, and offer a pleasant opportunity to take in some late afternoon sun.

The success of a house with this degree of detail depends primarily on the people who do the work, and we were fortunate to find some craftsmen who really made a difference. In particular, the complex notching of varied truss members required considerable skill and concentration. Jamie Arnold was the foreman, and did virtually all of the extensive on-site carpentry as well as much of the finish work. We were fortunate to find Gary Broyles to do the shop work—doors, built-ins and furniture. He has the very valuable knack of being able to combine excellent craftsmanship with the realities of time and budget.

In every carefully detailed project there is one essential ingredient that motivates the design and construction processes—the desire of the owners to create a special home. In this case, that desire was backed up with the concern and patience necessary to see the design and construction through to completion. □

Finishes and fixtures, European style

Most of the interior finishes in the house were chosen to add a modern, crisp touch to the rusticity of the structural frame. In order to keep the interior bright, the clients wanted white wall surfaces, but none of us thought we'd like the contrast between smooth drywall and the rough spruce. To get a bit of texture on the walls, we used a fiberglass wall-covering material called TASSO (Mirror of Sweden Inc., 117 E. Ocean Ave., Lantana, Fla. 33462) that's used frequently in Scandinavian countries but is little known in this country. It's fire-resistant and comes in a variety of weaves that resemble translucent burlap. TASSO is simply pasted over the drywall with standard wallpaper paste. Painted white, it added the perfect texture and maintained the brightness of the walls (photo right).

From Danish catalogs we chose a variety of simple yet elegant light fixtures, and David and Nanna picked them up in Denmark during a visit to her family. The clean design of the fixtures (by Louis

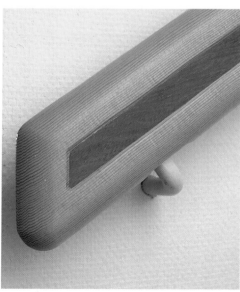

Purpleheart is used as an accent on this handrail. When first cut, its color lives up to the name; it later fades to brown. The wall covering behind it is a Swedish import called TASSO.

Poulsen & Co., Nyhavn #11, 1004 Copenhagen K, Denmark) and the subtle ways in which they release their light is highly refreshing, and was well worth the extra effort it took to get them. (We made sure the fixtures were UL listed.) For cabinet hardware we turned to the "hi-tech" products of HEWI (HEWI Inc., 6 Pearl Ct., Allendale, N. J. 07401). Made of high-quality nylon, these handles and accessories are simply designed, well made, pleasant to the touch and add bright spots of color to the wood and white walls. Cabinet hinges and drawer slides are Austrian (Grass America, Inc., P.O. Box 1019, 1202 Hwy. 66 South, Kernersville, N. C. 27284), and furniture hardware came from Häfele's great catalog (Häfele America Co., 203 Feld Ave., P.O. Box 1590, High Point, N. C. 27261). Plumbing fixtures and trim were generally of European manufacture (by Grohe America, Inc., 2679 Coyle Ave., Elk Grove Village, Ill. 60007, and by Ifö Sanitär, AB S-29500, Bromölla, Sweden). —G. M.

Cozy in Any Weather

Creating comfortable spaces in a home that faces New England's harsh winters and hot summers

by Linda Moody

The house that my husband and I built in rural Massachusetts (photo above) continues the evolution of New England architecture. It began with the first saltbox designs. The early settlers expanded the basic gabled-roof house design by adding more rooms at the back to make living indoors through the long, harsh winter easier. Completed in 1988, our house has typical New England features: wood clapboards, two-over-two windows and gables to maximize second-floor space. The colors we selected for the exterior come from nature: cedar stain on the wood

clapboards, bright hunter green for the trim. The house is practically camouflaged in spring, summer and fall in the screen of oak, black birch, maple and shagbark hickory trees.

Nature influenced the design of our house in other ways as well. Like the early settlers before us, we had to contend with the New England weather. I designed the house to be both warm in the winter and cool in the summer.

The garden room—We began by siting the house so that its long axis faces 15° off true south

(drawing p. 30). The saltbox shape works to buffer cold northwesterly winds. The roof comes down low on the northwest, from a 12-in-12 pitch to a 4-in-12 pitch, thus channeling prevailing winter winds up and over the house. We then located most of the windows on the south and east elevations; the north has only one window. We used mostly double-hung, single-pane windows with true divided lites and exterior glass storm panels set into the wood sash. The storm panels kick up the R-value to about that of insulating double-pane glass. Triple-pane glass, though it has a greater R-value, reduces solar gain, and we wanted to use the sun's energy to help heat our house.

The house's siting also dictated the layout of rooms, especially our garden room (top left photo, facing page). Located on the southwest corner of the house, the garden room is a two-story passive-solar sunspace. It has about 90 sq. ft. of south-facing, double-pane casement windows (which, unlike double-hung windows, can be opened completely) and a stone floor. The floor, a combination of bluestone and crushed stone, has high thermal mass to help regulate indoor temperature: It slowly absorbs and stores the sun's heat and then disperses it at night. The floor consists of 6 in. of crushed stone over a layer of 2-in. rigid insulation that lies over several feet of clean gravel. The insulation prevents stored daytime heat from escaping downward.

Some of the plants sit on the stone floor in pots and in flats. Crushed stone, in addition to having great thermal mass, allows water to filter downward and evaporate, so these plants can be watered without worrying about floor damage or cleanup. And instead of wood baseboard, I laid up a course of colorful Great Wall tiles, which were hand made in China. Each tile looks like a watercolor painting. I used more of these tiles on a kitchen countertop.

The garden room is an oasis in all seasons, and it has given rise to a new family tradition. On New Year's Day, we gather there and plant seeds in flats for our gardens. This makes spring feel a little bit closer, and indeed with this room, plants and flowers always feel a part of the house.

On the second floor, the master bathroom (right photo, facing page) features a whirlpool surrounded by double-hung exterior windows and three more casement windows that open to the garden room. The windows overlooking the garden room create the feeling of bathing in a quiet pool in the woods and allow the garden's solar heat to reach the upstairs bedroom through the bath.

Lighting enhances comfort—The house's design also takes advantage of natural light. The kitchen and the bedrooms face east to pick up the morning sunshine. The kitchen has solid-maple and Great Wall tile countertops, walnut and maple cabinets and a wood ceiling. With early morning sun shining in, the room is cheerful and homey.

Skylights in the kitchen and in the living room let sunlight into the house. In winter, with the leaves gone from the trees, the low sun shines through the doors of the west-facing porch and beams on our massive brick masonry woodstove, highlighting its rustic colors and giving a sense of warmth and comfort to the interior. The porch screens feature my own touch-fastener-type system, making them easy to remove for maximum winter light.

My intention with the house's design was to have an open floor plan but still allow for intimate spaces to make it cozy. So the floor plan includes several bump-outs, giving us special places, like the piano nook in the living room and the reading alcove off the dining room. The

SPECS
Bedrooms: 2
Bathrooms: 2
Heating system: Masonry woodstove
Size: 2,500 sq. ft.
Cost: $66 per sq. ft.
Completed: 1988
Location: Pepperell, Massachusetts

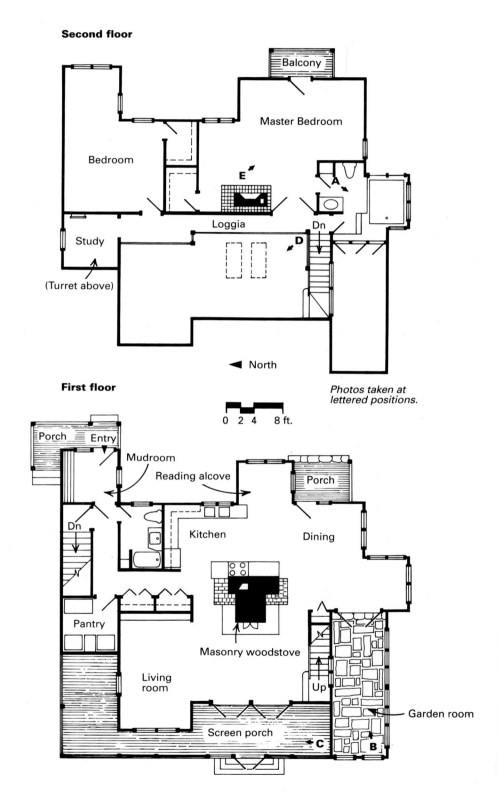

Second floor

First floor

Photos taken at lettered positions.

0 2 4 8 ft.

◄ North

An irregular footprint. *The house was sited to collect sunshine in the garden room; elsewhere, windows in bump-outs and a screen porch on the west elevation create a variety of lighting experiences.*

Drawing: Jeff Bellantuono

Walled-in pond. On the second floor, over-looking both the garden room and the sylvan exterior, this bathroom contains a whirlpool. Photo taken at A on floor plan.

With rocks and stones and trees. Inside the garden room, bluestone and crushed stone store the sun's heat and radiate it at night. This heat enters the second-floor bathroom through casement windows at the top of the far wall. Photo taken at B on floor plan.

Like the wind touching the sail. On the west elevation, the screen porch catches cool summer breezes coming off the Nashua River. The porch also shades this side of the house to control summertime overheating. The double French doors open into the living room. Photo taken at C on floor plan.

A variety of spaces. The living room, viewed from the loggia, is designed to be an entertaining area that is open to the kitchen and, through two sets of French doors, to the screen porch. Its expansive feeling contrasts with the intimacy of the piano nook at the far end of the living room. Photo taken at D on floor plan.

Bedrooms face east. Besides letting morning sunshine into the master bedroom, this triple French door unit offers a panoramic view that, combined with the cathedral ceiling, enhances the spaciousness of the master bedroom. Photo taken at E on floor plan.

reading alcove is surrounded by windows; it's a friendly, sun-filled spot to sit and read during the long, cold winter.

Varying ceiling heights and planes also makes each space different and lends intimacy to the open floor plan. The kitchen has a low ceiling of T&G, V-grooved 1x6 pine. This room is open to the living room (photo facing page), which has a pine cathedral ceiling with operable skylights that help keep the entire house cool. An upstairs balcony/hallway, or loggia, overlooks the living room.

The master bedroom (photo above) has a cathedral ceiling with a skylight. A triple French-door unit topped with a transom and a half-round window leads outside to a balcony overlooking the gardens. Being able to see the outdoors upon entering makes this room feel larger. This is a trick used in condominiums that have limited square footage.

Holding onto the heat—You enter the house through a mudroom that acts like an air-lock entry. The mudroom is small, about 8 ft. by 8 ft., but it's enough to buffer the cold. Many original New England farmhouses featured mudrooms as a buffer between heated indoor air and the cold outdoor air.

The brick masonry woodstove at the center of the house provides most of the heating. A masonry woodstove, sometimes called a Finnish or Russian woodstove, is different from a traditional fireplace or metal woodstove. A masonry woodstove recaptures the heated gases that escape the burning fire and stores this heat in the stove's prodigious thermal mass. Through a series of

runs and baffles, smoke goes up, then passes down across the enclosed firebox and goes up again. The stove burns extremely hot, but the brick surface never gets so hot that it burns your hand. Because the brick mass is almost always warm in winter, animals and humans seek it out as a cozy spot during the cold and dreary New England winter.

We elected to build a masonry woodstove because we liked fireplaces but knew they were terribly inefficient. We wanted an efficient heat source but didn't like the way a metal woodstove heats up and cools down quickly, nor did we want to deal with the amount of residue a woodstove creates in the chimney flue. Our masonry woodstove is efficient and clean, and we rarely have to use our backup, oil-fired forced hot water system.

Summer cooling—The house is designed to keep cool through a combination of ventilation and shading. Although the setting winter sun penetrates the house to illuminate the masonry woodstove, the roof's overhangs provide shade during the summer. Building a substantial roof overhang was one way to keep our house cool. Both the soffits and the rakes overhang 2 ft. These large overhangs make it unnecessary to close the upstairs windows during summer storms because rain rarely reaches the upper portion of the house.

The west elevation of the house has a large screen porch (bottom left photo, p. 31) that provides shade where summer overheating potential is greatest. The gable roof on this side of the house changes from a 12-in-12 pitch at the top to

a 4-in-12 pitch at the plate where the porch framing begins. The porch roof was originally designed to come down lower, but when we were building the porch, we realized a low-hanging roof would obscure the best part of the view. Raising the ridge height and the eaves wall provided a steep enough pitch on the porch roof and opened up the view.

The west-facing screen porch catches the cool summer breezes coming off the nearby Nashua River. Two sets of French doors connect the living room to the screen porch and allow the cool air from the porch to circulate through the living room.

Along with the operable skylights in the cathedral ceilings, a turret above the second floor expels rising hot air at the high point of the house while drawing cool air from the porch and the garden room, where open windows and shading from deciduous trees control the temperature. The result is convection air movement, where rising hot air is replaced by cool air.

You must climb a ladder from a second-story study to reach the turret, but once there you have a 270° view around you through more single-pane, double-hung windows. A skylight in the hip-roof cathedral ceiling offers great views of the stars at night. The turret even has a pine floor. Although this room measures 8 ft. by 8 ft. (the floor opening is about 2 ft. by 3 ft.), the house sits at the highest point of the lot, so you feel as if you are sitting on top of the world when you're in the turret. □

Linda Moody is an architect in Pepperell, Mass. Photos by Rich Ziegner.

A Cascade of Roofs

Multiple gables, long overhangs and metal roofing dominate the design of this house in Georgia

by John Phelps

The mountains of northern Georgia rise and fall through dense hardwood forests brushed with mountain laurel. While driving through these rural mountains, I'm always struck by the similarity of the building styles and materials that make up most of the farmhouses, the tenant-farmer houses and the barns. Galvanized metal roofs, board-and-batten siding, double-hung windows and simple gable roofs are common to almost every building in the area (at least every building that isn't a house trailer).

I got a chance to design a house using these styles and materials when Dick and Gee Mitchell called to tell me they had bought land in the mountains of White County, Georgia.

I wanted the house to fit in with the local architecture, but I knew the house also had to fit the Mitchells comfortably. They wanted a two-bedroom house they could use on weekends. And later in their lives, when they retired and their children were grown, they would build a larger house on the property and turn the first one into a guest house for their kids and, they hoped, their grandchildren.

A room they didn't know they needed—The 25 acres of land that the Mitchells bought rise steeply from a narrow road to a ridge and then slope back down the hillside to the headwaters of the Chattahoochee River. They wanted to disturb the site as little as possible and remove only a few trees. The driveway would be nothing more than a narrow path. A compact footprint would minimize site disturbance. The Mitchells also wanted to take advantage of the mountainside view from as many directions as possible.

To accommodate the Mitchells, I devised a compact, cross-shaped plan that would allow one-room, 12-ft. wide wings that could open in several directions to the view. This plan is divided into four parts (floor plan p. 36).

The front door in the south wing would face uphill, allowing one to enter the house almost from ground level without having to walk up a lot of steps. Because the Mitchells are early morning people, I put the bedrooms in the east wing so that the rooms would catch the early sun. The kitchen and the utility room are in the west wing, and the living room faces downhill to the north, with windows on the north, east and west sides. The staircase, the hallways and the bathroom are

A series of roofs. **Three gables, one atop another, add variety and style to the front of a vernacular house tucked into the mountains. Photo taken at A on floor plan.**

located in the core of the building where the four wings cross.

I designed the house around the 12-ft. square core. I wanted the house to step up gradually from each end of the four wings and reach the highest point directly over the core of the house where the wings intersect. The guest bedroom is stacked over the master bedroom, which forms a two-story mass on the east wing. Perpendicular to that wing, along the north/south axis, I added a two-story space for the foyer and the staircase to the second floor. Because the living room is the largest and most important space in the house, it is opened up as a two-story room with a second-floor balcony. When the one-story kitchen was added to the west wing, all the spaces Dick and Gee had asked for were in place. But something was missing.

If the gable roofs I had in mind were going to work, I had to resolve how they would come together. Because there are three different ridge heights, a cross-gable configuration wouldn't work. So I added a room the Mitchells didn't know they needed: a 12-ft. square, third-floor study over the core of the house. Perfect. Now the gables stepping up from below all stop at different levels against the four walls of the study.

The gable roof above the study culminates the sequence of roofs that start at the front porch (photo above), two floors below, and serves as a structure against which to end those roofs. The study also can act as a belvedere to vent hot air up and out of the house in the summer.

Opening up the interior with trusses—The only space in the house that needed to be more

Opening up the living room. The author designed 4-ft. wide bays that flank the east and west sides of the 12-ft. wide living room. The bays are framed with separate shed roofs. Photo taken at B on floor plan.

Gable overhangs.
The author
designed gable-
end truss details
at the overhangs
to echo the living-
room trusses.
Photo taken at D
on floor plan.

than 12 ft. wide was the living room, which would also be used as a dining area when the Mitchells had guests. A good-size dining table would be kept against one wall and moved out when family and friends came to visit. To get the additional space, I added 4-ft. wide, single-story bays to the east and west sides of the two-story living room. From the exterior, looking at the gable end of the living room, the bays would appear as small sheds on both sides of the room.

These flanking bays allowed me to do several things. First, I could lower the ceilings on both sides of the living room, creating intimate sitting and eating spaces. Second, in the eaves walls above the flanking bays, I could add clerestory windows that would fill the upper volume of the room with light.

Because the living room would be the focal point of the house, I decided to try something other than straightforward balloon-framed walls and a conventional stick-framed roof. Something more interesting was needed—something that might add another dimension to this little room.

I wanted to use 2x10 rafters to frame the shed roofs over both sides of the living room. (More on these oversized rafters later.) Normally these shed rafters would run from the outside wall of the bay, up to a beam inside the living room and stop there. I found that if these rafters didn't stop at the beam but were extended into the upper volume of the living room's two-story space (photo p. 35 and drawing facing page), a large, inverted V would be formed inside the room. The rafters meet at the center of the room, about 4½ ft. below the ridge beam of the roof above. What I had could become the two top chords of a roof truss if I added the chords at the bottom to span the 12-ft. wide space. To complete the truss, all I needed were king posts (vertical members running between top and bottom chords at the center of the truss).

Because the peak of this truss would be 4½ ft. below the ridge beam of the roof above, the king posts could extend above the top chords and help support this ridge beam. I had never seen this in a truss before, and it was something that led to the next set of decisions: what size members to use and how to connect them.

Holding it all together—Truss-joint connections made with bolted steel plates are expensive. I have used them before, and problems invariably crop up with misalignment, ugly welds, mismatched bolt holes and just generally poor craftsmanship. Without plates, I knew my best bet for both simplicity and beauty would be to frame the trusses with multiple 2x members that would overlap each other and be both nailed and bolted together at the intersections.

The living-room truss top chords are single 2x10s (drawing facing page). One 2x10 would extend from the shed-roof framing every 4 ft. through the living-room wall, into the upper volume of the living room and meet its counterpart from the opposite side at the center of the room. From this truss peak, I then dropped a 2x6 king post down between a pair of 2x8 bottom chords.

SPECS

Bedrooms: 2
Bathrooms: 2
Heating system:
Propane-fired hot air
Size: 1,448 sq. ft.
Cost: $89 per sq. ft.
Completed: 1992
Location: White
County, Georgia

*Photos taken at
lettered positions.*

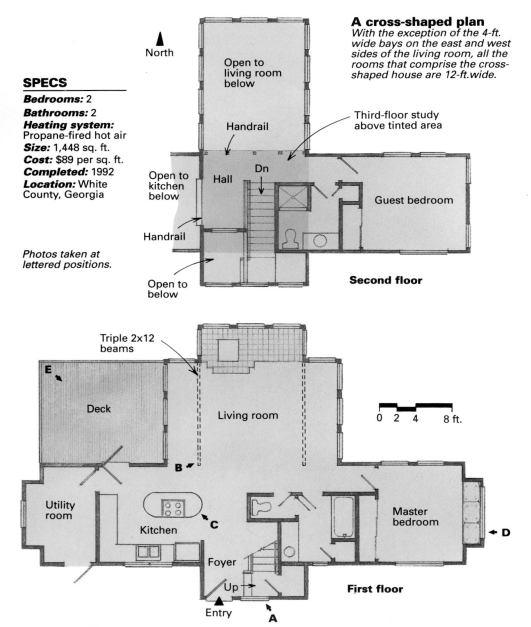

North

A cross-shaped plan
*With the exception of the 4-ft.
wide bays on the east and west
sides of the living room, all the
rooms that comprise the cross-
shaped house are 12-ft. wide.*

Open to
living room
below

Third-floor study
above tinted area

Handrail

Dn

Open to
kitchen
below

Hall

Guest bedroom

Handrail

Open to
below

Second floor

Triple 2x12
beams

E

Deck

Living room

0 2 4   8 ft.

B

Utility
room

Kitchen

C

Master
bedroom

D

Foyer

Up

Entry

A

First floor

Drawings: Gary Williamson

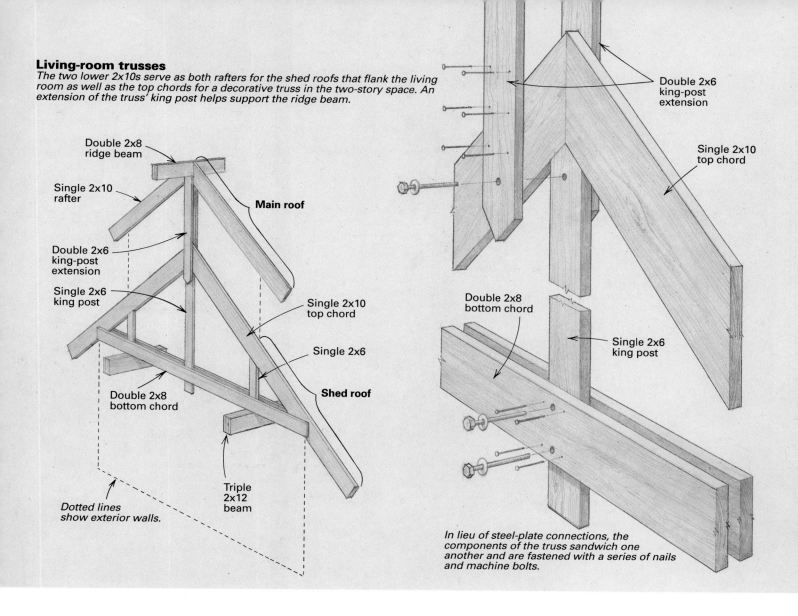

Living-room trusses
The two lower 2x10s serve as both rafters for the shed roofs that flank the living room as well as the top chords for a decorative truss in the two-story space. An extension of the truss' king post helps support the ridge beam.

Double 2x8 ridge beam

Single 2x10 rafter

Double 2x6 king-post extension

Single 2x6 king post

Double 2x8 bottom chord

Dotted lines show exterior walls.

Main roof

Single 2x10 top chord

Single 2x6

Shed roof

Triple 2x12 beam

Double 2x6 king-post extension

Single 2x10 top chord

Double 2x8 bottom chord

Single 2x6 king post

In lieu of steel-plate connections, the components of the truss sandwich one another and are fastened with a series of nails and machine bolts.

To extend this king post to support the ridge beam of the roof above, two 2x6s were lapped on each side of both the 2x10 top chords and the top of the single 2x6 king post below. From there, these two 2x6s were extended to sandwich each rafter pair of the roof above.

To complete the living-room roof framing, the bottom chords of the trusses rest on beams made of tripled 2x12s, which are exposed along the east and west sides of the living room. Visually the beams help delineate the space of the flanking bays. On one end of the room, the beams die into a wall, and on the other end they sit on posts made of a 2x4 nailed on each side of a 2x8.

The look of the exposed trusses was repeated in the kitchen (bottom photo, p. 38) by using doubled 2x8 tie beams 48 in. o. c. Single 2x6s were set vertically between the two 2x8s in the middle of the tie. The 2x6s were extended up to the ceiling where they were cut to fit under the intersection of the two rafters.

Large rafters and deep overhangs—From the beginning, I wanted the gable roofs to be the most prominent feature of the house. Deep overhangs emphasize these roofs and keep most of the rain off the wood walls below. In the summer, when the sun is at its highest, the overhangs

also shade the rooms from intense sunlight. The overhangs at the gable ends are supported either by cantilevered beams or by wall brackets built from multiple 2x members. At the peak of each 2-ft. gable overhang, small trusses were used both to stiffen this part of the roof and to echo the look of the living-room trusses (photo facing page).

Excluding the overhangs, the span of each of the numerous gable roofs on the house is only 12 ft. To frame these roofs, 2x6 rafters 24 in. o. c. would have been fine had I not wanted 3½-ft. overhangs.

I wanted to use 2x10, #2 southern yellow pine for the rafters for three reasons. First, the extra depth of the 2x10s (as opposed to 2x6s) adds stiffness to the overhangs. Second, more of each rafter is exposed below the fascia (top photo, p. 38), which calls attention to the roof edges and strengthens their emphasis as a decorative element. Third, 2x10 rafters would allow me to use 8-in. thick fiberglass batts to insulate the high ceiling areas. The actual width of a 2x10 is 9¼ in., which allows a 1¼-in. airspace above the insulation for ventilation of the roof framing.

These 2x10 rafters were way oversized for the living-room truss top chords, but that did not matter. I was using these trusses to make the living

room an exciting place, as well as to hold up the roof. The other truss chords in the house were deliberately oversized to be proportional to the 2x10s. This oversized stock also provided large areas for nail and bolt placement where the 2x members overlapped.

Galvanized metal roofing—Metal roofs can fool you. In the mountains of Georgia, all you see are barns and farmhouses covered with metal. Years ago these roofs were shiny silver, but they have started to rust and have turned a beautiful reddish brown. I wanted to use this material on the Mitchells' house to help give it a local character. What a great material! Farmers use it on their barns, so you think it must be cheap and easy to install. Wrong.

The galvanized steel roofing I was looking for is made by the Wheeling Corrugating Company (1134 Market St., Wheeling, W. Va. 26003; 304-234-2338) and produced in my area at Wheeling's Fort Payne, Alabama, mill.

The pattern is referred to as 5-V roofing because, you guessed it, there are five V-shaped bends in each piece. It is made in thicknesses of 29 ga., 30 ga. and 31 ga. and is available in almost any length. The 29-ga. roofing weighs only 77 lb. per square. Each sheet is 26 in. wide with

Oversized rafters. The 2x10 rafters cantilever 3½ ft. from the top plates of the walls. The long overhangs emphasize the multiple rooflines and shade the sidewalls during the summer. The galvanized metal roofing used on the house is similar to the material used on many of the local farm buildings. Photo taken at E on floor plan.

Continuing the look. In the kitchen, doubled 2x8s were used as tie beams. A vertical 2x6 is sandwiched between the 2x8s and is toenailed into the intersection of the rafters. Photo taken at C on floor plan.

two V-shaped ridges along each side and one in the middle. The roofing sheets overlap 2 in. per side, giving 24 in. of coverage per sheet. The sheets require a 6-in. end overlap between them. The 5-V roofing is attached to the roof deck with nails that have a vinyl gasket under the head. 5-V roofing can be cut using a circular saw with a steel-cutting or Carborundum blade.

Getting the metal roofing up and in place was more than the roofer had bargained for. In long lengths the material is flimsy at best. And in some places the roof was 40 ft. high. The first day saw metal roofing flying down the mountain in the wind. Calm, windless days were roofing days from there on. Because the roofing is installed vertically (rather than horizontally), staging made of roof brackets and planks would not have worked. To get the 5-V in place, a ladder was put on the roof, roped over the ridge and tied off on the other side of the house. The ladder then could be slid along the roof plane, from ridge to eaves, parallel to each new piece of 5-V.

In Atlanta, 5-V roofing costs approximately $34 per square; it's not cheap. And what you do not think about when you see barn roofs is that almost without exception, they are straight runs of metal covering large, simple surfaces. There are rarely hips, cheeks or sidewall flashings with which to contend. These details run the cost up even higher. Way up. Also, as one

roofer put it, "Don't forget, if a barn leaks, it's not the end of the world. Houses can't leak." Labor and flashing for the small, fairly complex roof of the Mitchells' house ran the cost up to $85 per square.

The cost may seem exorbitant, but you get a maintenance-free material that will last for at least 50 years. It is possible to paint 5-V with a galvanized primer and finish coats, but painting adds to the cost and eliminates the main advantage of using the material: If you just put the 5-V up and leave it alone, the roof will gradually weather from a bright silver to a dull gray, then it will gradually change to a rusty, reddish brown.

Roof vents and lightning rods—For the ridge vents, I wanted to use something that would really emphasize the ridges. More roofs—little ones this time—were set on top of the ridges and served as ridge vents. These vents are referred to as Boston ridge vents (see *FHB* #63, pp. 43-44). They were framed with 2-ft. 6-in. long 2x4s set on edge and nailed to 1x4 furring strips, which were, in turn, nailed to the roof deck. These ridge vents were held back 2 ft. from the end of the main roof to align with the exterior walls below.

Because the house is on a mountain and has a metal roof, the Mitchells were concerned about lightning. I had never used lightning rods and had no idea if they were needed. The National Fire Protection Association (NFPA, 1 Batterymarch Park, Quincy, Mass. 02269; 617-770-3000) has in its Lightning Protection Code, NFPA 78, a very helpful formula to determine the degree of risk. Numerical values are assigned to each of six different categories: structure type, construction type, relative location, topography, occupancy and contents. Lightning frequency also is measured numerically for different geographic zones of the country. Some best guessing is required for a few categories, but by plugging the numbers into the formula, I determined that lightning rods were needed.

To install the lightning rods, uninsulated braided cable conductors were run through the stud walls to connect the rods on the roof to a metal ground rod set in the earth. The ground rods, the cables and the roof-ridge saddles (the Y-shaped bracket that holds the rod to the roof) were installed by the electrician before the metal roofing went on. The roofing had to cover the saddle. The roofer, being the last man on the roof, then installed the lightning rods on top of the saddles and attached the ornament and red glass balls down over the rods. A rod was located on each end of each ridge vent. Material cost for the five rods, the cables and miscellaneous accessories came to $2,000. The hardware was manufactured by the Independent Protection Company, Inc. (P. O. Box 537, Goshen, Ind. 46527-0537; 219-533-4116) The lightning rods add a somewhat whimsical finishing touch to the roof. □

John Phelps is a principal of Phelps & Sullivan Architects, Inc., in Atlanta, Ga. Photographs by Jefferson Kolle.

Louisiana Country House

Behind the traditional façade is an uncommon tribute to the sun, the river and the site's first inhabitants

by Errol Barron

Like most house projects, this one began with a particular site. It is a ten-acre stretch of land along the banks of the Little Bogue Falaya, a slow-moving tributary of the Bogue, which flows into Lake Ponchartrain north of New Orleans. This river was well known by my client and college friend George Riser, who had frequently walked along its banks near his first house in Covington, Louisiana. Riser spent his free time studying local plants and birds near the river. His purchase of this familiar territory along the Little Bogue, as the locals call it, was inspired by its isolation, its dense and varied foliage and by its known association with an ancient Indian culture. But Riser did not have any inkling of what a house built here might look like, where it would stand in relation to the river, or what he would discover during its construction.

Building a house always begins with an idea of change in both a piece of land and a person's life. Often, in a commercial architecture practice, it is difficult to work in such a personal manner as one does when designing houses. But working with Riser, I saw again how, much more than shelter, a new house promises a new setting, new views, more space, and offers a chance to give shape to the owner's—and the architect's—views of life and to the spirit of a site.

Riser wanted an efficient house of about 2,500 sq. ft. that would suit his needs as a collector of artifacts and an avid observer of nature. It was important that the house have a variety of outdoor spaces—high, low, screened and open. The living room had to be large enough to host the monthly meeting of the Covington Book Club, whose most well-known member is writer Walker Percy. And Riser especially wanted more light than he had in his present house.

While a new house offers opportunities for experimentation and innovation, it must also acknowledge the deep and inescapable past of its predecessors. Individual houses are not really new but are part of an unbroken chain of building ideas that are as old as the materials used to express them. Both Riser and I were

The public face of this Louisiana house takes its side-facing gable, "tin" roof, and high-roofed porch from local folk houses. The sketch below shows the two-part design as a rectangle facing north and a sun-tracking semicircle facing south. The blue arrow indicates a pool and the pink circle marks the fireplace.

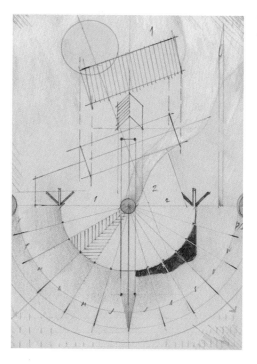

aware of the stylistic demands of an area like southern Louisiana.

Choosing the right spot—Our first step, picking the precise location for the house, took a long time. After wandering over the site for almost a year, Riser kept returning to the same ridge, a small piece of high ground projecting like a nose toward the river and overlooking two ponds. He did not know until later that he was following the same maneuver that the site's original occupants must have taken centuries before. After Riser chose the ridge, he invited me to to walk with him and sketch the site to get a feel for the topography. I, too, became enthusiastic about the ridge for its year-round views of the ponds and winter view of the river, and for its wildlife and the multitude of trees, including pines on the ridge; live oaks, beeches and hickories near the river; and a 40-in. dia. *magnolia grandiflora*, the largest we've seen in the wild.

Not long after our walk, I gave George two books I admire. One was *The Place of Houses* by Charles Moore, Gerald Allen and Donlyn Lyndon, and the other was Christopher Alexander's *A Pattern Language*. Riser read the books with complete fascination. From the first book, we worked out a program of services needed, spaces to provide and how they would be arranged. The simple and accessible logic of Alexander's book was immensely appealing to Riser and he read enthusiastically. Meanwhile, I sketched out the first attempts to submit the forces of the site to geometry.

A two-faced scheme—I immediately divided the house into two parts. As I sketched out the environmental influences of the site, I found that the compass points and movement of the sun coincided with the best views. The ridge runs north/south, so an east-west half circle drawn on the site would begin with the rising sun to the east and would move clockwise past a pond to the southeast, the river due south, another pond to the southwest and finally end with the evening sun (drawing left).

To claim the ridge from nature, the forceful gesture of a circle seemed necessary, almost

Half the south-facing semicircle is the living room (photo above). Small windows allow light and views to other rooms. The house has a variety of outdoor spaces, including a large screened porch, a quarter-circle terrace and a roof deck (from which the photo below was taken). The mildew on top of the curved, stuccoed-concrete beam prevails on many surfaces in this damp environment. Markings in the terrace imitate designs found on 1,500-year-old pottery dug up on site during excavation.

like driving in stakes for a campsite tent. I defined the half circle with columns, and assigned the principal public spaces of the house to this area. A traditional rectangle would make up the other part of the house facing the driveway to the north. Remaining rooms would go into the rectangle, which we saw as the more conventional, less aggressive space.

With *A Pattern Language* by his side, Riser experimented with this plan and sent me many overlays. I began to fear, however, that unbridled experimentation with too many patterns would weaken the design and destroy our original concept. So we staked out the plan on the ground, both agreeing quickly that the simple, original composition fit the site well.

As we finally built the house, the one-story half circle contains indoor and outdoor living rooms and the two-story rectangle contains the more private domestic spaces of kitchen, bathrooms, bedrooms and study (floor plans, facing page). The major axis of the half circle is rigorously lined up with the compass points, but the rectangle tilts off axis to line up with the driveway. A wedge makes up the difference between the two shapes. It contains a stair, a dining room and a screened porch facing south and west.

We called the front part of the house "generic" because it imitates in a general way the traditional forms of local architecture: boxy shape, tall porch, front steps and gable roof (photo previous page). We called the rear a sundial because its geometry and its 12 columns are based on the movement of the sun. A hall divides the half circle into two exact quarter circles spaced about 6 ft. apart; the 12 columns throw a powerful pattern of shadows into the spaces they encircle.

Half of the sundial is the terrace, an outside living room that overlooks the hillside and the river. I liked the idea that the contours of the ridge might become part of the composition, so I heightened this effect by stepping the terrace down with concrete risers and filling the treads with earth and plants (bottom left photo).

To stabilize this assembly of parts, we positioned a fireplace almost at the center of the half circle, which also makes it the focus of the quarter-circle living room (top photo). Inside the house, the rooms are organized about a spine, a long hall that is aligned with the rear part of the house but that begins just inside the front door. When you enter the house, you quickly realize that the rest of the house is nothing like the front: the floor tile isn't aligned with the door and the hall/spine takes off at an angle to the entry hall. This is the first clue that something is not quite normal.

A look down the entry hall, which abuts the fireplace, reveals an exterior pool that drains due south down the hillside (bottom photo, p. 43). The source of its water is a 1,400-ft. deep artesian well that produces clear water at a constant 70°. The well water is cycled through a heat pump to provide both heating and cooling. We were intrigued by the notion of giving the natural elements of fire and water prominent positions in the plan and liked the

Bottom drawing: Errol Barron and Stephen Monette

Second-floor plan

11. Study
12. Open to below
13. Master bedroom
14. Roof deck

1. Entry hall
2. Kitchen
3. Dining
4. Living room
5. Hall
6. Pool
7. Terrace
8. Screened porch
9. Sitting alcove
10. Guest bedroom
11. Study
12. Open to below
13. Master bedroom
14. Roof deck

First-floor plan

North

0 4 8   16 ft.

View of pond
View of river
View of pond

**Bird's-eye view
from the southwest**

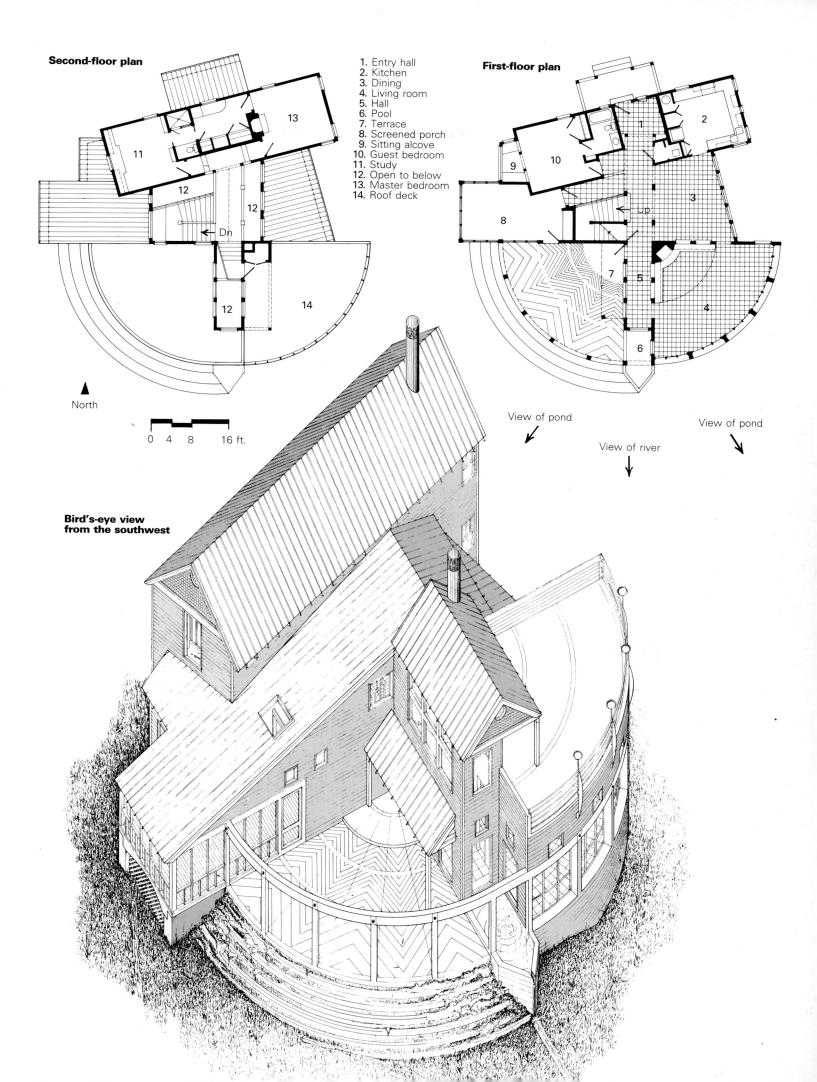

romantic idea of heat rising and the well penetrating the earth.

Digging footings, finding history—The only given for the house was that the floor be above the flood plain, which was 25 ft. above the river. Since an interstate was built several miles south, forming a kind of monumental dam, the natural drainage of rivers and runoff to Lake Ponchartrain has been reduced. Shortly before beginning construction on the house, Riser visited the site after a major storm and discovered that only the tip of the ridge was uncovered by water. We would have to bring in fill to raise the level of the entire house.

Based on the recommendations of friends, Riser selected Balanced Builders from Bush, Louisiana, to construct the house. Partners Steve Owens and Buddy Weaver tried to sub out as little as possible, preferring instead to build the house from foundation to finish. Rather than begin laying out the house with a transit, we started in a more primitive fashion, with a pocket compass. It was important that the semicircle have a true east-west axis. Owens felt that the legs of a compass were too short for staking this axis, and as construction began around the summer solstice, he set stakes during sunrise and sunset to mark the rising and setting of the sun. He pulled a string between the stakes and set his compass at the middle of the string. The line lay east/west.

As excavation began, my earlier campsite analogy turned out to be more than idle musing. One day after a rainstorm, Weaver was clearing the site in preparation for digging footings and saw a fragment of an arrowhead at his feet. Riser had heard that banks of the Little Bogue had been part of a hunting ground for early Indians, but the number of pottery shards and arrowheads that turned up so surprised him that he shut the project down for further examination. For two months, Riser and professional archaeologists from several universities carefully excavated the site, which yielded several hundred shards of pottery, many with a distinctive line-filled triangle pattern, as well as 75 to 100 stone tools and arrowheads. Riser, who has since become an established avocational archaeologist, is still cataloging these objects.

The site hadn't been a permanent one for the early Indians, so contained no burial grounds, but from the 4th to the 7th centuries it had been an intermittent camp for Indians fishing and hunting along the river. In those days, the river ran closer to the house site, where its relic channels, now the two oxbow ponds, lie. We found satisfaction that the instinctive pull toward this site as a place to inhabit was the same today as it had been so long ago. This invested the house with a palpable sense of history.

A raised slab—When digging for relics was complete, digging for the house began. We knew that the first floor would be entirely finished with Mexican tile, and felt that a raised slab would make a stable, moisture-proof base. Wood-framed floors over crawl spaces in the south frequently have condensation problems, which can cause problems for tile floors.

To build the foundation, Owens and two other masons built what is locally called a chain wall, a reinforced concrete block wall with a concrete-block bond beam on top. The lower courses of block are 12-in. thick, but to provide adequate bearing width for the 5-in. thick reinforced concrete slab, the top course of block is 8-in. wide. Because of the sloping site, the chain wall varied from 3 ft. to 5 ft. tall and it took more than 400 yd. of fill to bring the grade to the level of the slab. The slab is supported by block piers and exterior and interior walls but not actually by the earth, which was compacted just enough to act as formwork for the bottom of the slab.

To ensure a steady reference point for building the two curved quarter circles, Owens had cast a 22-ft. long 2-in. dia. steel pipe in concrete at each radius point and marked lines by means of a fine steel cable looped around the pipe. The 12 columns at the perimeter of the circles were built from concrete block topped with a cast-concrete beam. Columns and beam were parged for uniformity of color and texture.

Practical details fit the ideal—In a house concerned with geometry and symbols, there remained practical questions of what materials to use. To simplify what we felt might become a somewhat raucous composition, we decided to use the humble Louisiana tin roof (this roof is actually ribbed 24-ga. galvanized steel) and to sheath the entire house in traditional wood clapboards, called weatherboards in these parts. To withstand the fiery sun and pervasive damp, we used clear heart redwood clapboards and to avoid splitting, which redwood is prone to, we drilled the ends of the clapboards before nailing them. Traditionally, cypress would have been the norm, but good cypress is gone now, and the "growback" cypress available today tends to split badly during installation and to cup and warp afterwards.

Riser preferred stain to paint, so we primed the clapboards front and back with stain before installation and stained them after they were in place. To reproduce the look of a traditional bleaching oil mixed with creosote (creosote is no longer on the market because of its toxicity), we used two different layers of Cabot stain: the first, a grey-white called Seagull; the second, a light grey called Driftwood. This gave the clapboards a weathered look that came close to the color of light pine bark. The fir window and door trim was painted white and the undersides

The dining room is part of the wedge that fits between the semicircular rear of the house and the rectangular front. Natural materials, such the Mexican tile and beaded pine ceiling, are a warm contrast to the cool plaster-coated drywall and white-painted window frames and sash.

of rafters and decking were painted a light blue, the color used on many soffits in the south because its similarity to the color of the sky discourages mud daubers seeking protected nesting places. No matter what finish you use in the damp Louisiana woods, however, the exterior woodwork will mildew. Only yearly washings with bleach will keep a house clear of mildew.

Although we chose major materials early, we also chose not to overplan. We left the actual species of woods and types of finishes unspecified because I have found that the decisions arising during construction are some of the most magical ones. As a house goes up, the owner sees how the house will actually look, and he is able to make decisions he couldn't earlier. We all made an agreement early in construction that we would weigh three factors before making each decision: practicality, economics and aesthetics.

One serendipitous change to the materials came about as the siding was going up. On a site visit I noticed patterned shingles in the gables. "This wasn't on the drawings," I said to Owens. He smiled and told me it was a nice detail he'd seen on many houses in the region. All I could do was agree—it *was* nice and it fit the house well.

On the generic side of the house we used double-hung windows with simple divided-light patterns in the upper sash (Marvin Windows, Warroad, Minn. 56763). Balanced Builders made the remainder of the windows on site, including the many small fixed-glass windows and the large fixed and casement windows in the curved living-room wall. Before Owens and Weaver built the windows, however, Riser and I spent considerable time looking at elevations and selecting the exact locations and sizes of the windows. The small windows served two purposes. One was to break up the expanse of the elevations both inside and out (photo facing page) and the other was to allow glimpses of light and foliage from the inside and to capture the changing patterns of the sun as it moves around the house. Riser kept telling me that these windows were unnecessary but I kept lobbying until he eventually gave in, probably from exhaustion. He is happy now that he did.

Where the budget allowed, we used local wood inside. Owens and Weaver built the stair, upstairs floor and the beaded dining-room ceiling out of humble Southern yellow pine, which I had thought would be painted until I saw the quality of the wood after it was sanded and varnished, and after the balustrade, treads and thresholds were pegged with mahogany (top photo). Building the stairs, windows and doors for this house inspired Owens and Weaver to add a full-fledged millwork shop to their business.

The drywall was finished with a skim coat of plaster. Its cool white color was selected as a contrast to the wildly colorful wooded site, but in the generic portion of the house we painted the walls a warm, glowing peach.

One detail we did have pinned down from the beginning was the Mexican tile floor

A Southern yellow pine staircase with mahogany pegs and rail leads to the master bedroom, at left in the photo above, and the roof deck. A view from the front door (photo right) ends at a pool of artesian-well water that drains down the south slope to the river.

(photo facing page). The secret to success with such a soft tile is in cleaning and finishing it. Muriatic acid can soften Mexican tile, so Weaver cleaned the tile with a mild cleaner made especially for Mexican tile and finished it with a clear penetrating sealer. The subtle finish gives the smooth, unglazed tile an association with the earth below it.

To honor the Indians who had been there first, the slab-on-grade terrace is scored to match the patterns on the pottery fragments unearthed during the excavation for the foundations. To give it a handmade look as on the pottery, Owens scratched the pattern into the setting concrete with a stick. □

Errol Barron is an architect in New Orleans, Louisiana, and teaches at Tulane University.

Simplicity with Style

A hillside house and a realistic budget combine visual drama with a basic floor plan

by Duo Dickinson

It's easy to throw money and space at design problems. Many architects do that on the drawing board, and projects end up staying projects and never getting built, as budgets are left in the dust. It's only by being responsive to the client's needs and the site's characteristics that an architect or builder does his job at the highest level of skill and integrity. Designing and building a custom home means encountering unpredictable problems. But if you can keep your head about you, those problems can be turned around to serve the

needs of your clients, and occasionally, the art of architecture.

Multiple uses—The people who contacted me one winter afternoon in 1986 wanted to build a second home on a small plot of land facing a lake in New Jersey. Not an unusual proposition, but these were not typical clients. The soon-to-be-retired couple wanted a house for the summer months, while their son, a busy New York litigator, desperately wanted a year-round weekend getaway. Although nei-

ther party alone could afford a second home, a partnership arrangement could bring them what they wanted.

A previous hip injury to one of the parents mandated an easy-access, self-sufficient suite at street level, but with minimal openings to the street. The son needed his own bath and accommodations separate from the rest of the house. The budget dictated that everyone share the kitchen and laundry. Both parties wanted a separate guest suite for relatives and friends. Overriding all of these requirements was the

Photo: Otto Baitz

desire for a minimum-maintenance house. And of course, everyone wanted water views.

A year-long design process followed. My sketches and crude models were gradually replaced by detailed drawings and a relatively precise model. It would take between 2,000 and 2,500 sq. ft. to meet everyone's needs. With basic construction costs in the northeast U. S. of nearly $100 per square foot, we assumed that we could build this house for about $200,000—if we were clever.

A difficult site—The main stumbling block was the site's steep slope. The lot was problematic at best, and potentially unbuildable given the budget. Setback requirements limited the buildable area to a 40-ft. by 40-ft. rectangle. The site also dropped a full 18 ft. over that area. This one-quarter acre lot in a district zoned for one-acre sites meant that we were "grandfathered" on a site that didn't comply with the present code. And the local zoning code permitted a height of only 35 feet. Fortunately, in-street sewers, water and power were accessible; otherwise there would have been little chance of getting water in and waste out of such a steep, impermeable site.

The big view—Beyond its aggressive slope, the site's most impressive aspect was the large lake it addressed. The slope faced due west, limiting the chance for passive-solar gain. But given the particular occupancy requirements, this was not a major drawback.

A simple siting move greatly enhanced our opportunities for catching the big view. On my first visit to the site, in winter when the trees were leafless, I saw that by twisting the house orientation by about 15° (as opposed to paralleling the lot lines), we could look right up the "throat" of the lake, which would more than double the view of the water. But this move would further tighten the available area of buildable land.

Flexibility—Some architects might cringe at such limitations; but the success of this project shows that tight siting conditions, limited budgets and oddball owner requirements need not create the legendary budget-busting, schedule-voiding, aesthetic-stomping results. There is one simple solution, and it's not the quality of the architecture or drawings: a good builder is the key. Our builder, Doug Raymond of D&J Construction, was the hero of this job. His constant can-do enthusiasm was a crucial factor in the success of the project.

What makes a "good" builder in a project such as this? It can be summed up in one word: flexibility. It's tough enough to build an architect-designed home for one set of clients with a generous budget on a benign site. Building a nontraditional house for nontraditional clients on a nontraditional site is quite another matter. Broad shoulders are needed to respond to the inevitable design changes. In fact, several changes in the scope of work made the construction schedule extraordinarily tight. A small crew could have built the

Floor plan

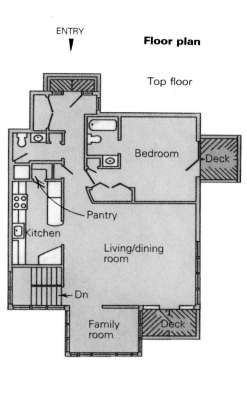

Top floor

ENTRY

Bedroom

Deck

Pantry

Kitchen

Living/dining room

Dn

Family room

Deck

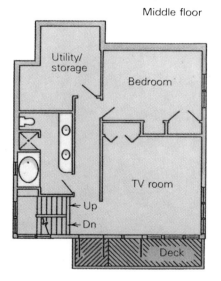

Middle floor

Utility/ storage

Bedroom

TV room

Up

Dn

Deck

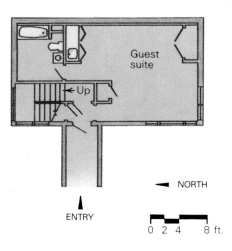

Lower floor

Guest suite

Up

NORTH

ENTRY

0 2 4 8 ft.

original house design in six to eight months. The final design ended up taking the better part of nine months.

A simple box—The basic house requirements and budget were best served by a three-story house descending the hillside (photo facing page). We minimized the construction costs by designing the house as a simple box, and gained visual appeal and better views via the simple "tack-ons" of a family room and three decks. The top floor would be completely above grade and would include the parents' suite and the common areas. The middle level was given over to the son, and the lowest level became the guest suite (floor plan, left).

Large rock out-croppings had originally—and wrongly—led us to believe that ledge was close to the surface. In fact the biggest change in the project's scope came with the happy discovery that ledge did not kick in until a full level below the uppermost finished grade. The design needed to change to allow the middle floor to back into the hillside, all the way to the site's east setback limits. This move let me add a middle-floor TV room in which son and parents could gather, as well as a storage room. Only the guest suite—already half-buried three feet below finish grade to satisfy the zoning's vertical limit—was now limited in depth by the existing ledge. To incorporate the changes, I had to do a quick and complete redesign for client review, then get the information to the builder and the local building department. Though it is always easier to make a house larger than smaller, the added space did squeeze the budget.

House upon a house—The house's most prominent feature is its cantilevered family room. Aesthetically, this attached form is a house upon a house. Functionally, its popped-off space separates a casual use from the more formal living area. Experientially, its three exposed sides give a feeling of being nestled amid the leaves of the trees, with a visual focus across the lake.

How did we build it? Simple wood framing could not tolerate the load of a 10-ft. cantilever without some type of stiffening or support. In the neighborhood, we saw many spindly two-story columns, most out of plumb, some bowed and post-braced with diagonal struts. Erosion had built up the lower levels of these steeply sloped sites, and some columns were being buried in the rising "tide" of finish grade. Not surprisingly, their bases showed signs of rot or rust.

So without columns, the question was how to stiffen such a large cantilever. Knee braces work well, but we wanted a deck below the family room. Hanging the structure from the roof or wall with steel cables or tie rods would present problems also. We wanted a tall, open space behind the wall that the room was attached to, so creating enough structure to provide support for a hung solution would be quite expensive. And because we would need to attach diagonal hangers as close to the out-

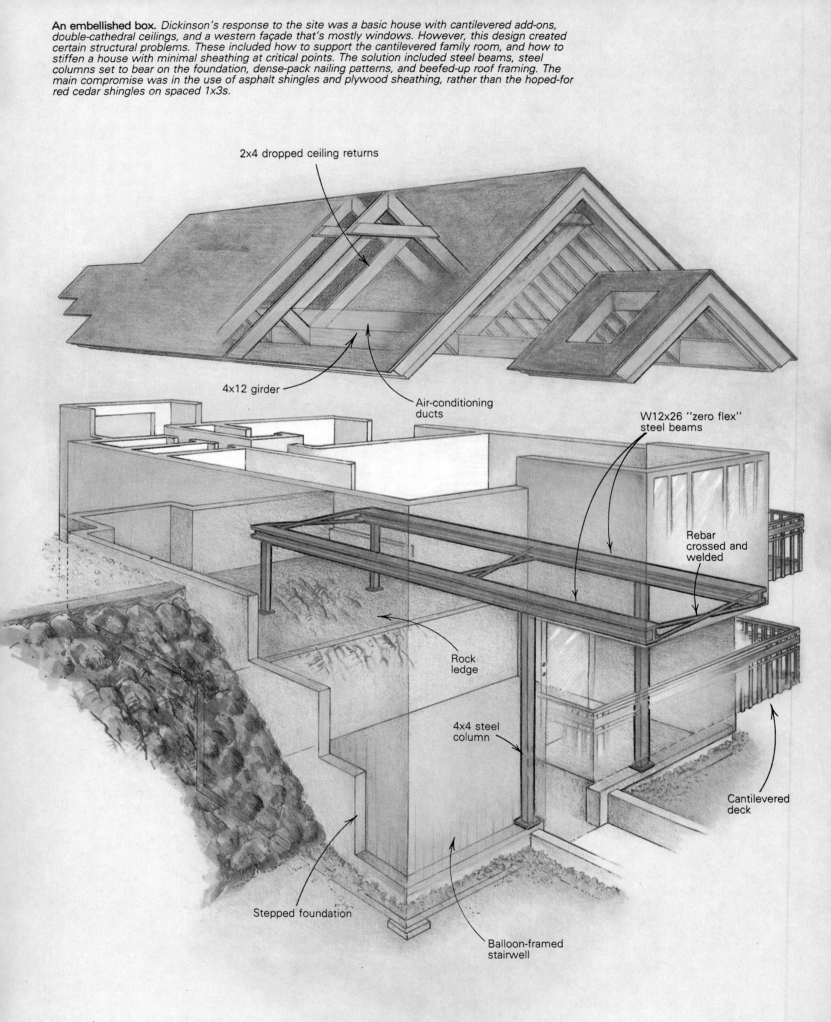

An embellished box. *Dickinson's response to the site was a basic house with cantilevered add-ons, double-cathedral ceilings, and a western façade that's mostly windows. However, this design created certain structural problems. These included how to support the cantilevered family room, and how to stiffen a house with minimal sheathing at critical points. The solution included steel beams, steel columns set to bear on the foundation, dense-pack nailing patterns, and beefed-up roof framing. The main compromise was in the use of asphalt shingles and plywood sheathing, rather than the hoped-for red cedar shingles on spaced 1x3s.*

2x4 dropped ceiling returns

4x12 girder

Air-conditioning ducts

W12x26 "zero flex" steel beams

Rebar crossed and welded

Rock ledge

4x4 steel column

Cantilevered deck

Stepped foundation

Balloon-framed stairwell

ermost corner of the cantilever as possible, they would cut across the flanking windows of the extended space.

In the end, we chose a conceptually simple design—a straightforward cantilever supported by steel beams (drawing facing page). Because of the significant structural loads generated at the spring point of the cantilever, we used steel columns there and ran them down through two stories to bear on the foundation.

We used an even simpler secondary set of cantilevers to frame two of the house's three decks, designing the floor framing to project beyond the exterior wall and to bear on a dropped header. This guaranteed that our decks would not obstruct views from the floors below. These continuous cantilevered joists had to be pressure-treated lumber to prevent rot and decay. But we wanted the cantilevered joists for the middle floor deck to bear all the way back on the lower foundation wall—a total span of 20 ft.

Around here, pressure-treated Southern yellow pine can only be easily found in up to 18-ft. lengths. Our solution was to buy untreated 20-ft. 2x10s and send them out ourselves for treatment. This cost more, but it was covered in Raymond's original price—and the service was available through the local lumberyard supplier.

Simple cantilevers are very easy to frame and are maintenance-free if done properly. It's important to design the interior side of the cantilever to resist upward thrust. On a simple extended joist cantilever, I use prefabricated steel joist hangers, with one installed normally to handle downward loading, and a second installed with the bottom side up to resist upward pressure. These decks were cantilevered out 5 ft. When exceeding that length, I narrow the joist spacing from 16 in. to 12 in. and/or increase the size of the joists from 2x10 to 2x12.

Water infiltration is another concern with cantilevered framing. In this house, a strip of flashing extends from behind the siding out over the deck framing. In addition, the place where each joist penetrated the exterior wall was sealed with silicone caulk.

Designing for stiffness—Another prominent feature of the house was the space we created in the top-level common areas. We wanted a completely open wall with enough

Dropped ceiling returns created two ceiling peaks and provided an overhead chase for air-conditioning ducts. Despite the lofty ceiling, the floor plan is fairly compact; efficiency dictates the use of small spaces.

The use of simple cabinetry contained costs in the kitchen and baths. The angled tops of the cabinets match the pitch of the cathedral ceilings. The kitchen borrows its view from the stairwell.

windows to catch the big view, as well as a column-free top floor with a cathedral ceiling.

This presented another structural dilemma. Windows preempt sheathing and the stiffness it affords, so the problem was how to have stiff corners *and* large, wraparound windows. We stiffened our roof and gable wall in three ways. First, we used "dense-pack" (6 in. o. c. into the framing) nailing patterns around the windows and the corners of the roof facing

the lake. We were especially concerned with the stairwell, which is essentially a balloon-framed corner of an otherwise platform-framed house (drawing facing page). After our engineer, Martin Gehner of Branford, Connecticut, reviewed the plans, we eliminated one window from the stairwell glazing. This added some sheathing, and thus some stiffness, at the joint between the gable wall and the cantilevered family room.

To further stiffen the structure, we attached collar ties about halfway up our simple gable-roof framing, one per set of rafters. Finally, we used dropped ceiling returns to create two ceiling peaks within the overall roof form (top photo, left). In addition to creating a visually active ceilingscape, the additional framing stiffens the roof and limits the volume of interior air, reducing the cost of heating and cooling. And hiding the collar ties greatly simplified the ceiling drywall work. The dropped ceiling also created a small attic space over the kitchen side of the house (bottom photo, left), which serves as a mechanical chase for the top floor's air-conditioning ducts.

Catching the view—I specified stock Marvin units for about 90% of the windows. In response to the large westerly view, however, we wanted clerestory fixed windows above these stock units. These windows needed to "touch" the ceilingscape and to match the angled ceiling planes. I specified custom Marvin units. To ensure a perfect fit, we asked Raymond to make full-size plywood templates of the window openings after the rough framing was complete. The clients and I also wanted to make the stair into a view platform, so we treated the windows as a wall of glass coursing down the angle of the stair (photo p. 48).

In a three-story house, the stairs had best be nice or you'll resent every level change. In addition to its function as a link between the three suites, we designed this stairway as a place for a great view of the lake. The foot of the stair begins five feet from a doorway that leads to grade. This design permits direct lake access, keeping most of the level change within the building.

With all of this glass, you might ask, what visually connects the various window and door units and accommodates the fancy framing? Trim, inside and out. Consistent trim widths and detailing visually fuse the separate units into large patterns. All trim completely spans the individual windows and doors it connects. This many wall openings could have degenerated into chaotic, competing groups; instead, they form a simple, coherent design.

Spending where it counts—Although cost was a paramount concern, I reminded my clients that there are two types of costs—long-term and short-term. Spending a little more up front can greatly lower the long-term maintenance costs. For the long term, we used materials whose surface was more than skin deep, such as clear, rot-resistant woods. The siding is 6-in. clear T&G red cedar, run vertically. Red cedar shingles on the cantilevered family room form a visual counterpart to the siding. All exterior trim is clear redwood. Deck rails and decking are clear cedar, which though still naturally rot-resistant, is less expensive than redwood.

All exterior wood was finished with clear wood preservative. Unlike cedar shingles, vertical siding does not allow for a "self-draining," non-coated solution. But if it's recoated every three to five years, the siding should last the life of the house. Without a preservative, some form of solar or bacterial decay would ultimately stress the exterior skin to the point of failure.

Although we originally specified red cedar roof shingles, which if properly installed last upwards of 50 years versus the 25-year lifespan of asphalt, the need for roof stiffening meant that we couldn't use the 1x3 wood sheathing required for proper ventilation of wood shingles. For strength, we used plywood sheathing with dense-pack nailing and asphalt shingles.

We used zero-maintenance stucco at the peak of the gable because of the difficulty of reaching the 30-ft. high gable wall from the steeply sloped site around the house. Even though the rake boards and eaves in that area will need periodic maintenance, I feared that the joint between the family-room roof and upper gable wall would suffer the most abuse, and would thus need the most maintenance.

The site is landscaped with perennial plantings and stone berms, so there's no need to mow or garden. I had hoped to avoid gutters (as they need continual maintenance) but the run-off from the eaves was simply uncontrollable, creating little raging rivers during rainstorms. So we were forced to add gutters and leaders set to splash blocks, which directed the torrent away from the house. Chalk that up to a necessary compromise.

And so it goes on a custom-designed job. Engaged clients have legitimate input, ethical architects offer suggestions and respond to the client, and open-minded builders coordinate and respond to an ever-changing scope of work.

Interior finishes—All common areas have 2½-in. red oak flooring with a three-coat clear urethane finish. Walls and ceilings are painted ½-in. drywall. In the baths and kitchen, we used stock tile and simple custom plastic-lami-

Stepping down. The wall of glass at the balloon-framed stairwell seems to follow the angle of the stair. The stairway links the three levels of the house and provides a great view of the lake.

nate cabinets (bottom photo, p. 47).

On the top two floors, we grouped the rooms around a central hallway, rather than running a hallway down one side. This let each square foot of circulation space perform double duty. Efficiency also dictated a kitchen pantry for high-density storage, a stacked washer and dryer, and a fairly precise use of minimally sized areas, such as the breakfast counter in the kitchen (top photo, p. 47).

Four heat zones allow for localized heating and cooling. Air-locks with double doors at each entry mitigate air infiltration. Insulation includes a layer of 1-in. rigid urethane foam under all cathedral-ceiling surfaces and plenty of fiberglass in the roof, including in the dropped ceilings. In addition there are R-19 fiberglass batts in the walls. The significant percentage of half-buried and buried space further increases the structure's thermal efficiency. Skylights and south-facing glass in the living room and bedroom provide at least some afternoon passive-solar gain, though the bulk of the glazing faces west.

No cracks, one regret—In any house that steps down a hill and uses a variety of structural systems (steel and wood, balloon-framing and platform-framing), there is always a danger of uneven settling or movement. But there have been only a few hairline drywall cracks caused by the normal shrinkage of the wood framing. There have been no leaks, and no signs of settlement. Three laminated cabinet doors have warped, but an extra hinge pulled them back flat.

Any regrets? One. In striving to contain costs and guarantee a relatively seamless Corian kitchen countertop, I specified a separate sink rather than an integral unit. The separate sink did save a few hundred dollars, and because Corian sink units are made in different lots at the factory they seldom form a perfect color match with the stock counter pieces. Unfortunately, this command decision was the wrong one; a grime-collecting seam formed around the sink, and the owners eventually replaced it with an integrated Corian unit. I ate this cost, as no one (including me) remembered if I had given the clients the option of eliminating this high-maintenance item by spending more and having a potential color mismatch.

Flexibility is the key to the custom-building process, whether that means a whole floor redesign due to subsoil conditions or a revision of the sink specs. □

Duo Dickinson has his own architecture firm in Madison, Connecticut, and occasionally teaches at Yale and Roger Williams College.

Natural Selections

A house in North Carolina borrows shapes, colors and details from the landscape

by Kim Tanzer

Before our clients Bob and Mary Peet had even begun to search for an architect of their new house, they had chosen a site and selected a landscape architect. This sequence gave the architecture firm I worked for, Dail Dixon Associates in Chapel Hill, North Carolina, a sense of the importance they placed on the land. From design to construction, we studied the language of forms found on the site and tried to translate that language into the design of the house itself.

Bob and Mary Peet's narrow two-acre site is part of a mature forest, with access through a small subdivision on the eastern edge. A few house lots border north and south, and a ridge runs the length of the site from east to west, ending in a wooded knoll (bottom drawing, next page). From this knoll the land gently tumbles downhill west and northwest toward a distant stream. In this zone of modest drama is a grove of mature white oak trees, which mask the border between the Peets' property and the thousands of acres of Duke Forest, a perpetually protected property.

Living next to Duke Forest is important to the Peets. In an area growing as rapidly as that

The hip roof and hip skirt of the house imitate both the terrain and the vernacular houses of the area. Corrugated fiberglass covers the roof of the pressure-treated walkway that runs from the garage to the front door. Standard cedar lap siding, asphalt shingles and manufactured windows kept costs down during a building boom.

around Research Triangle Park in central North Carolina, a permanently protected natural edge is as comforting as it is rare. And both Bob and Mary are professional botanists who look at the forest not only as a beautiful view, but as a laboratory.

Through his relationship with "his trees" we quickly came to understand Bob's enthusiasm and precision. After receiving the initial survey, which showed the diameter of each tree to the nearest two inches, Bob resurveyed, noting diameters to the nearest hundredth of an inch. He also marked through trees that he felt were unimportant, despite their size. Like most professionals, Bob and Mary are both more precise and less romantic about botany than an amateur might be.

The Peets are exceptionally articulate and methodical. They questioned our decisions and researched alternatives. At first, Dail and I found this difficult, but as we became more comfortable working with the Peets, we came to respect and even anticipate their intense interest in details. Bob and Mary, on the other hand, became more and more willing to trust our judgment, especially once the house was under construction.

Respect for the terrain— The most prominent feature on the site was the wooded knoll, and it seemed obvious to Dail and me to place the house on it. But Jock Wick, the landscape architect hired by the Peets, had a better idea. He suggested that rather than obliterate the knoll by placing the house on it, a more subtle approach would be to tuck the house beneath the "brow of the hill," as Frank Lloyd Wright might have done. Our rule, then, was to put architectural elements near, not over, important site features. Wick also suggested that major interior spaces step diagonally down the hill to relate to the view of the oak grove, and that the south wall of the house form part of an outdoor room. We kept this in mind as we worked out the design.

During schematic design, Wick had to give up his position as landscape architect of the Peet house so we helped Bob and Mary select a second firm, Hunter-Reynolds-Jewell, from Raleigh. By the time Sam Reynolds and his colleague Jory Johnson were hired, we had almost finished working drawings. It was difficult for them to come into the project after most major decisions were made, yet they were able to carry out the fine-tuning that the project required. Reynolds and Johnson carefully adjusted the placement of the house within the area specified by Wick, moving a layout stake ever so slightly to frame a view of a particular tree through a window or to allow another tree to soften a corner of the house. They also suggested we twist the garage away from the house to open a view of the entrance from the drive (photo, previous page).

Whereas Dail and I spent most of our design time in the office working with new forms,

the landscape architects initially spent most of their time on the site, working with existing physical features. I found their hands-on approach to laying out the driveway interesting. They knew the drive would run roughly along the ridge, and they walked back and forth with Bob, looking for a path that would minimize tree-cutting. As they refined the route, Reynolds noted several site features he hoped would enhance the path. A small knoll to the left of the drive became an initial point of focus for cars turning in and could be highlighted with bulbs

and wildflowers. A cluster of sourwood trees leaned over the path, providing a sense of enclosure. And nearer the house, a gnarled hickory tree bent over the drive, forming a gateway to the entry garden. Selective clearing and planting around these elements was the only landscape design intervention needed here.

The owners speak—Earlier, we had looked through house-design magazines with the Peets to discover their reactions to styles, colors, window types and details. We found, for instance,

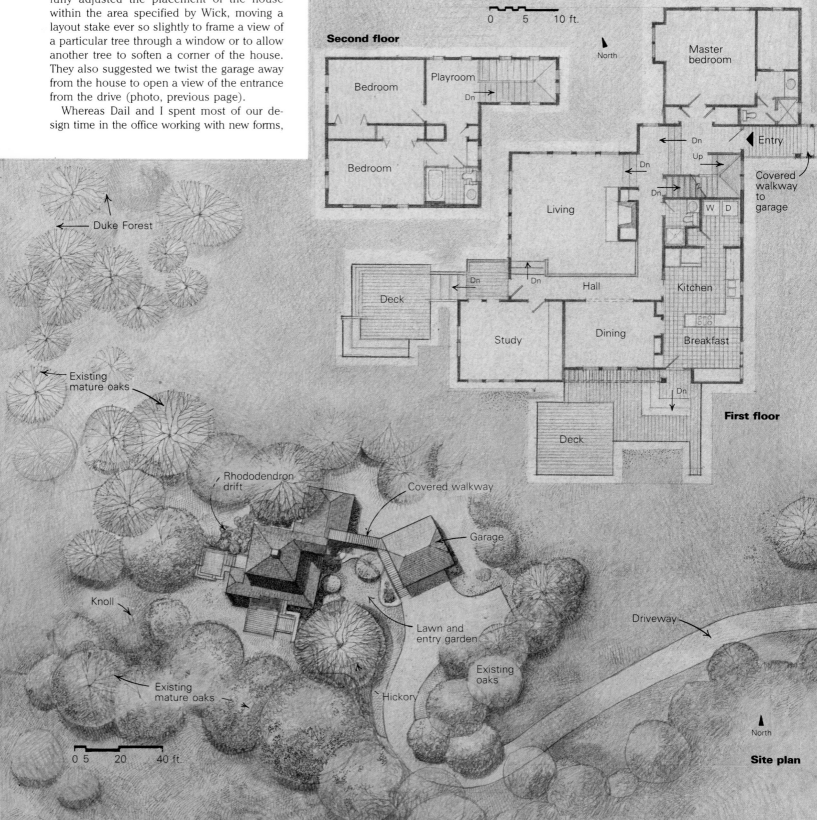

0   5   10 ft.

Second floor

North

Master bedroom

Bedroom
Playroom
Dn

Bedroom

Dn   Entry
Up
Dn
Covered walkway to garage

Living
W   D

Dn
Dn
Hall
Kitchen

Deck

Study
Dining
Breakfast

Deck
Dn

First floor

← Duke Forest

← Existing mature oaks

Rhododendron drift
Covered walkway

Garage

Knoll

Existing mature oaks
Lawn and entry garden

Existing oaks

Driveway

Hickory

North

Site plan

0 5   20   40 ft.

that Bob didn't like floor-length windows and that Mary liked low-maintenance plumbing fixtures, such as self-rimming sinks and brushed metal fittings that don't show spots. One of our most helpful design tools was a seven-page program statement that Bob wrote. Whenever he thinks about house plans, he said, he first considers the orientation of the rooms and what he will see from the windows. Bob viewed the study as perhaps the most important room in the house, and it had to have views of the forest. It would be a library, studio and laboratory for two, inspired by Bob's memory of a photograph of Darwin's study, where there was plenty of room to spread papers, pile books and accumulate specimens.

The program statement gave Bob and Mary a voice in absentia. We read it through many times and tried to accommodate as many preferences as possible. For example, we felt the living room should be about 11 ft. tall to feel comfortable, but because of Bob's dislike of tall rooms, we ran trim around the room at 9 ft. across the window heads. This visually reduced

the room's height, and to accentuate this, we lowered the soffit over the hall (photo below).

From our discussions, we discovered that Bob didn't like to see roofs below when looking out windows. But we felt that for the house to sit comfortably in the land, the central two-story space should be hugged by one-story rooms. Our solution was to place small square windows high in the upstairs rooms (photo p. 49). The view out is to the tree canopy above, not the roofs below. These high windows also allow privacy upstairs.

Imitating the landscape—The Piedmont region of North Carolina is a romantic landscape, with changing views and varied lines of sight. The sky is partially obscured by trees and land forms. The ground is varied and discontinuous. Geologically, the Piedmont is a region of old mountains weathered into gently rounded hills, with dense foliage and rocky outcroppings. We wanted to imitate this land mass with the building's mass, to suggest that in some way it had been formed by the same agents.

We also wanted to borrow from the spatial qualities and textures of the forest. Duke Forest is largely deciduous with several layers of plant life. The highest layer (60 ft. to 80 ft. tall) is a canopy of oaks, hickories and pines. Next is an understory of dogwoods and sourwoods (15 ft. to 25 ft. tall). Lowest is a shrub and groundcover layer. The highest point of the house is the chimney, which caps the central hip roof. In the same way that the land cascades away from the knoll, shed roofs fall from the hip-roof form, ending in hipped gables over the study and master bedroom. We thought that hipped gables on the lower levels and the garage would better imitate the roundness of the landscape than gabled ends would. We did use an "uneroded" gable on the stair tower to provide a sense of openness for the entrance (photo p. 49).

We also tried to imitate the textures of the forest—the filigree of branches, leaves, light and shadow. Rather than imitate nature literally, as in Art Nouveau architecture, where handrails and window mullions may look like vines, we

A band of trim 9 ft. above the floor serves to case window heads and to lower the apparent height of the living room. The large windows bring the view of the forest inside. The view is filtered by divided lights above and by the balustrade around the elevated hall.

wanted to abstract certain characteristics of the landscape and use them to guide our decisions about proportions, scale, shape and complexity. Decks are placed unobtrusively on the ground like so many fallen leaves, and the dining-room roof overhang is cut away to make a trellis, like the lacework of the branches overhead (photo left).

We wanted the act of walking through the house to be like walking in the forest. As you walk in these woods, you move gently up and down, stepping to one side or the other, looking ahead through the trees, then close to the ground, then far to the sky. There appear to be no clear paths, so that the act of negotiating, of finding a foothold here or catching a view there, becomes a dance with the landscape.

To bring this experience inside, we provided contrasting paths, places and views instead of long halls, symmetrical axes and grand vistas. We made the living room the center of the house and wrapped a hall and all other spaces along two sides of it (floor plans p. 50). The living room is located to the northwest so you can look from any space on the first floor through the living room to the oaks and forest beyond. The windows are so large that the oak grove feels almost like part of the room. The study, with its sloping ceiling, bookshelves, and private entry, feels secluded, like a den in the woods. The dining room, which is open on one side to the hall and living room, and on the other to the southern woods, filters sun and shade (bottom photo). To break up views both inside and out, we used divided lights in the exterior windows of the living room, a railing between hall and kitchen, and framed openings to the hall from the surrounding rooms.

Making the most of colors and patterns found in the forest, split-faced concrete block imitates stone, pressure-treated decks are placed on the ground and step unobtrusively to the leaf-covered forest floor, and the roof over the dining room is cut away to make a trellis that catches the sun.

Interior colors that come from nature add warmth to the moderate use of natural materials, such as the oak rail, cedar soffit, oak flooring and stone fireplace (photo below). The living-room palette, for example, was chosen from colors found in a piece of bark, the green dining room from the color on the underside of a new maple leaf, and the yellow kitchen from a fallen birch leaf (photo right).

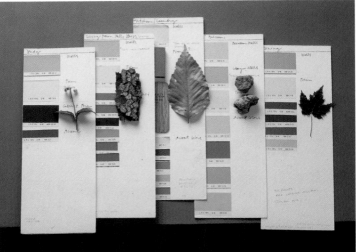

Juggling details—After the Peets approved our schematic design, we added another member to our team, builder George Cole. Cole gave us a rough estimate on the schematic drawings and was able to help with design not only as a builder but as a detail designer as well. Our discussions with Cole ranged from the cost per linear foot of a particular trim profile to its ability to visually "hold the corner" of a wall.

In 1986, when we were designing the Peet house, local residential building costs were taking off. For several other residential projects we found that a builder's final bid could run as much as 30% higher than his preliminary cost estimate, due to the inflation of bids from subcontractors and suppliers who had more business than they could handle. To avoid surprises later, we tried to control cost through design.

First, we designed a scheme that could be built in phases but that would look complete at any stage. The garage, entry trellis, two exterior decks, and landscaping were independent units that could be added as money be-

came available. Although these features would be important to the integration of the house with the site, we hoped the placement and massing of the house would make a good beginning. Fortunately, we didn't have to test this assumption because the Peets found the resources to pay for the complete project. George Cole and his crew completed the house, while builders Lewis Caraganis and Dave Tompkins built the garage, covered walkway and terrace.

Our second means of minimizing the impact of inflation was to make the house easy to build using the standard North Carolina building vocabulary. We used a conventional concrete-block foundation, 2x4 wood framing and common materials, such as 1x6 lapped cedar siding with 5/4 trim, asphalt shingles, drywall, standard windows and doors, and standard cabinet details.

Where we modified these conventions, we did so cautiously but, we hoped, in significant places. For example, the interior trim on the first floor is built up of standard molding sections arranged in a slightly off-standard way. We used a backband as a cap for 1x6 casing at each door head, uncapped 1x4 casing at the jambs, and more backband to cap the 1x6 base. The balustrade has a stained-oak rail and painted 2x2 balusters. A painted 2x2 crosspiece fits between every other spindle, forming squares where the balustrade runs horizontally (photo right). This square is repeated in the shape of most single windows and in the divided lights over the picture windows in the living room.

Rather than cover the rafter tails with fascia and finish off the overhang with a soffit—the way most builders finish houses around here—we left the rafter tails exposed and painted them (top photo, facing page). Cole cut standard soffit-type vents in short strips and fit them in the frieze board between the rafter tails.

Because each of us involved with this house respected the other's expertise, we were less defensive about our own skills. For example, Sam Reynolds expressed concern about choosing plant materials for two botanists. He came to see that while Bob and Mary had a more complete scientific understanding of the taxonomy, habitats and diseases of plants, he knew better how to design with plants. Often, Reynolds would describe in general terms the plants he had in mind and what purpose he saw for them in the design, but he would leave the final selections to the botanists and to Southern Green, the landscape contractor from Chapel Hill.

Colors from nature—Our final round of decision-making was to choose colors. The practical problem we faced was a familiar one. We needed to incorporate the earthy colors of some of the Peets' furniture and to consider Bob's interest in primary colors, yet we wanted to move beyond their existing color palette. Rather than select colors from paint chips, we looked for colors found in the site itself.

I collected a variety of rocks, bark and leaves, identified the individual colors that

Both painted and natural wood meet at the stair. A simple balustrade is made up of an oak rail and painted 2x2-stock balusters and crosspieces. Backband caps the 1x6 base.

made up each each object and matched those colors with paint chips and material samples (middle photo, facing page). To our delight, we found that nature combines colors in ways that are both wildly imaginative and wonderfully compatible. We proposed to the Peets that since these colors worked together on the site, they would work together inside the house. We identified each palette with a room or group of rooms based on existing furniture, on the mood we hoped the room would convey, and on the availability of the finishes. Bob and Mary appreciated the subtlety of the colors and the method of selection and, with a few revisions, approved our finish schedule.

Kitchen finishes are based on the colors of a fallen beech leaf, with taupe quarry tile and beige grout, off-white trim and Corian countertops, stained golden-oak cabinets,

and light, bright-yellow walls. We followed the colors found on the underside of a new maple leaf for the dining-room palette, with muted gray-green walls, dusty white trim and burgundy accents (bottom photo, facing page). And the living room, the L-shaped hall and the children's playroom draw colors from a chunk of beautiful silvery-beige bark with rust highlights. As the Peets buy new furniture and art, and eventually repaint or recarpet, they can refer both to the color palettes devised for the house and, of course, to the landscape itself. □

Kim Tanzer is an assistant professor of architecture at the University of Florida in Gainesville. She was a project architect with Dail Dixon Associates in Chapel Hill, North Carolina. Photos by Jerry Markatos.

A House Among the Oaks

A carpenter turned designer plans a house with simplified construction details in mind

by Greg Belt

The trees dominate the house, not vice versa. The author didn't want to design a house that would overwhelm the land. In the center, the common rooms are fronted by a long porch. The guest rooms are across the breezeway to the left. Photo taken at A on floor plan.

I was a carpenter long before I designed my first house. And now, although I have had formal training in architecture, I still approach many aspects of a project from a carpenter's point of view. Having spent ten years in restoration and renovation work makes it difficult for me to look at design solely in the abstract. As I design something, I imagine myself building it.

For this reason, materials that are unpleasant to work with or a building process that seems unduly complicated will literally send me back to the drawing board. If a building detail calls for a tool or a skill that is unlikely to be available on a typical construction site, I think more evaluation of the plan is in order. A detail might well be worth some extra trouble, but if a simpler approach can accomplish the same thing, I view that as a superior answer.

These biases were reinforced several years ago when I designed and built a home for my parents. Their land is in the foothills of the San Rafael mountains in California's central coast area. The house sits at the upper end of a small valley that is shaded by a handful of ancient oak trees (photo above) and sheltered by two north-south ridges. Unlike many of their neighbors, whose houses look across at each other from their hilltop sites, my parents decided to build in a valley and have their views look down the valley and up at the hills. My parents' site doesn't feel the brunt of the wind that the houses on the hilltop experience, but the greatest attribute of their site is the intimate scale of the valley and its oak trees.

My job was to create, at a reasonable cost, a habitat that would be in harmony with the valley. Throughout the design I tried to be led by simplicity. I sought solutions that could be built in a straightforward and economical manner but that would still capitalize on the beauty of the building material and the technique of construction. High priority also was given to long-term ease of maintenance and to passive provisions for light, heating and cooling.

The house comprises three sections— My first concerns with the site had to do with the sheer physical mass of the house. There was a danger of a large building dominating both the oak trees and the natural topography of the little valley. My design strategy was to divide the house into smaller elements—a compound of connected structures—according to their use and purpose (photo facing page). The reduced scale of the separate pieces helps to fit the house in among the oaks, and the division of the home allows the natural axis of the valley to continue through the house more freely than a more consolidated plan would have allowed. Further, the separate pieces could vary in foundation height to follow the contour of the land better.

The logical division that evolved separated the home into three parts (drawing facing page). The first and smallest provides guest accommodations and is located on the west side of the valley next to the driveway. Two mirror-image guest rooms are separate from the main house and

Photos this page, facing page: Earl Richmond

Building the house in three parts reduced its mass. In the foreground, separated by the broad stair, are the two guest rooms. The middle section, capped by a clerestory, holds the living room, kitchen and gallery. Behind that is the owners' bedroom suite and library. Photo taken at B on floor plan.

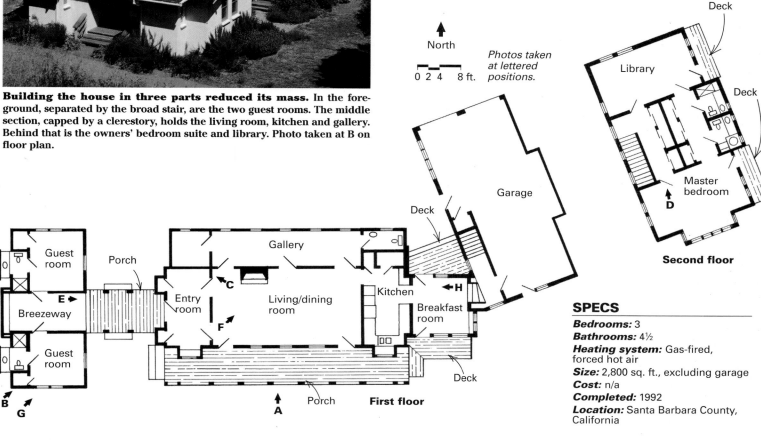

Separate parts have different uses

To reduce the mass of the house, the author separated it into three parts. The common areas of the house are sandwiched between the guest rooms and the owners' rooms. Separate wings afford privacy to the owners and their guests. The owners' rooms, with a garage below, are set at an angle to the rest of the house and are built into the hill to accommodate the valley's slope.

North

0 2 4 8 ft.

Photos taken at lettered positions.

Deck

Library

Deck

Master bedroom

D

Second floor

Garage

Deck

Guest room

Porch

Gallery

Entry room

C

Living/dining room

Kitchen

H

Breakfast room

E

Breezeway

F

Guest room

Deck

B   G

A   Porch   **First floor**

Deck

SPECS

Bedrooms: 3
Bathrooms: 4½
Heating system: Gas-fired, forced hot air
Size: 2,800 sq. ft., excluding garage
Cost: n/a
Completed: 1992
Location: Santa Barbara County, California

separate from each other. The rooms share a common roof, but they are separated by a breezeway that leads from the front door (photo p. 56) to the driveway, making it a convenient location for unloading and loading baggage.

Separating the guest rooms from the main house serves other purposes besides scaling down the mass of the house. It affords visitors privacy from the rest of the home. Also, because each room has a separate space heater and hot-water circulating pump, those utilities can be supplied to the rooms on an as-needed basis.

The second, central part of the house is the ceremonial section. It consists of an entry room; a tall main room for living, dining and entertaining; and the kitchen and breakfast room (bottom photo, p. 59) at the far eastern end. Aside from the door between the kitchen and dining room, all the interior doors are topped with transoms to link the spaces visually.

This tall, central section of the house is capped with a clerestory and flanked by two lower side

aisles, the north one enclosed into the gallery and the south one open to form the front porch.

The third part of the home, to the east, is the only part that is a full two stories high. To diminish the impact of its height, this section is half-sunken into the side of the hill. The first floor, one wall of which is an 8-ft. retaining wall, serves as the garage with storage and work space. The upper floor provides library and living quarters for the owners. The sunlight and views down valley are given to the master bedroom, whereas the northern light at the upper-valley end serves the library. Between the library and the bedroom is a core area of closets (bottom photo, p. 57) and bathrooms. Both bedroom and library open to private decks on the hillside to the east.

Exposed trusses have multiple benefits—To open and enrich the interior spaces of the house, I used exposed, site-built roof trusses throughout. Aside from the obvious engineering benefits of the trusses—they hold the house together—there

are aesthetic benefits that can be appreciated on a couple of levels. My hopes were that a person seeing the trusses could appreciate them for their structural beauty, the same way you might find beauty in a suspension bridge. On another level, the Douglas fir and the hardware used to make the trusses also have a beauty of their own (photo p. 58).

Opening up the roofs with exposed trusses also provided opportunities for venting the living areas. In combination with operable transom windows above the interior and exterior doors, the high awning windows in the clerestory and the venting skylights in the master-bedroom wing allow summer heat to move toward the roof ridge and out of the house.

The details of the roofing connections were kept straightforward and consistent. As a designer I considered steel trusses or timber-framed trusses, but the carpenter in me opted for dimension lumber with bolted connections. The design of this truss system was influenced by a

Butted trim is made by alternating thick and thinner components. The shadowlines created by butting ⅝-in. thick trim (above), such as the baseboards and side casings, into ¾-in. thick pieces, such as the plinths and baseboard corner blocks, mask any imperfections in the joinery. Photo taken at C on floor plan.

A core area of closets separates the master bedroom from the library. Shoji-screen type closet doors (right) slide on tracks. Operable transoms above all the interior doors add to the passive ventilation in the house. Photo taken at D on floor plan.

Roof trusses support the breezeway. The trusses that are above the breezeway (facing page) between the guest rooms and the front door have similar details to those inside, but they are smaller in scale. To reduce the height of its roof, the breezeway steps down from the guest rooms. Photo taken at E on floor plan.

similar system written up in *Fine Homebuilding* (*FHB* #6, pp. 18-21). Four-by rafters, ridge beams and king posts are connected by prefabricated steel brackets and through-bolted. Two 2x collar ties then embrace the rafters and king posts of each rafter bay, one on each side, and are bolted through as well.

Using the steel brackets allowed a structurally engineered connection of uniform and completely predictable appearance to be easily achieved in every part of the home. These same details were used outside in the breezeway. The truss details also influenced the design of the fly rafters, which are the overhanging rafters on the gable ends.

Decks and porches are transitions from the outside—My parents are avid gardeners and bird watchers. Weather permitting, they spend much of their time outdoors. Almost 1,000 sq. ft. of decks and porches are incorporated into the house. All but one of the exterior doors open either onto a deck or a porch.

To enter the house, you step from a gravel path onto a 4x12 cedar step, then up onto cedar decking and finally up one more step into the house. In this rustic setting this sequence helps to keep some dirt outside, but it also helps to soften the abrupt change of environment from the natural to the manmade.

The heavy cedar steps are fastened with ½-in. anchor bolts that are set into a concrete footing. Steel spacers ⅜ in. thick were used under the step at each connection to allow the wood to dry. Once the footings were in place, the making of these steps was simple and relatively foolproof. If one of the steps ever rots, replacement will be simple.

The details for the railing across the front porch and along the breezeway between the guest rooms and the front door were created to highlight the materials as well as the system of construction. I wanted a railing that would be comfortable enough for people to sit on, and at the same time it had to be light enough in form not to block the view down the valley. Last, I wanted to use standard-dimension lumber and keep all joints simple to make and self-draining.

Curved stucco eliminates exterior casings, thus reducing exterior maintenance—My parents wanted a structure that didn't require much maintenance. Outside, we chose stucco for its fire resistance, its capacity for integral coloration and its plasticity. By wrapping the stucco into a bullnose at the door and window openings, we could eliminate most exterior trim (top photo, p. 59). This detail saves material and labor initially, but it also saves the future maintenance of all that trim.

The bullnose was accomplished by setting windows and doors with 2x4 jambs into thicker 2x6 exterior walls. The 2-in. difference between the jambs and the studs gave me room for the bullnose. I cut a plywood template to the radius of the curve into the jambs and gave it to the plasterers who applied the stucco.

Expansion joints in stucco are not a requirement for residential construction in California,

A large room fills the middle section of the house. The horizontal band of trim at the height of the transoms' head casings lowers the eye to the living area. The clerestory above evacuates hot air and lets light into the room. The frosted-glass door beyond the dining area screens the kitchen. Photo taken at F on floor plan.

at least not yet. But I used the expansion joints with the hope that they would minimize the initial cracking that always occurs in stucco walls. I also hoped they would reduce rupture cracking due to earthquakes.

Since the house was built, we have had several small quakes. There have been no rupture cracks, but there is really no way of telling whether the expansion joints have helped. Still, they cannot hurt. Aside from their structural benefits, I think the joints in the stucco created by the expansion joints serve as an attractive visual break on the otherwise planar surface of the exterior walls.

Butt-jointed interior trim is quick to install—All the interior trim, including the doors, jambs and transoms, is vertical-grain Douglas fir. As with many of the details in the house, I was after ease and speed of installation as well as simplicity of line and joinery. Using trim of different thicknesses was the answer to all requirements.

I ordered trim stock in two thicknesses: ⅝ in. and ¾ in. The trim is applied in a sequence of alternating thicknesses: Each piece of ⅝-in. trim is sandwiched between pieces of ¾-in. trim (top photo, p. 57). If you picture a cased door with baseboards running to both sides along the floor, the sequence of thicknesses runs like this: ⅝-in. thick baseboard butts into ¾-in. thick plinth. From there, a ⅝-in. vertical flat casing runs up the side of the door to a ¾-in. head casing. In the inside corners, the ⅝-in. baseboards butt into ¾-in. corner blocks with the top end grain relieved in a 45° bevel.

The beauty of alternating thicknesses is that all the joints between pieces can be butt joints. The shadowline formed by the thicker piece next to the thinner piece masks any slight imperfections there might be in the joint

All the trim stock was prefinished in natural Watco oil, then cut to length. We used a router table on site to ease the newly cut edges of the thicker members and to chamfer the top edges of the plinths and corner blocks. While the trim was going up, I asked everyone to follow a consistent nail pattern. When we were finished, the nail holes were left unfilled. The deliberate pattern of the nails throughout adds to the appearance of the trim work whereas random, patternless nailing would have appeared unfinished. □

Greg Belt is a designer and general contractor in Lompoc, Calif. Photos by Jefferson Kolle except where noted.

Stucco with expansion joints curves into the windows. To reduce exterior maintenance, window casings are eliminated by curving the stucco into the window jambs. Although not required by residential building codes, the author opted for expansion joints in the stucco. The joints serve as a visual break to otherwise flat walls. Photo taken at G on floor plan.

A half-wall blocks the counters from the breakfast table. The cabinets are trimmed with fir accent strips to match the rest of the wood. To the left of the table, a small deck gets morning light. Photo taken at H on floor plan.

A Contemporary Farmhouse

Complex shapes, unusual materials and a surprising color scheme enliven this house in the Sierra Nevada foothills

by Charles Miller

Tree-top view. *The presentation drawing of the Coverts' house shows the distinct elements of the rural compound and how they are joined. At the left, a classic farmhouse with a wraparound porch faces west. This part of the house, which contains the kitchen, the family room and the master bedroom, is connected at the entry to the barnlike bedroom wing. At the far east end, a shed roof covers the garage and the carport. The many trees on the site made the triangular sunscreen over the living-room window unnecessary.*

Builder Jake Covert remembers well the first time he worked with architect Cathi House. She had designed a large, formal residence to be built in Hillsborough, California, an affluent suburb south of San Francisco, and Jake won the contract to build it. While studying the foundation plans, he fixed his eyes upon the dimensions that showed the distance between the stemwalls. They were detailed to ⅛ in. Jake was a seasoned builder and had never seen such specifications. So he called the architect and asked why on earth the footings had to adhere to such tight tolerances. House met him at the site and walked him through the logic of it, explaining that the house was designed on unit modules that included ⅝-in. drywall and precisely cut tiles and stone. Making sure the foundations were on the money would make it easier for contractor and subcontractors alike.

Satisfied that this architect knew what she was talking about, Jake faithfully executed the plans. The parts fit together as expected, and the house eventually was given the grand award for best custom home in its class of 1989 at the National Association of Home Builders convention.

Many houses later—Fed up with the congestion and the pollution of the Bay Area (and with the endless hours it takes to satisfy the clients of a custom builder), Jake decided to make a change of scene and career. He and his wife, K. C., bought a wooded lot in the northern California foothills of Nevada City. But before he got out of the business entirely, Jake wanted to build his own house. Who should design it?

By now Jake had built a half dozen projects designed by House + House, the San Francisco architectural firm piloted by Cathi House and her husband, Steven. Jake had seen firsthand the interaction between the architects and their clients. He liked the way they could satisfy the obvious requirements of the project while addressing the not-so-obvious ones. By unanimous vote, the Coverts commissioned House + House to design their home.

Asked what special requirements the Coverts brought to the table, Cathi shrugs and says, "For the most part, everybody has the same list. They need a kitchen, a dining room, a place for the family to gather, and bedrooms and bathrooms. What's harder to do is to make a house that satisfies their unspoken needs." The key to that, of course, is getting to know the clients.

The Coverts are informal people who appreciate serenity. They like to have their Bay Area friends come and stay the weekend. Jake is also an accomplished finish carpenter, and he takes pride in finely wrought details. These factors played important roles in shaping their house.

Designed to ramble—While considering the informal part of the equation, Cathi settled upon the idea of creating a fictional compound of rural buildings that had been connected gradually over the years into a rambling house (drawing facing page). Houses that grow in such an unplanned fashion often are more satisfying than those that appear to be more methodical, for the same reason Fenway Park is a lot more interesting than Riverfront Stadium.

At the west end of the Covert house is a classic New England farmhouse with a wraparound porch (floor plan below). At one end the ground floor has an inglenook for a woodstove and a couple of chairs. At the other end is the essential space for a family that likes to entertain—a big kitchen (top photo, p. 64) with lots of windows that overlook the surrounding forest and plenty of counters on which to prepare food and to lean against. The master bedroom (left and top right photos, p. 62) is over the kitchen.

The living room/bedroom wing of the house is in a simpler, gabled piece of the building designed to look as though it might have once been a barn. It is intersected by a steep (18-in-12) gable roof that creates dramatic spaces upstairs for Jake's office and daughter Katie's bedroom. Son Schuyler gets around with the help of a wheelchair, so his room is on the ground floor—which is on the same level as the adjacent decks, porches and paved floors of the garage and the carport. A shed roof off the north side of the house covers the garage and the carport and carries on the theme of the ever-expanding farm buildings.

The farmhouse wing and the living-room/bedroom wings of the house are not perpendicular to one another—rather they are 15° off square. The wings are joined by a two-story flat-roofed link that serves as the formal entry on the ground floor (top left photo, p. 63) and as K. C.'s sitting room on the second floor (drawing p. 62). The off-square intersection of the two wings is very apparent in the exposed framing in the entry (middle right photo, p. 62). Cathi says the topography of the site leant itself to placing the two wings at odd angles to one another. But then she quickly adds, "Almost all of our houses have a similar break from perpendicular in them. It makes for surprising spaces that become special because they are unusual. If the site hadn't presented the 15° angle, I would have found some other reason for it to be there."

Local color—When Cathi visits a site for the first time, she brings a shopping bag. As she studies the terrain, she collects twigs, leaves, lichens, flowers, rocks, bark and a sample of the topsoil. She puts the specimens in the bag, tags the bag accordingly and sets the collection aside for later reference to help develop a color scheme.

Each part of the house has its own cladding to distinguish it from the others, but the materials are closely related to keep the compositions visually bound. For example, the farmhouse wing is covered with smooth 1x4 redwood siding, and the barn is finished with rough-sawn red cedar 1x10s. The tower that flanks the entry is covered with rough-sawn cedar 1x4s and 1x10s, providing a visual transition between the entry and the tower (drawing p. 63). The chimneys and the generous expanse of sidewalls are finished with corrugated galvanized sheet metal (bottom right photo, p. 63)—the kind typically used for barn roofs. When used as siding, this material has chameleonlike qualities. In raking light it sets up a visual pattern akin to vertical venetian blinds. In diffuse light galvanized siding becomes a soft mirror that reflects the colors of the surrounding landscape (bottom left photo, p. 63).

Once the finish materials have been selected and the orders placed, samples can be put on the table. Cathi then retreats to the quiet of her office conference room, puts on some soothing music and spreads out the contents of the

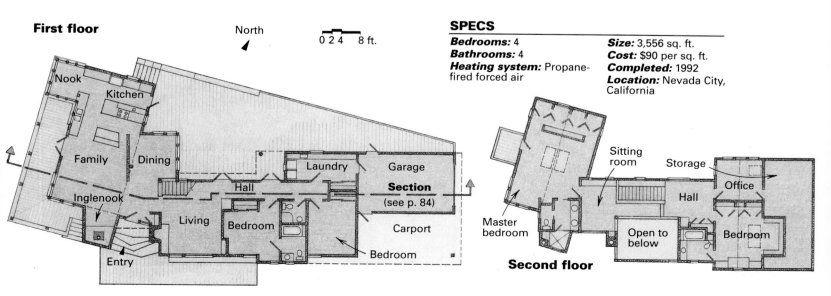

First floor

North

0 2 4 8 ft.

Nook
Kitchen
Family
Dining
Inglenook
Living
Bedroom
Laundry
Hall
Garage
Section
(see p. 84)
Carport
Bedroom
Entry

SPECS

Bedrooms: 4
Bathrooms: 4
Heating system: Propane-fired forced air

Size: 3,556 sq. ft.
Cost: $90 per sq. ft.
Completed: 1992
Location: Nevada City, California

Sitting room
Storage
Office
Master bedroom
Hall
Open to below
Bedroom

Second floor

Drawings this page: Vince Babak

A freestanding headboard screens the closet in the master bedroom.

Behind the headboard.

Exposed framing in the entry.

Suspended stairway.

Inside, pattern and light. *Closet, shelves, a vanity and banks of drawers are concealed behind the freestanding headboard in the master bedroom. The doors on the left lead to* *a tiny deck over the wraparound porch. In the entry, bold patterns of floor joists and beams define the off-square confluence of the two wings of the house.*

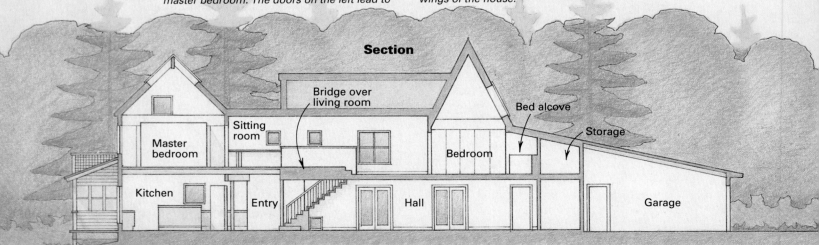

Section

Master bedroom

Sitting room

Bridge over living room

Bed alcove

Storage

Bedroom

Kitchen

Entry

Hall

Garage

Drawings this page and facing page: Vince Babak

A chimney flanks the flat-roofed entry.

Deck living on the backside.

Rough-sawn siding meets metal.

Massive trim in bold colors.

Delicate framing over the porch.

Familiar shapes, surprising siding. *A flat-roofed, two-story box connects the two wings of the house. It's mostly glass, framed with teal-colored boards and a cranberry door. The cedar siding is stained a mossy green to tie it to the local landscape while the softly reflective corrugated metal siding changes colors and pattern as the light changes throughout the day.*

Elevation

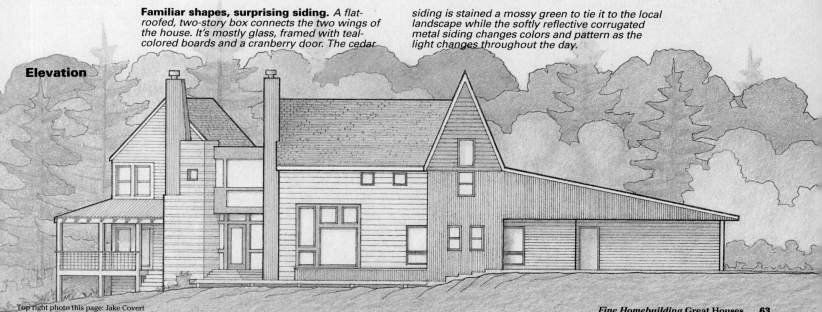

Counters everywhere. A broad counter between the stove and the refrigerator makes a handy place to stage ingredients. Separate counters for cleanup, prep and making espresso keep congestion to a minimum. The light-filled nook in the far corner holds the breakfast table.

shopping bag. She makes up paint samples that match the colors of the site from a well-stocked library of watercolor, acrylic and latex paints.

The sea-foam greens of the lichens and the moss and the burgundy red of manzanita bark were the most exciting colors to emerge from the bag. Cathi applied the colors in a number of ways. For example, the rough-sawn cedar siding is tinted green with Olympic Smoke Blue #908 semitransparent stain (PPG Architectural Finishes, One PPG Place, Pittsburgh, Pa. 15272; 800-235-5020).

The kitchen cabinets are colored with a glaze of green latex paint over vertical-grain Douglas fir plywood (bottom photo, this page). The painter, Vern Olson, mixed the paint in a one-to-one ratio with Floetrol, a paint conditioner typically used to minimize brush strokes (The Flood Co., P. O. Box 399, Hudson, Ohio 44236; 800-356-6346). Olson brushed on the mix, then quickly wiped it off with rags. The cabinets are finished with three coats of water-white nitrocellulose lacquer.

Experimenting with the reds, Cathi poured a dish of red latex paint and pumped it full of black until it approached the bark color. Then she

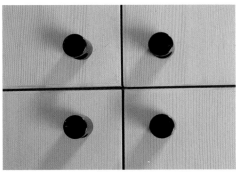

Cabinet detail. The kitchen cabinets are Douglas fir pickled with green latex paint.

spread it on a sample of the Douglas fir flooring and wiped off the excess. The result was a deep red—the color of mahogany—but with the golden overtones and the pinstripe grain of quartersawn fir. It was beautiful, but trying to get this color on the floor would prove difficult.

First of all, the Coverts hated it. It was too red. It was too dark. It was too much. How about something a little lighter? K. C. had professed a fond-

ness for pine flooring, so they made some samples. Cathi won't settle on a material or color if there are lingering questions about it. So they went through more samples that were all pronounced boring. Finally they all agreed that burgundy stain on Douglas fir was the right choice for the floors (photo facing page). Then they had to reproduce the sample on a grand scale.

Trial by staining—Much of the ground floor of the house is covered with the 1x4 fir flooring. It starts in the farmhouse portion of the building, runs through the entryway and the dining room and continues down the hall to emphasize the connection between the two wings of the house.

The Coverts had planned all along to take care of the labor-intensive details themselves, and staining the floor fell into this category. The sample they had to match had been made with latex paint. Why not simply duplicate it with the same ingredients? They quickly discovered why they couldn't. Latex paint dries too fast. If you've got large expanses of wood that need staining, it's tough to avoid lap marks where the stain dries differentially. The staining would have to be done with oil-base colors, which dry much slower and are therefore more controllable.

The Coverts started their search for the right oil-base stain by trying Benjamin Moore rosewood and mahogany semitransparent stains on fir samples. Too red. They tried walnut. Too brown. The concoctions didn't seem to have enough pigment in them to get the deep, rich burgundy color they sought. So they added universal colorants to the brews, which upset the chemistry of the stains and prevented them from drying.

Meanwhile, the local hardware store paint department took up the challenge. The folks there set up a rack of fir flooring samples and started mixing. Staining the floors was taking on a life of its own. Contractors dropped by daily to offer advice. Jake, approaching the end of his patience, boiled a bottle of California burgundy into a syrup and painted it on a hunk of fir. Too pale.

After 200 or so samples, they still hadn't found the right color. The results of their combined attempts were three 1-gal. buckets of different stain, each so tinkered with as to be of undetermined composition. In a last-ditch attempt before turning to vinyl and carpet, Jake dumped all three cans into a 5-gal. bucket and wiped the mix onto a sample. Incredibly, the mix was right.

Once the Coverts started applying stain, they couldn't stop until the floor was done—the job lasted from 7 a. m. to 1 a. m. Three coats of Sikkens Cetol TFF protect the floor (Akzo Coatings, Inc., P. O. Box 7062, Troy, Mich. 48007-7062; 800-833-7288). This is a water-based finish, and the technical staff at Sikkens says it will adhere to an oil-base stain so long as the stain has alkyd resins in it—no linseed oil allowed.

Complexity and pocketbook—Complicated intersections in the structure will enrich a house, but someone has to pay for them. Jake knew what to expect, and he was still surprised by how much extra it costs to build a house when it ventures out of the familiar realm of the perpendicular. He says framing anomalies in this house added about 50% to the cost of the framing.

Some thorny parts were: the battered walls on the chimney tower to the left of the front door; the wall framing where the flat-roofed entry link engages the master bedroom, where all the studs were of different lengths and required compound miters on their top ends; Jake figures the prow overhangs on the steep gables (top right photo, p. 63) cost about $1,000 each; the trimmerless windows in the corners (photo right) required steel hangers to carry the headers, which in turn had to be notched around the hangers to prevent bumps in the drywall wrapping.

The drywall wraps around the windows, however, are an inexpensive alternative to wood jambs and casings (Jake estimates about $50 savings per window). They're in keeping with the minimalist trim in the house and the soft gray of the aluminum window frames. The 78 double-glazed, argon-filled low-E aluminum windows cost $7,300—less than half the price for the cheapest wood windows Jake investigated.

On the exterior the aluminum windows are framed with hefty pieces of painted trim on the wood-sided portions of the house (bottom mid-

Two-story living room. Douglas fir stained burgundy covers most of the floors on the first level. The high window has no corner trimmer, allowing its jamb to be flush with the wall.

dle photo, p. 63). Where they occur in the corrugated siding, the windows are trimless, but they are separated from the metal siding by a bead of silver-colored caulk to prevent galvanic reaction.

Jake's target was $75 per sq. ft. for the finished house. It came in closer to $90, and that figure doesn't include his time as the general contractor. Jake and K. C. are not sorry they had to spend the extra money; it just reminded them that custom work costs more than ordinary work.

Now that the house is 99% complete, Jake can start working on finishing touches, such as the suspended stair (bottom right photo, p. 62). Cathi was sure to include a lifetime of trim details and built-in furniture in the working drawings to keep Jake busy should he lack for a project. □

Charles Miller is managing editor of Fine Homebuilding. Photos by the author except where noted. David Haun helped detail and plan the house.

At Home in the Redwoods

Open, vertical spaces inside make this single-story house feel as tall as the trees around it

by Robert H. Hersey

Navarro, at the western end of the Anderson Valley, is just 20 miles from the northern California coast. Summers here are warm, but the hottest days are tempered by the cool ocean air that creeps into the valley. My clients and good friends Sid and Fran Gage had long taken weekend trips to this area to escape their busy lives in San Francisco, and eventually they began looking for a place to build a second home.

One day Fran called me: "We've finally found a site that looks right, but it has so many big redwood trees that we're not sure where to start." Later, while looking over the site, we found ourselves in a clearing in a redwood grove near the top of a ridge. We were actually standing in a large natural room with walls formed by the huge tree trunks around us and a roof created by the foliage canopy that surrounded the clearing high above the forest floor. At once, I began envisioning the house as borrowing space from that large outside room (photo above).

Land contours dictate the house plan—The clearing we found in the redwood grove was at the top of the main ridge where it sloped steeply to the south. A secondary spur, or shoulder, ran off the ridge toward the west. Here, the house could receive sun from the clearing yet look out under the surrounding redwood branches for beautiful long views of Anderson Valley.

The Gages' requirements were fairly simple. They wanted individual, bunk-room spaces for the kids; a guest room that might double as an office; and a separate master-bedroom area with private bath. The kitchen, dining-room and living-room spaces were to be in a large central room. Both Sid and Fran enjoy creating wonderful gourmet meals, so the kitchen and dining areas would form the heart of the house.

As I sketched over the topographic survey of the site, certain aspects of the house evolved off of the contours (floor plan, facing page). The main ridge and the spur form two axes that run at right angles to one another, and the entry to the house is located at their intersection. From that point the master-bedroom wing steps down the slope on the spur, which is the most private, exclusive part of the site. The other bedroom wing with the guest room and kids' rooms runs up along the main ridge at a right angle to the master-bedroom wing. The main living spaces

Nestled in a ridge-top redwood grove. The tall trees create a natural outdoor space that the house captures and enhances. Photo taken at A on floor plan.

Stepping lightly down the slope. *Designed to fit into a clearing in a redwood grove, this house is built on three levels (shaded light to dark as the levels get lower) that follow the natural contours of the land. The two bedroom sections are at right angles to each other and are connected by a large central room oriented due south, down the steepest part of the slope, toward views of the valley and distant ridges.*

SPECS

Bedrooms: 4
Bathrooms: 2
Heating system: Electric, with woodstove supplement
Size: 2,200 sq. ft.
Cost: N/A
Completed: 1993
Location: Navarro, California

Photos taken at lettered positions.

0   2   4   8 ft.

North

Deck

Woodstove hearth

Master bedroom

D

Outdoor dining area

Kitchen

Deck

B

Dish pantry

Deck

Woodstove hearth

Bedroom

E

Living room

C

Dn

Up

Bedroom

Entry

Guest bedroom

Mudroom

A

Driveway

Inside spaces seem as tall as the outside.
Ceilings slope skyward over tall, narrow windows to accentuate the vertical feeling of the room. Photo taken at B on floor plan.

The heart of the house. Spreading the kitchen along one wall allows the owners to enjoy the company of their guests while they prepare meals. Photo taken at C on floor plan.

are perched over the slope inside the angle created by the two bedroom areas but with the outside wall facing south. Southern orientation gains the greatest amount of sun for the areas where most of the daily activity occurs. It also directs the living room toward valley views.

Roof planes slope toward the treetop canopy—I developed a number of strategies to capture and to enhance the space of the natural room formed by the redwood grove. The first and most obvious is the use of sloping roof planes that also form the ceiling planes. These planes begin low and protectively along the two main axes of the house, the north and east walls, and rise toward the south and southwest, uninterrupted until they reach the opposite wall of the building (photo facing page). In the large central room the ceiling reaches a height of 16 ft. At their lowest point, the ceilings are 8 ft. high. All of the ceilings over the interior spaces have the sense of soaring toward the canopy outside. Instead of using wide expanses of glass, I decided to group together narrow 24-in. window and door units to underscore further the vertical feel-

ing of the interior spaces. The windows run all the way up to the finished ceiling, and roof overhangs have been minimized for unhindered views of the trees.

A roomy kitchen is the social center of the house—When Sid and Fran are preparing a meal, they delight in having all of their guests around sharing wine, conversation and comments on the culinary activities. The kitchen (photo above) was designed to allow all of that to happen comfortably while leaving ample room for the Gages' tag-team cooking. We debated whether or not a counter should separate the kitchen from the rest of the space. But a counter seemed to isolate the kitchen more than the Gages wanted, so it was taken out of the house plan.

The work area of the kitchen runs the entire width of the main room. To soften the view of the kitchen from the living room, the cabinetry was designed like furniture with expressed legs and open shelves under a laminated maple countertop. The countertop is inlaid with 6-in. tiles at both ends, around the sink and around

the stove, leaving an open wooden chopping surface in between. The same tile is used as a backsplash, rising up behind the cooktop to meet the hood. A slotted maple shelf caps the backsplash area and provides convenient knife storage as well as a place for small kitchen items. To civilize the open kitchen, I hid the dish pantry with a pot sink, dishwasher and dish storage out of sight at the low end of the kitchen.

An open corridor overlooks the living room—The wall of the main room opposite the kitchen is formed by the bedroom wing, which is four steps above the level of the main room. The corridor that runs along the wall to provide access to the bedrooms was turned into an open gallery (photo facing page). This treatment enhances the narrow passageway and adds visual interest to the main room. The bedrooms have fairly small floor areas, but with their tall, sloping ceilings, they seem much larger.

Each bedroom is designed for bunk beds and a modest seating area, but each has a sleeping loft accessible by ladder. The loft in the guest room is a bit larger and serves as Sid's computer

Making a living from leftover logs
by Roe A. Osborn

When the Anderson Valley was logged around the turn of the century, the timber supply was thought to be inexhaustible. Consequently, when the giant redwoods were cut down, loggers often left the larger, less uniform lower sections of the trees lying in the woodlot in favor of the straighter, easier-to-manage upper sections of the tree trunks. Today, a lot of these discarded logs are still lying where they fell, and most are in surprisingly good shape, a testament to the durability of old-growth redwood.

Brian Usilton, who milled the redwood used for the decks, the siding and the exterior trim of the Gages' house, has made a living for the past decade by harvesting this unlikely natural resource. Usilton has purposely kept his business small, producing only 4,000 bd. ft. to 5,000 bd. ft. of salvaged lumber per week, or enough for about a half-dozen houses in a year.

Usilton's salvage operation consists of a Wood Mizer bandsaw mill (8180 W. 10th St., Dept. CC64, Indianapolis, Ind. 46214-2400; 800-553-0219), a heavy-duty log-moving truck and an assortment of other log-handling implements (photo below). At one time he trekked into the woods in search of logs to salvage, but now he purchases logs from people who wish to have them removed from their land. As a trained arborist, Usilton is committed to preserving the environment and does his best to minimize disturbance to a site when he is removing logs.

Usilton shies away from second-growth redwood, which he claims exhibits little of the rot-resistant characteristics of old-growth redwood. All of the wood Usilton mills surpasses strict grading requirements. In addition, Usilton uses every bit of waste. He even mixes the sawdust with manure for a successful organic planting medium.

Some salvage companies in the Anderson Valley go after "sinkers," redwood logs so dense that they sank to the bottom rather than floating down the river to lumber mills. Sinkers, however, require up to a year of air-drying before they can be milled, and the wood produced requires additional drying before it can be used.

Other salvage operations go after "runaway" logs that rolled down slopes into inaccessible places such as canyons or ravines while they were being dragged from the woodlot. Enterprising salvagers will even use helicopters to retrieve these logs.

—*Roe A. Osborn is an assistant editor for* Fine Homebuilding.

A new life for old redwood. When redwoods were cut down at the turn of the century, irregular logs such as the one in the center of this photo were left behind. Small salvage operations mill these discarded logs into high-quality lumber.

room. The main entry for the house sits at the vertex of the two bedroom wings. A mudroom entry was included next to the main entry. During the dry summer months, this room is usually bypassed, but in wet winters the mudroom becomes the main entry. Here, outdoor shoes are traded for indoor, and wet, muddy outer garments are shed. The mudroom has a concrete floor with a drain and also serves for storage.

Sid and Fran wanted their master bedroom to give them the feeling of waking up in the trees (photo above). The room, which is at the end of the building, has tall windows on adjacent walls. The orientation of the bed is the same as the main room of the house, so not only do they wake up with views of the tree canopy above but also of the valley and of the distant ridges, visible below the branches.

Two antique cabinets set the tone for the interior—When the house was in the early design stages, Sid and Fran acquired two beautiful old French cabinets at a local auction. One was a hutch that was just right for the open kitchen, and the other a wardrobe for the entry. These two pieces not only influenced the planning in

Waking in the trees. The master bedroom, which is at the most private end of the house, gives the owners the feeling of sleeping in a tree house. Photo taken at D on floor plan.

Deck at dusk. The deck follows one side of the house as it steps down. Lights on the ends of the posts illuminate the tree canopy after sundown. Photo taken at E on floor plan.

these areas but also set the tone for the interior materials and colors. The Gages wanted the interior materials to be light in color because despite all of those tall windows that let in light, the house is still surrounded by redwoods.

Sid and Fran had seen many houses during their visits to the area and had become familiar with the building materials most commonly used. They decided that the materials and finishes that were indigenous to the area would work well for their house, too. The floors are Douglas fir finished with clear Watco stain (Flecto, 1000 45th St., Oakland, Calif. 94608; 800-635-3286), and the ceilings are knotty, rough-sawn cedar. The Gages decided against wooden wall paneling, which is common in the area, in favor of white, plastered walls. However, instead of being smooth, the finish on the walls is varied and rough, which creates a rustic, textured feel. The character of the finish was so attractive that we decided not to paint it except in the bathrooms, where it was sealed against moisture.

All of the cabinetry and interior woodwork, including the custom window and door frames, was made out of clear, straight-grain Douglas fir in the nearby town of Philo. Contractor Charlie

Hochberg supervised the woodwork fabrication, and with his talented crew did a masterful job of a tricky installation. All of the interior woodwork was finished with clear Watco.

The custom light fixtures in the bedrooms were created by my wife, artist Susan Hersey (photo above left). They are composed of handmade paper sprayed on wicker frames. The elegant, rustic design of these fixtures and their earthy colors complement the house well.

An outside deck unites the inside spaces— The entry of the house is at grade on top of the ridge, but the side of the house facing the valley is suspended in the air high above the steep slope. Sheltered from the northwesterly breezes and facing the southern sun, this side is perfect for an outdoor space. We created a series of decks that step down around the trees and along the house as the house follows the contours of the ridge (photo above right).

The decks provide sunny sitting areas as well as a place for the barbecue and an outdoor dining room just outside the kitchen. Connected by short flights of steps, these decks form a passageway along the tree side of the house. On

the decks, you're always in the redwood grove with the trees rising on one side and the house with its tall windows and long board-and-batten siding rising on the other side.

I decided to extend the rough-sawn deck posts up to varying heights beyond the rail to emphasize the vertical, relating the deck structure to the surrounding tree trunks. Each of these deck posts is topped with a custom low-voltage light fixture that illuminates the branches above. In the evening, the deck itself borrows light that spills through the windows.

All of the deck material, the exterior siding and the trim of the house was made from recycled old-growth redwood (sidebar facing page). Because of the forest-fire danger, we chose a galvanized-steel roof finished with a baked-on polyester finish. We thought blue would go well with the redwood siding as well as the tree trunks and the green canopy. The custom post lamps and the sheet-metal cap on the deck railing also pick up the complementary blue color.   □

Robert H. Hersey is an architect who lives and works in the San Francisco area. Photos by Roe A. Osborn except where noted.

Japanese Influence on a Western House

A courtyard garden and an exposed timber frame are
among the inspirations from another culture

by Judith Landau

Like most clients, Peter and Annette Lancy arrived for their first design conference with a box full of books and magazines. But unlike other clients, the Lancys had tagged many pictures of Japanese houses. One stunning image showed a spacious room with shoji screens drawn back to reveal a garden framed by a sweeping roof and its supporting columns. Another photograph showed an elaborate network of roof beams, one of which had been fashioned from a gracefully arched tree trunk. Annette was enchanted by the serenity of the Japanese rooms, and Peter admired the sophisticated joinery required to connect the timbers.

Because the temperate coastal environments of the Pacific Northwest and Japan are similar, it seemed likely that traditional Japanese architectural forms included design solutions that would work equally well on Bainbridge Island in Washington. Low-pitched roofs to shed rain, broad eaves to protect wide expanses of windows and doors, and verandas that bridge indoor and outdoor spaces are features that would work well in the mild Northwest climate (photo below). But other than these obvious physical features, which I admired for their simplicity and primitive strength, I knew very little about the construction of a Japanese house. And while I intended to borrow only a few ideas, I felt my efforts wouldn't be successful unless I understood how the Lancys planned to use their house and how a Japanese house is organized.

What the owners really needed—As our discussion moved from design philosophy to specific requirements, I learned that Peter and Annette planned to raise sheep and llamas on their property, so the house had to function as a farmhouse—sturdy and easy to clean. Wood floors, for example, were out of the question because their two dogs might damage them. The Lancys wanted a formal living/dining room for family holidays and three large bedrooms to accommodate visiting children and grandchildren.

Peter and Annette expected to spend most of their time in the kitchen/family room, but Annette would need generous studio space for spinning and storing wool. There would also have to be plenty of wall space for their art collection and lots of shelves for all their books. Peter grows orchids, so he hoped we could find a space where heat and humidity could be monitored.

The gently rolling terrain of the Lancy's eight-acre property slopes to the south and the east. Two meadows had been carved out of second-growth fir and alder. The house would share the land with two small barns that would shelter the sheep and the llamas. Except for small gardens adjacent to the house, most of the land would be fenced for pasture. The site finally chosen for the house was a nearly level meadow encircled by clusters of trees. I envisioned a house that would follow the circular pattern of the trees.

If the rooms were linked together around a courtyard garden, the courtyard could become

Exposed timbers on the exterior. As in a traditional Japanese house, the timbers on this house in Washington are exposed on the outside. Between the two gables lies the courtyard garden around which the house is organized. Photo taken at A on floor plan.

A timber-framed pergola. Although the front door is hidden from visitors on first arrival, a rock path clearly leads the way. And the glass entry doors framed by a stout pergola leave no doubt that one has arrived at the main entrance. Photo taken at B on floor plan.

an outdoor room at the core of the house. If the rooms were not wide, and if there were window and door openings placed on at least two sides of every room, the interior would get plenty of light. The house that was taking shape in my imagination shared some features with a traditional Japanese house. A garden placed at the center of the house and movable shoji screens (wooden frames with translucent rice-paper panels) to dissolve the barriers between interior spaces and the landscape are common elements in Japanese house design.

Units of measure—In his book *Measure and Construction of the Japanese House* (Charles E. Tuttle Co., 1985), Heino Engel suggests that the Japanese were the first to apply a standard unit of measure to a building system. The standard unit (called ken) is the distance between supporting posts, and this distance controls the scale, the proportion and the form of a building. Traditional Japanese carpenters were so familiar with the system that they could create an entire house from a floor plan drawn by their clients. And they could manipulate spaces, knowing that the scale and the proportion of every room would be in harmony with the rest of the building.

If I wanted to borrow from the Japanese tradition, I would need to approach the design systematically. I decided to organize the floor plan on a 4-ft. module, which is compatible with Western building materials. Dimensions of 4 ft. by 8 ft. and 4 ft. by 12 ft. nicely accommodate stress-skin panels and plasterboard. Posts cen-

tered on 4-ft. grid lines leave regularly spaced openings for windows and doors. Multiples of four can also make good room sizes—12 ft. for bedrooms and kitchens, 16 ft. and 20 ft. for living rooms, 8 ft. for bathrooms and 4 ft. for halls.

I arranged the designated room areas on the grid and drew sections showing approximate post and rafter locations. I worked between the plan and the sections, using the grid to establish wall and ceiling heights. It was exciting to see how the plan remained cohesive as rooms changed sizes and shifted positions.

The U-shaped plan that finally emerged (drawing below) is composed of three large rectangles and two smaller ones offset, as they might be in a typical Japanese house where the offsets help define outdoor spaces. One rectangle—the living/dining room—is one step lower in response to a slight change in the grade.

Rooms are linked to each other by an interior corridor that has several functions. The corridor acts as a circulation axis that bridges the three main zones of the house. It adds 5 ft. of living space to the edge of the kitchen/family room and eventually becomes the library when it reaches the bedroom wing (photo right). In a Japanese house it is typical for both the edge of a room and the veranda to serve as a corridor that links the rooms of the house together.

Western vs. Eastern timber framing—Although I was satisfied with the floor plan and with the way interior details had begun to take shape, I knew it would be a challenge to design a

A hallway of books. An extensive library lines the hallway outside the main bedrooms. Although the bookshelves steal space from the bedrooms, the books buffer sounds from the kitchen, lend a marvelous texture to the walls and make easy work of reaching for a bedtime story. Photo taken at C on floor plan.

SPECS

Bedrooms: 3
Bathrooms: 2½
Heating system: Hydronic radiant floor
Size: 3,780 sq. ft. (includes garage/shop)
Cost: $135 per sq. ft.
Completed: 1991
Location: Bainbridge Island, Washington

Photos taken at lettered positions.

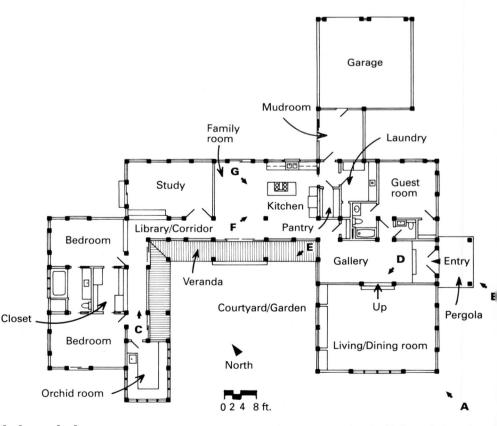

A U-shaped plan. *Inspired by a semicircular cluster of trees on the site, the U-shaped plan of this house coalesced with the creation of a central garden courtyard. This plan separates the public and private areas of the house and permits views and access to the courtyard from both areas.*

Drawing: Jeff Bellantuono

Natural timbers in the ceiling. The entrance to the living/dining room is marked by a taiko beam, cut from the arched trunk of a madrone tree. Beyond this sensual entry, above the acid-etched concrete floor, a peeled cedar log helps support the purlin and common rafters in the roof, similar in detail to a Japanese roof. Photo taken at D on floor plan.

Veranda view. A plank-floored veranda flanks the courtyard garden. Strategically placed skylights in the veranda roof allow sunlight—which is a precious commodity in the Northwest—to reach the kitchen through the glass doors. Photo taken at E on floor plan.

suitable frame for this house. Western-style timber framing originated in northern Europe. As it is practiced today, this framing style uses widely spaced posts (up to 16 ft. apart) braced by diagonal members. The frame is revealed on the inside but covered on the exterior by sheathing.

The opposite is true of a traditional Japanese timber frame, in which the posts are spaced more closely, have no diagonal braces and are exposed both inside and outside the building.

The wall of a traditional Japanese house consists of horizontal and vertical wood strips, covered with bamboo lath and plastered with a mixture of mud and straw. To resist lateral forces, such as those applied by strong winds or earthquakes, a Japanese house relies primarily on the flexibility of the frame and on the wall material installed within the frame. The Japanese approach of engineering a timber frame to withstand a force by moving with it is similar to the martial arts practice of redirecting an opponent's thrust back to its source.

For the Lancys' frame, I looked for ways to create Japanese impressions using Western construction methods and materials that our company understands. To that end, we put more posts into the wall than is typical, using them to define each window and door opening. In prominent places, we used peeled cedar logs to help support the roof, thereby introducing an element that suggests a Japanese roof structure (photo p. 75).

By the way, the 12-in. dia. cedar logs were cut locally, peeled, cleaned and kerfed to prevent radial checking. Kerfing, a common practice of Japanese carpenters, involves making a straight cut into the heart and along the full length of the timber. Wedges are driven as far as they will go into the cut, then they are tapped in farther as

Cabinets like furniture. Inspired by Smallbone, a British cabinet company, these Douglas-fir cabinets look more like furniture than the particleboard boxes found in most kitchens today. The 6-ft. island is capped by a black granite countertop, and the main counter is oiled maple. Photo taken at F on floor plan.

the timber dries. We faced the cut, with its wedges still in place, toward the ceiling where it was out of sight.

Finishing the exterior—On most of our timber frames, we use stress-skin panels, which are structural panels made of rigid insulation and waferboard, applied to the exterior face of the frame. But on the Lancy house this technique would have concealed the frame on the outside. I was unwilling to compromise the honesty of the frame by adding trim to imitate the frame on exterior walls. There was only one solution: the panels would have to be fitted between the timbers. Essentially, we replaced the traditional bamboo, mud and straw with polyurethane insulation and waferboard.

We used 2x4s, routed into the edges of the panels, to connect the panels to the frame. Expanding urethane foam serves as a gasket between the two. The 4½-in. thick panels left enough timber edge exposed to finish the interior and exterior walls with drywall and stucco. The insulation value of the house does not seem to have been compromised very much. Although we lost the continuity of the panel, we gained the mass of the timbers.

Protecting the exposed Douglas-fir frame from the weather will be an ongoing challenge. Because the Lancys elected not to add an ultraviolet protective stain to the frame (they liked the natural color of the wood), it will be necessary to reapply a protective oil coating about every two years.

In a Japanese house the color of the exterior walls would be determined by the kind of earth used in the infill mixture. Because we did not have that option, we colored the latex stucco a rather dark gray with a greenish cast, a color we hoped would help the house recede into the Northwest landscape.

A tour of the inside—The walkway to the house follows a meandering rock path that begins at the edge of the meadow and leads past a landscape of low pines to the timber-framed pergola that flanks the glass entry doors (photo p. 72). When the rock path crosses the threshold, it expands to form the floor of the entry, two steps below the gallery's polished concrete floor.

The Lancys wanted a radiant-floor heating system and had expressed interest in a tile floor. More than 3,000 sq. ft. of tile would have taken a big bite out of the construction budget, so I suggested concrete as an alternative. We discovered an acid etching compound that, when applied to finished concrete, gives it a transparent color (Kemiko Stone Tone Concrete Stain, Epmar Corp., P. O. Box 3925, Santa Fe Springs, Calif. 90670; 310-946-8781). The transparency allows variations caused by the minerals in the concrete to show through. When the surface is sealed and waxed, it resembles glazed ceramic tile. Because it was scored into rectangular blocks, our floor pattern suggests Japanese tatami mats with their dark tape binding.

The living room combines sitting and formal dining areas. Low cabinets, designed to store prints and ceramic sculpture, line one wall. Wood for all of the cabinetry in the house was taken from the same resawn Douglas-fir timbers used in the structure.

Clearly, the large amount of glazing in the Lancy house is a major departure from the Japanese tradition. The windows were designed to fit into the frame without sills. They slide open in the wall plane and are placed low on the wall. In spite of its broad eaves, the house is filled with light. We made sure of this by adding skylights in strategic places. Skylights in the veranda roof (top photo, facing page) let light shine through the glass doors and into the kitchen. Fourteen other 2-ft. by 2-ft. skylights were placed between rafters on the north and west slopes of the roof.

Although the Lancys are fond of shoji screens, their lifestyle precluded the use of these fragile panels. So we settled for sandblasted glass panels with wooden grids in the clerestory spaces above windows and doors (photo below). In a Japanese house panels called ramma are found in this space. Our grids are designed to be removed easily for cleaning.

The kitchen cabinets, arranged in an L shape around a 6-ft. island, are a complete departure from any Japanese influence (bottom photo, facing page). Because a modern kitchen has no precedence in a vernacular house, we approached the kitchen from a craftsman's perspective and made the cabinets seem more like furniture. They were built by Michael Hamilton, the cabinetmaker who runs our company's cabinet shop, and modeled after cabinets Annette had seen in a catalog from Smallbone, the British cabinet company.

At the center of the house, both literally and figuratively, the kitchen is a cheery spot, lit by doors and windows on two sides and by skylights in the roof. Peter and Annette spend much of their time in the kitchen—eating, reading and talking. And as the room most likely to hold a spot of sunlight, the kitchen is also where the Lancys' dogs are usually found, curled up and asleep on the floor. ☐

Judith Landau is a designer who, with her husband, Charles Landau, runs Timbercraft Homes in Port Townsend, Wash. Photos by Kevin Ireton.

Another view of the kitchen. **Along one edge of the kitchen, a lowered ceiling marks the 5-ft. wide circulation corridor that links the main parts of the house (unless sleeping dogs block the path). In the clerestory spaces above windows and doors that look onto the courtyard garden, wooden grillwork behind sandblasted glass lends another Japanese touch to the house. Photo taken at G on floor plan.**

Live Large, Look Small

Bungalow details bring a big house down to earth on a spectacular site

by David Hall

In the Pacific Northwest it's not uncommon to find building sites with pleasing views of water and mountains. But when Henry Klein and I made arrangements to meet Dinah and Wilbur Kukes at their site on Washington's Lake Whatcom, we weren't prepared for such an exceptional location. Rising steeply from its shoreline and surrounded by water on two sides, the site commanded dramatic views that were framed by the trunks of towering evergreens. Walking the property, we found the remains of an old family camp. In varying states of decay, small

guest cabins were nestled near the cliffs and among the forest vegetation. Back from the sandstone banks and the weathered trees, a larger cabin occupied the clearing where the Kukes wished to build their new house.

In an area where summer cottages had been the rule, the Kukes wanted a year-round house that could hold their family of five while affording space for entertaining large groups of people. In spite of these significant size requirements, our clients wanted their place to have an informal, unimposing personality, honoring the rus-

tic character of the cabin that would have to be demolished to make way for the new house. So our challenge as architects was to create a house that would look small but *live* large, enclosing plenty of space without dominating its setting.

The house was built by Gerritt Dykstra and completed in 1990. Seeing it today (photo below), we can comfortably remember our fears about overdeveloping such a beautiful site and feel reasonably good about the solutions we found. Whether your viewpoint is from the water or from the woods, it's hard to believe you're

Views inside and out. Concrete pods, undercut to give a floating impression, lead to this lakeside home from a boathouse. Facing page: The view from the dining room into the living room is shown. Although separated by a half wall and a curving counter, the kitchen is within easy reach. Photo taken at A on floor plan.

A covered entry. Small in proportion and rich in detail, the covered entry evokes the small scale and informal personality of a Bungalow-style home. The ridge of the entry roof is glazed with single-pane, ¼-in.-thick wire glass. Photo taken at B on floor plan.

looking at a 6,500-sq. ft. residence. By massing the house carefully, choosing good materials and incorporating traditional details from Bungalow- and Craftsman-style houses, we were able to downscale its presence.

A three-part plan—Dinah wanted the kitchen to be the center of the house. She envisioned a large, open space, easily accessible from both the living room and the dining room (photo p. 79). A pantry would be included in the kitchen plan, with a laundry room close by. Dinah also insisted that the children's bedrooms and the family room be separate from the master bedroom and the living and dining areas.

As plans developed, the house evolved into three parts: the main house, the children's wing and the garage. It made sense to face the main house and the children's wing south and east, where they'd get the best views of the lake. The two-wing, L-shape form of the living area was an easier fit on the site than a larger, all-inclusive structure would have been. Only one facade is visible, or partly visible, from most viewpoints, thanks to the trees. This massing gives the impression of a smaller place.

We were able to give the Kukes the room and the features they wanted in two levels (floor plan, left). The children's wing includes a large TV room downstairs, as well as a bedroom and a three-quarter bath. Upstairs, two bedrooms share a bath. Bay windows on both levels help bring in the view. Each bay has a built-in window seat, with storage space beneath it.

In the larger main wing, bay windows give way to dormers and gables that overlook the lake through large, semicircular windows. Below these windows, the south and west walls carry windows and glass-paneled doors. The master bedroom has its own dormer view; but the owners can also step outside their bedroom onto an indoor balcony that overlooks the living room, which has its own light-filled dormer.

The upper-level plans also show a study and an office located over the garage. This extra room was found during construction, when we realized the attic area was big enough to finish off as living space. To gain access we added a door at the end of Wilbur's walk-in closet.

The garage is conveniently close to the kitchen and joined to the main house by a gabled roof extended to form an enclosure between the two buildings. Early in the design process this space simply was a passageway. But as plans developed, so did the potential uses for this indoor/ outdoor room. Finished with shingled walls, exposed aggregate floors and a T&G hemlock ceiling, the room is the next-best thing to being outdoors in a region famous for wind and rain. With this in mind, we added a brick fireplace and a barbecue against a garage wall at one end of the

This expansive floor plan sports several unique features. On the first floor, the main house is linked to the garage by an indoor/outdoor room enclosed on one side by two window-filled garage doors. For privacy, the master bedroom and the children's wing are not accessible to each other on the second floor. Each has its own staircase.

Photos taken at lettered positions.

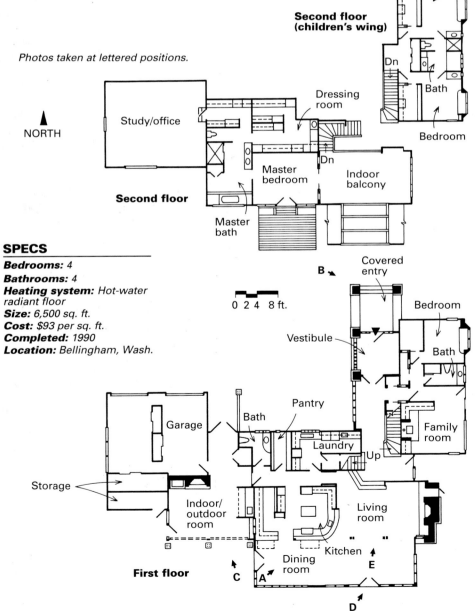

NORTH

Second floor (children's wing)

Bedroom

Dn

Bath

Bedroom

Dressing room

Study/office

Second floor

Master bedroom

Dn

Indoor balcony

Master bath

SPECS

Bedrooms: 4
Bathrooms: 4
Heating system: Hot-water radiant floor
Size: 6,500 sq. ft.
Cost: $93 per sq. ft.
Completed: 1990
Location: Bellingham, Wash.

B

Covered entry

Bedroom

Vestibule

Bath

0 2 4 8 ft.

Garage

Bath

Pantry

Family room

Laundry

Up

Storage

Indoor/ outdoor room

Living room

Kitchen

Dining room

First floor

C

A

D

E

It's not the garage. Framed by a cedar trellis, the large double opening gives ample access to an unheated indoor/outdoor room located between the garage and the kitchen. Even when they're closed during bad weather, these garage doors can still bring in great views. Photo taken at C on floor plan.

space. In the room's south wall we installed two garage doors with glass lites (photo above); whether opened or closed, the view isn't compromised. A cedar trellis stands just outside these doors ready to support newly planted vines.

Borrowing from the bungalow—With its tapered pillars, projecting beams, exposed rafters and small gable roof, the main entry recalls the comfortable proportions and well-crafted details

that typify the classic Bungalow-style home (photo facing page). This small roofline creates a sheltered vestibule that's much appreciated during frequent rains and carries out from the large house a cozy and friendly greeting.

Following the entry's lead, we borrowed other Bungalow- and Craftsman-style details to reduce the scale of the house and at the same time gave it a rustic, lodgelike feel. Red cedar shingles—used frequently on bungalows—seemed a wise

Skylights in the eaves. Single-glazed skylights outside the living room allow for a broad and nearly transparent eave overhang. Photo taken at D on floor plan.

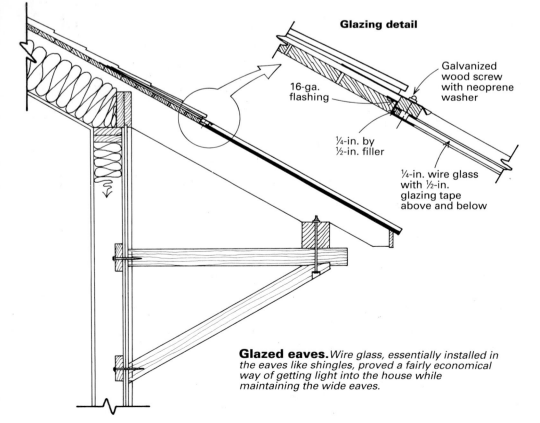

Glazing detail

16-ga. flashing

Galvanized wood screw with neoprene washer

¼-in. by ½-in. filler

¼-in. wire glass with ½-in. glazing tape above and below

Glazed eaves. *Wire glass, essentially installed in the eaves like shingles, proved a fairly economical way of getting light into the house while maintaining the wide eaves.*

choice for exterior siding. We specified 24-in. long Royals instead of standard 18-in. shingles. The use of Royals allowed an exposure of 11 in. instead of the 5-in. to 8-in. exposure recommended with 18-in. shingles, which reduced the number of shingle courses and, in turn, reduced the scale of the house.

On every fourth shingle course all around the house (on the entry pillars also), we used a 3-in. exposure. This treatment (one of many decorative shingle effects found on Bungalow-style houses) wraps the building in horizontal lines that counter the vertical reach of the walls. Stained to a natural cedar color, this wood cladding will help the house blend in with the weathered tree trunks and stone outcroppings that distinguish the site.

The wide eaves and the broad gable overhangs found on many bungalow houses work well on the Kukes' house. From a practical point of view, the overhangs shelter the sidewalls, the doors and the windows during frequent rainy periods. Aesthetically, extended rooflines seem to reduce the size of the living spaces they shelter, much the same way that a large hat seems to diminish the head that it covers.

But roof overhangs limit the amount of light that can reach indoors. This problem is most serious with wide eaves and during winter. Fortunately, we found an effective, fairly economical way to get light into the house while maintaining wide eaves. By locating our skylights in the eaves (photo and drawing left), outside the heated space, we were able to use single-glazed, ¼-in. thick wire glass, a lighter and less-expensive alternative to insulated glass or manufactured skylights. Each wire glass lite is installed like a shingle, fastened to the roof sheathing under the upper shingles and supported by the rafters and the continuous 6x6 beam that anchors the rafter tails at the eaves. The 6x6 is supported by 4x4 sidewall braces that are left exposed. Glazing tape and metal flashing complete the eave skylight detail, which is used off the living room and off the indoor/outdoor room. With some variation, we adapted our single-glazed skylight to cap the ridge of the covered entry roof (photo p. 80)

We continued to draw inspiration from the Craftsman style inside, exposing structural elements and using wood to add warmth and well-crafted details. The exposed king-post trusses break up the living room's cathedral ceiling without blocking light or views. The balcony that overlooks the living room is supported by two 6x14 glulam beams that, in turn, support 6x8 joists. The balcony's hemlock decking is also left exposed, doubling as the ceiling of the space below. Doubled 6x6 columns frame the view from the entry hall (top photo, facing page) and support one of the balcony beams. Simple but elegant, the balcony and the main stairway railings have balusters made from hemlock closet poles.

The brick fireplace occupies the east wall of the living room and offers physical and visual warmth. Made of salvaged brick, which is less uniform in texture and color than new brick, the fireplace and its chimney enhance the home's rustic demeanor. In our design we allowed the chimney to stand free of the living room's east wall, leaving room for another semicircular window in its gable. This decision made the chimney part of the view, so we designed decorative projecting headers that give the brickwork an engaging Queen Anne character.

Outside the house—Landscaping plays a strong part in unifying the house with its site. On the southeast corner of the house, a cedar deck links the children's wing and the main wing to outdoor areas. Our deck-railing design incorporates a bench seat (photo below).

Undulating walls of dry-stacked river rock tie the house to the site naturally. These walls were created by using large rock "anchors" beneath progressively smaller rocks. Landscape architect Richard Haag successfully integrated the rock deposits with patios that were made of exposed aggregate concrete and bricks. Native plantings will eventually soften the rock outcroppings, giving this well-crafted masonry work an even more natural appearance. Haag's work is also evident on the north side of the house. But on the south side he managed the difficult job of resolving the steep grade that exists between the house and water's edge. Grass-crete pavers are cut into the sandstone bank, providing stepped trails down to the lake. Grass-crete is cast concrete block that has openings in it to allow plantings or grass to grow through it. Thyme is beginning to fill the voids between pavers.

For access to an existing boathouse, Haag designed a series of randomly sized concrete pods that appear to float on the water (photo p. 78). The floating illusion is created by stepping back the lower edge of each pod by about 6 in. These stepping stones have a brushed aggregate finish and help the owners get out on the water. ☐

Architect David Hall is a partner in the Henry Klein Partnership, located in Mount Vernon, Wash. Photos by Charles Miller except where noted.

Doubled-up supports. Doubled 6x6 columns frame the entry hall in this view from the living room. On the stairway and the balcony, doubled hemlock closet poles masquerade with elegant effect as railing balusters. Photo taken at E on floor plan.

Varied shingle courses. Broad and narrow exposures "to the weather" combine to diminish the scale of shingled sidewalls. Beyond the three bay windows of the children's wing (east elevation), a cedar deck extends around the southeast corner of the house.

Living by the Lake

A separate bunkhouse, connected by a porch, affords privacy for three generations

by David O'Neil and Sheldon K. Pennoyer

An invitation to the lake. The entryway porch that connects the main house and the bunkhouse draws visitors forward by framing an enticing view of Squam Lake beyond. Photo taken at A on floor plan.

Squam Lake sits within the outwash plain of New Hampshire's White Mountains. To the north and the west, the lower profile of the Rattlesnake Range surrounds Squam Lake, giving scale and character to its many bays and inlets. The edge of the lake is strewn with granite boulders and slabs left by the receding glacier and softened by a millennia of successive winter freeze-ups. Beyond the shore, an old forest grows with an abundance of white pine and oak interspersed with smaller poles of birch and alder, all garnished by delicate mountain laurel (top photo, this page). At night, across the water one can hear the crazed call of the loons. Squam Lake's inhabitants and summer visitors have worked hard to preserve its wildness; it was not by accident that this lake was chosen for the filming of *On Golden Pond*.

On the southern shore of Squam Lake, at the outlet to Dog Cove, our clients Frankie and Dennis Whitehead wanted to build a house that would accommodate their extended family—grandparents, children and grandchildren. They wanted a summer house that would suit the relaxed life they lived while on vacation.

When we met the Whiteheads and walked their Squam Lake property with them, we saw that their lot was long and narrow. To the west, there is conservation property that can never be built on, but to the east there is a neighbor's house that's intrusively close. We had to convince Dennis and Frankie not only that we could give them their lake views, their sunlight and the post-and-beam character they admired, but we also had to convince them that we could provide the sense of seclusion they wanted.

As if all this weren't enough, the Whiteheads also wanted sleeping quarters for their many

grandchildren, but their budget precluded building a fully finished six-bedroom house. Fortunately, we solved the two toughest problems—privacy and sleeping capacity—with a single idea.

Enter the bunkhouse—We have spent a lot of time in the Adirondacks and have admired the work of late 19th-century architect William West Durant, who helped create the Adirondack style with his designs of the great camps—large summer retreats of the wealthy.

The 19th-century camps were usually comprised of a series of buildings, each with its own function. In a compound there might be a kitchen-dining camp, a living-room camp with bedrooms arranged around a balcony on the second floor, a camp for the hunting and fishing guides, a woodshed, an icehouse, a boat house and several privies.

Inspired by the notion of a compound, we suggested building a separate bunkhouse (photo facing page)—modeled after the guide's camp—to provide a space for the grandchildren to sleep. To keep costs down, the bunkhouse would have a rustic finish—open stud walls and a woodstove for the occasional chilly summer mornings. The

Apart, yet connected. On the left, the grandchildren's bunkhouse is separate from the main house, where the whole family congregates for meals and other common activities. The footprint formed by the two buildings and the porch creates two outdoor courtyards. Photo taken at B on floor plan.

A buffering bunkhouse. *A separate bunkhouse for the grandchildren screens the neighboring house from the main house. The arrangement of the buildings creates two courtyards, at least one of which is always protected from the wind and the sun.*

SPECS

Bedrooms: 3 plus bunkhouse

Bathrooms: 2½

Heating system: Oil-fired forced hot air

Size: Main house–2,350 sq. ft. Bunkhouse–715 sq. ft.

Cost: $88 per sq. ft.

Completed: 1990

Location: Squam Lake, New Hampshire

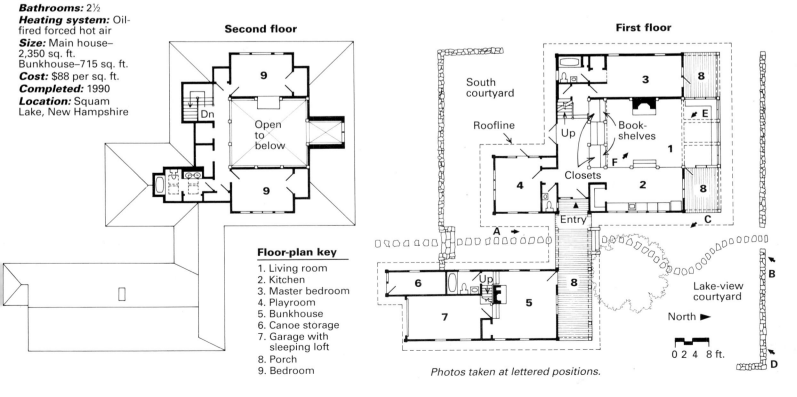

Second floor

First floor

Floor-plan key

1. Living room
2. Kitchen
3. Master bedroom
4. Playroom
5. Bunkhouse
6. Canoe storage
7. Garage with sleeping loft
8. Porch
9. Bedroom

Photos taken at lettered positions.

Drawing: Jeff Bellantuono

Buffering bunkhouse. A separate bunkhouse for the client's grandchildren screens the neighbor's house to the left and affords a little privacy for the grandparents from the children. The covered porch leads to the entry of the main house. Photo taken at C on floor plan.

Fundamentally camplike. A large sheltering roof with deep overhangs, big hip dormers and a chimney made of native stone all hearken back to an earlier style. Great pains were taken to keep the floor levels and the porches close to the ground. Photo taken at D on floor plan.

bunkhouse would also contain space for canoe storage until a boat house could be built at the water's edge.

Aside from downsizing the main house, building a bunkhouse provided a separate space for young grandchildren that would give them some independence. And while it was close enough to the main house in case of emergency, it also gives the Whiteheads a little peace and quiet from rambunctious children.

The bunkhouse also is a visual buffer between the neighbor's house and the main house, providing the privacy the Whiteheads asked for.

The main house and the bunkhouse are joined by a porch (photo above left). The footprint formed by the two buildings and the connecting porch creates two private outdoor courtyards, one facing south and one facing the lake (floor plan p. 85). Regardless of the sun's direction or the direction of the fluky winds that can blow around Squam Lake, one can find a protected outdoor area in which to sit.

The porch connecting the two buildings became the front entrance; it draws visitors forward by framing a perfect, inviting view of the lake beyond (bottom photo, p. 84).

Settling into the landscape—We tried to keep the house as close to the ground as possible to avoid a house that stuck way up in the air, looking as if it had just landed on the lot. The floor levels step down to accommodate the corresponding drop in the ground's elevation. Before excavating for the foundation, we established the building-elevation lines so that, wherever possible, the house's three porches would be only a single step above the forest floor.

The main house, the bunkhouse and the connecting porch all have the same eaves height. Keeping these eaves heights consistently low tied together the very different sizes of the two buildings and helped convey the notion of a great sheltering roof, which provides protection from the weather.

On the exterior, below the high-set windows that illuminate the kitchen counter, we installed a bank of flat panels to make the windows appear closer to the ground (right photo, above).

The array of columns supporting the main roof and the connecting porch are painted gray to blend in with the screen of trees standing between the building and the lake. Clapboards were left a natural color (left photo, above) to reflect the bed of pine needles that Frankie said would become their "forest lawn."

The heart of the house—We wanted to make good on our promise to give the Whiteheads the timber frame they had originally desired. But rather than using heavy timbers everywhere, which seemed inappropriate for smaller rooms and dormers, we decided to frame only the central living room in heavy timber. This space, recalling the living rooms of the great camps, is two stories high, with a focus on a tall granite fireplace (bottom photo, facing page).

This large, timber-framed room became the armature of the house. The kitchen, the entry hall and the master bedroom, with two guest bedrooms on the second floor connected by a balcony, surround the living room. This central space serves as a common room for dining, reading in front of the fireplace, or whatever else a multigenerational family might want to do while on vacation.

The outer layer of rooms was framed conventionally, providing a continuous, well-insulated exterior envelope, with the added benefit of using less-expensive dimensional lumber for dormers, eaves, porches and the bunkhouse.

Keeping the camp inside—As we developed the design, Frankie and Dennis encouraged our ideas about a simple floor plan and the use of natural materials. Instead of painted plaster ceilings, the tongue-and-groove pine of the porch ceilings and soffits was continued into all of the rooms surrounding the two-story living room.

We separated the hallway from the living room with wood-clad storage units set below the ceiling that serve as closets on one side and as bookshelves on the other. On top of these units, we concealed lights to provide a romantic source

Kitchen with a view. The long kitchen is three steps above the living room and is directly opposite the fireplace. An open balustrade mimics the second-floor balcony. A person working in the kitchen can still be a part of the family activities in the living room below. Photo taken at E on floor plan.

of uplighting for the wooden ceilings under the balcony. Only the walls surrounding the granite fireplace were finished in plaster to give the Whiteheads a better background on which to hang their family portraits and their collection of half-models of historic ships.

Frankie wanted a kitchen that was separate but within view of the heart of the house. So we located the kitchen three steps above the living room and directly opposite the fireplace (photo above). A wood railing, similar to the balcony above, partitions the different floor levels.

On the north end of the living room (photo right), an expansive view of the lake can be had through a bay of large, single-lite windows with smaller transom lites above. We wrapped a simple paneled window seat around the windows to serve as extra seating at large family dinners.

The process in retrospect—We were fortunate to have found clients who wanted a summer place that, in Frankie's words, "with simplicity and style blends into the landscape." To find the house, you must paddle your canoe in very close to the lake's rocky shoreline and peer up into the woods, where the house's triangular form sits quietly within its unaltered landscape.

David O'Neil and Sheldon K. Pennoyer are the principals of O'Neil Pennoyer Architects in Somerville, Mass. Photos by Jefferson Kolle.

Massive timbers, massive fireplace. The large common room in the main house overlooks the lake. All three generations gather in the room for meals and other activities. The window seat around the bay of windows serves as extra seating at large dinners. Photo taken at F on floor plan.

House on The River

Concrete piers, cantilevered steel and prefab framing support a rustic hideaway

by Steve Taylor

This story takes place on and because of the St. Lawrence River and, in particular, its majestic headwaters. Here, for a stretch of 60 miles, waters from the Great Lakes flow around more than 1,500 islands en route to the sea. These granite islands, formed during the close of the last Ice Age, are home to hardwoods and softwoods, summer sun and winter ice. The border between New York state and Ontario, Canada, winds through here now.

Most of the families in this river community have been coming here for generations. Dick and Carol Munro are no exception. My crew and I know them well because we've worked with them in the past, remodeling their house on Bluff Island and building an adjacent floating boat house for them, among other things. Based on our earlier work, the Munros asked us in the fall of 1988 to design and build for them a new three-season (spring-summer-fall) guest house a few hundred feet away from the remodeled main house.

Given the remote and unspoiled nature of the site, we knew that both the design and construction of this house would offer a challenge. In fact, neither turned out to be conventional; many of the sturdy, singular structural components that bond the house to the rugged terrain double as strong aesthetic elements, which produce the honest, rustic (but not rough) appearance that we were looking for.

Surveying the site—We picked the ideal spot for the guest house: a north-facing point that offers a panoramic view of open water and distant islands and captures magnificent sunsets during half the year. The point is thick with a mix of hardwoods, hemlocks and pines, with cedars holding the banks.

We hired local surveyors to produce a topographical map of the point showing elevation

Above water. Amply glazed to fetch views of the river, the house sits atop an undercarriage of rectangular steel tubing that cantilevers over the bank to support cedar decks.

Modular rusticity. The living areas are unified beneath shop-built bents, spaced 6 ft. 8 in. o. c. to accommodate stock Andersen windows. A native-granite fireplace with a glazed chimney cricket up top occupies one module. The stair (right in photo) leads to a loft over the dining and kitchen areas.

Bent detail

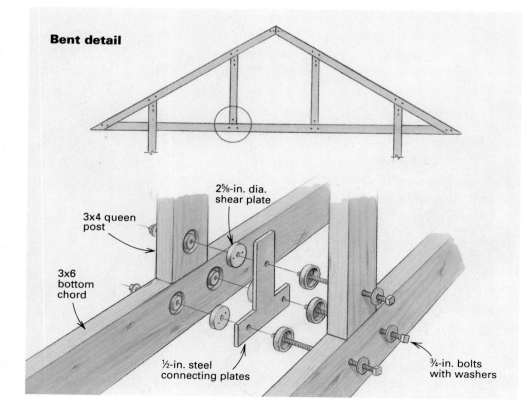

2⅝-in. dia. shear plate

3x4 queen post

3x6 bottom chord

½-in. steel connecting plates

¾-in. bolts with washers

changes in 1-ft. increments. The map cost only $650. On it we indicated the direction of sunrises and sunsets at the equinoxes and the summer solstice, as well as other significant features such as a gulley that bisects the point and drains rainwater and spring runoff from higher ground. We then drew a number of site elevations (sections through the land) to give us a thorough understanding of the site.

Open plan, modular layout—Based on this information, we decided to place the house at the top of the bank about 20 ft. above the river, bridging the gulley. This would provide the house with a relatively flat yard on the south side and superb views of the river to the north.

The house is L-shaped, following the configuration of the bank (floor plan p. 92). One wing is perpendicular to the river and contains a living room, a dining area, a kitchen and an open loft. The other wing, which is parallel to the river, holds a master bedroom and bath, a smaller bedroom and a second bathroom. The living room and both bedrooms open to the outdoors.

From the river, the house looks like a pavilion, with walls in the living areas composed mostly of glass (photo facing page). Decks cantilever out over the bank like pine boughs reaching for light. The roof overhangs are 4 ft. 6 in. wide, sufficient for sheltering an exterior cantilevered walkway on the north side of the bedroom wing and a generously glazed interior hallway on the south side. This hallway adds passive heating (circulated by convection) during early spring and late fall, when leaves are scarce and the sun is low in the sky. The kitchen, too, is bumped out under the eaves at the southeast corner of the house so that its south wall is directly in line with that of the hallway.

To add visual interest by creating repetitive structural elements, we laid out the house on a 6-ft. 8-in. module. This measurement was determined by the size of the standard Andersen windows that we selected to optimize the view plus the thickness of the shop-built truss/post units, or *bents*, that would support the walls and roof (more on those later).

Many of the finest homes on the islands, built around the turn of the century, have native-granite fireplaces, weathered or stained wood siding and cedar-shingle roofing. The interiors of these homes are typically wood-paneled, often with beaded pine. We chose to incorporate these materials into this house.

Charles N. Timbie of C. N. Timbie Engineers, Inc. in Lansdowne, Pa., worked out the structural details for the house. Laying out everything on the module, he designed a concrete-pier foundation that anchors the house to bedrock, cantilevered steel beams that support the floors and decks, and the bents.

Floating and hovering—Building on islands in the north country can be fun, but it isn't always easy—especially when you work year-round like we do. We figured the Munros' house would take nearly nine months to complete, so we planned to work on it straight through winter.

Our office and shop are situated next to a small dock on another island that is connected by bridges to the U. S. and Canadian mainlands. During most of the year, we use a scow (a flat-bottomed boat with square ends) and several smaller work boats for transporting workers and building materials to job sites. For transporting heavy equipment and other hefty loads, we hire two mighty Navy-surplus landing crafts.

These boats aren't of much use in winter, however, when the St. Lawrence River typically freezes over. That's when we use Hovercrafts or snowmobiles and sleds, depending on the condition of the river.

For winter travel to the Munros' site, we used a Hovercraft if we were likely to encounter both open water and ice. A Hovercraft is propelled by a snowmobile engine that drives a large fan and provides about 10 in. of lift. We traveled by snowmobile and sled in colder conditions.

Piers to bedrock—We broke ground in late September. Test holes revealed that bedrock lay beneath 8 ft. to 12 ft. of sand and clay—unusually deep for this area. Timbie specified a foundation consisting of 24-in. square concrete piers anchored to bedrock to resist and help thwart erosion of the bank. The south wall of the house lies on relatively flat ground, so it's supported by a

pair of concrete-block walls bearing on concrete footings 4 ft. below grade. A 13-ft. 4-in. wide gap (two modules) between the walls allows the gully to pass through. A concrete-block foundation also supports the fireplace and extends down to bedrock.

Foundation trenches were excavated with a backhoe. At each pier location, we drilled two ⅞-in. dia. by 8-in. deep holes in the bedrock and dropped a Chem-Stud epoxy capsule (The Rawlplug Co., Inc.; 800-243-8160) into each one. Then, using an electric drill, we spun a 22-in. length of ¾-in. galvanized threaded rod into each hole, breaking and mixing the epoxy capsules and bonding the threaded rods to the bedrock. The threaded rod extends far enough out of the bedrock to anchor 3-ft. square by 8-in. high concrete footings and to tie off ¾-in. rebar cages that extend up through the piers.

We formed the piers with Symons forms (Symons Corp., 200 East Touhy Ave., Des Plaines, Il. 60018; 708-298-3200), plywood-sheathed metal frames that are drawn tight at the corners with metal wedges. Brackets welded to the outsides of the frames accommodate 2x4 wales that align and reinforce adjacent forms. We rented the forms from a local tool-rental outfit.

Concrete was poured into each form to an elevation just below the bottoms of the steel floor beams that would sit on the piers. Anchor bolts embedded in the tops of the piers would secure the beams to the piers, and steel shims and a nonshrink-mortar grout would be used to support the beams at the correct elevation.

Cantilevered steel—With the foundation work in progress, Williams Marine Service (Ivy Lea, Ontario, Canada) fabricated and primed the 6x14 hollow structural steel beams. We chose ⅜-in. thick rectangular structural steel tubing over more conventional steel I-beams because tubing is stronger, an important consideration with beams that cantilever up to 13 ft. 4 in. Not only does tubing have the equivalent of two webs as opposed to the single web of an I-beam, but it's made out of higher-grade steel than I-beams (ASTM A 500 steel, which is rated at 46,000 psi, as opposed to ASTM A 36 steel, which is rated at 36,000 psi).

Also, I-beams have an industrial look, and we would have wanted to conceal them, which is a time-consuming and costly process. Tubing, on the other hand, looks more refined. We had each beam tapered at the ends for a length of one module, which makes the cantilevers appear more delicate.

The steel beams were loaded onto our scow, cleared through U. S. Customs and floated to the island, where they were installed by the excavator. The beams were fastened with the anchor bolts to the piers through predrilled ½-in. thick steel plates welded to the bottoms of the beams.

After the beams were installed, the prime coat was touched up, and two coats of Pettit's Marine Epoxy Paint were applied (Pettit Paint Co., Inc., 36 Pine St., Rockaway, N. J. 07866; 201-625-3100). Concrete blocks were then cut and laid on top of each pier to conceal the anchor clips and cradle the beams. That done, the exposed

Showering in the sun. Daylit by a skylight, the main bathroom features built-in incandescent lighting above and below the soffit, an Ifo low-flow toilet and a quarter-round shower.

Indirect incandescents. Interior soffits throughout the house are fitted with dimmable linear incandescent lighting fixtures concealed beneath plastic grilles. These fixtures are quieter than dimmable fluorescent fixtures, and the incandescent bulbs butt together for unbroken illumination.

concrete and block were troweled with Conproco Foundation Coat (Conproco Corp., P. O. Box 16477, Hookset, N. H. 03106; 603-626-5100), a fiberglass-reinforced concrete coating. We colored the coating to blend with the local granite. Though this product provides structural reinforcement for masonry walls, we applied it primarily for aesthetic reasons.

Insulation support—We fastened 2x6 pressure-treated plates to the top of the beam system with powder-activated, stainless-steel fasteners, then toenailed floor joists to the plates. Floor framing consists of 2x10 Western spruce joists for the house and 2x8 pressure-treated joists for the

decks, all spaced 16 in. o. c. The 2x10s are topped with a ¾-in. T&G plywood subfloor, and the 2x8s with 5/4x6 cedar decking.

We nailed 1x3 cleats near the bottoms of the 2x10s to support loose panels of ¼-in. tempered pegboard, which in turn support 5½-in. fiberglass batts. The pegboard protects the insulation, but allows it to dry out should it get wet.

Building bents—Meanwhile, back at our shop, Bill Strodel supervised the manufacture of parts for the bents. We settled on the use of bents for aesthetic reasons—namely, to reinforce the modular layout of the house. Built of Douglas fir, the two-layer bents consist of double 3x8 top chords;

double 3x6 bottom chords and posts; and double 3x4 queen posts and webs (drawing p. 89). Strong joints were achieved by running ¾-in. square-head bolts through custom-made, ½-in. thick steel connecting plates sandwiched between the layers. High-stress joints at the perimeter walls, eaves and other critical points are reinforced with two 2⅝-in. TECO shear plates per bolt (TECO, P. O. Box 203, Colliers, W. Va. 26035; 800-438-8326). Shear plates are circular metal connectors that ride in grooves cut in the timbers; the plates distribute compression loads and shear forces (for more on metal connectors, see *FHB* #43, pp. 44-49). The grooves are cut with a cutter head, a special tool resembling a hole

A transparent cricket

A cricket, or saddle, is a small gable that diverts rainwater around an obstruction, typically a chimney. We wanted to make the chimney cricket for this house out of glass to allow natural light to wash down the stone face of the fireplace. No millwork company we contacted wanted any part of the idea.

We found a glass company (Paragon Glass, Inc., 210 Factory St., Watertown, N. Y. 13601; 315-782-6300) that offered to make and install glazing for the cricket, provided we framed the opening. They would help us work out the framing details. We accepted.

The framing (drawing right) consists of two gable rafters, two valley rafters and a ridge beam supported on one end by a triple 2x header nailed on either end of a roof truss. The valley rafters are raised above the roof plane and machined at the tops to accept valley flashing and grooved near the bottoms to support the roof deck. The top of the ridge beam and gable rafters are rabbeted to receive the glazing panels.

The glazing itself consists of two triangular, double-glazed, 1-in. thick, low-e glass panels. The tops of the panels are ¼-in. tempered glass to withstand impact from above, and the bottoms are ¼-in. laminated safety glass that won't shatter and fall if it's broken. The panels are bedded in butyl glazing tape and supported at the valley rafters with aluminum clips. The skylight is flashed at the chimney, ridge and valleys with terne-coated stainless-steel flashing.

The final effect is of clean structural members that are glazed to let light in from above (photo above). The total cost of the glazing was $543.50, including installation, but not including our structural work. —*S. T.*

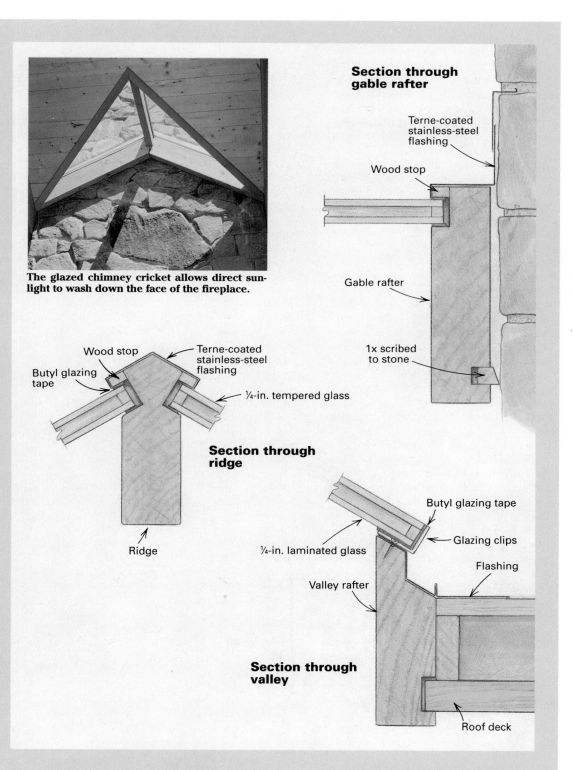

The glazed chimney cricket allows direct sunlight to wash down the face of the fireplace.

Section through gable rafter

Terne-coated stainless-steel flashing

Wood stop

Gable rafter

1x scribed to stone

Section through ridge

Wood stop

Terne-coated stainless-steel flashing

Butyl glazing tape

¼-in. tempered glass

Ridge

Section through valley

Butyl glazing tape

Glazing clips

Flashing

¼-in. laminated glass

Valley rafter

Roof deck

saw that's available from TECO. The ½-in. voids between the two layers are filled with strips of Douglas fir.

The bents were shipped in pieces to the job site, assembled and then raised with the help of block and tackle. Once all the bents were raised, we connected the bottoms of the posts to the rim joists with TECO prepunched truss plates and added temporary bracing where necessary. Finally, we installed a 3x8 ridge beam in precut notches at the tops of the trusses.

Closing in on winter—With the bents installed, we raced to get the house under cover before winter. Over the top chords, we installed exposed 2x6 T&G white-pine roof decking, 2¾-in. thick urethane foam insulation and 15-lb. felt. Large blue reinforced-polyethylene tarps were spread, tied and strapped over the whole thing for added protection. The finish roofing would be deferred until spring when it could be done more efficiently.

Meantime, mason Clyde LaGraves built the fireplace, which fills one module (photo p. 89). We picked the pinkish-colored granite for it—including a 700-lb. lintel stone—from a local quarry that closed more than 40 years ago. The mortar was colored to look old by adding 6 heaping tablespoons of dry, black cement coloring and 2 heaping tablespoons of dry, red cement coloring (both supplied by a local masonry supplier) to 5 gal. of water, which, in turn, was mixed with the mortar. We raked the joints so that the granite rocks are in relief.

Breaking ice—That December was the coldest on record: 21 days of below-zero temperatures. We loaded the wall insulation, flooring, paneling, trim and whatever tools and equipment we could think of (including heaters and enough propane for the winter) on the scow for one last boat trip to the island. On Dec. 14 and 15, we broke 7 miles of 2-in. to 3-in. thick ice in temperatures ranging from -4 F to -17 F. The balance of the millwork and other materials would be delivered later by snowmobile and sled when the ice cover was thick and sound.

Thin walls—Before freeze-up, we had managed to start framing exterior wall panels to fit between the bents. Now it was time to complete the walls and get some heat inside the house.

We framed both the exterior and interior walls with 2x3s to allow the wall posts to be exposed. The exterior walls are insulated with 2½-in. thick fiberglass batts (sufficient for a three-season house), covered on the inside with a 6-mil polyethylene vapor barrier and covered on the outside with ½-in. plywood sheathing and then with Tyvek house wrap.

The spaces between the bents were sized both vertically and horizontally to accommodate the Andersen windows. The doors, however, were another matter. The larger mill houses were not interested in making special doors for us. We were fortunate enough to have the Croghan Island Mill nearby (Bridge St., Croghan, N. Y. 13327; 315-346-1115), an heirloom that is still running on water power. They made all of the

exterior and interior door units to our dimensions at very reasonable prices.

With the walls roughed in, our finish carpenters applied 1x6 T&G white-pine paneling to the interior of the house and 1x6 T&G Western red-cedar siding to the exterior. The only exterior trim on the house is cedar boards milled to match the bent posts and nailed to the exterior siding directly over the hidden posts. This again reinforced the module. The soffit is finished with 1x6 white pine and continues from the exterior to the interior to provide a visual link between the outdoors and the indoors.

Back on top—Once the ice melted in early April, we resumed work on the roof. We removed the tarps, applied furring strips horizontally 5 in. o. c. over the felt and topped the roof with Western red-cedar shingles nailed to the furring. The valleys and gables were flashed with terne-coated stainless-steel flashing (TCS) made by the Follansbee Steel Corporation (P. O. Box 610, Follansbee, W. Va. 26037; 800-624-6906). This material is as workable as copper, but it doesn't leach and stain shingles like copper does. Its color, almost like pewter, blends well with weathered shingles. At this time, we also installed a custom-made, chimney-cricket skylight over the living room (see sidebar p. 91) and two Pella skylights, one over each bathroom (top photo, p. 90).

Linear lighting—Meantime, the finishing crew laid fir flooring throughout the house, built pine cabinets for the kitchen and bathrooms and prepared the tops of the interior soffits to accommodate cove lighting (bottom right photo, p. 90).

We chose ALKCO linear incandescent lighting fixtures for the cove lighting (ALKCO, Div. of

Jac Jacobsen Industies, Inc., 11500 West Melrose Ave., Franklin Park, Il. 60131; 708-451-0700). This dimmable lighting is considerably more expensive than fluorescent lighting (a 12-in. long fixture costs almost $40), but it's also considerably nicer. The light is warm, soft and continuous (the bulbs butt together tightly, unlike fluorescent bulbs), and the fixtures are much quieter than dimmable fluorescent fixtures.

Odds and ends—By late spring, the house was close to completion. The outside crew laid the decking and built cedar railings. The railing posts were laid out on the module to reflect the structural layout of the building. We designed the balustrade with an open slot at the top for easy viewing of the river below.

Augliano Painting of Clayton, N. Y., finished the siding and deck railings with Cabot's Bleaching Stain and the soffit with Clear Wood Finish, or CWF, made by The Flood Company. Inside, they applied clear finishes only: Watco Danish Oil on the wall paneling, ceiling, bents and cabinetry; and polyurethane on the flooring. Doors were finished with Pratt & Lambert Solid Hide Oil Stain, in a color matching the "Terratone" color of the Andersen windows.

Landscaping was kept to a minimum. We did some planting and seeding to cover our tracks and to give back to nature some of what we had taken. We planted native flora only: cedar, pine, maple, birch and juniper. A wet spring made this somewhat difficult. Bud Constance, who sowed the seeds, was thinking on his feet, however. He wore snowshoes so he wouldn't sink up to his knees in soggy soil. □

Steve Taylor is a designer/builder in Thousand Island Park, N. Y. Photos by Bruce Greenlaw.

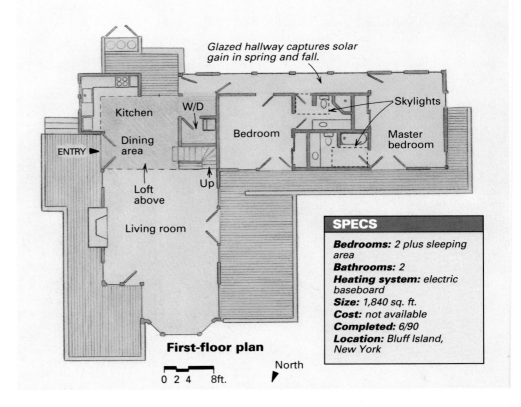

Glazed hallway captures solar gain in spring and fall.

Kitchen
W/D
Skylights
Bedroom
Master bedroom
ENTRY ▶
Dining area
Loft above
Up
Living room

First-floor plan

0 2 4 8ft.

North ▶

SPECS

Bedrooms: 2 plus sleeping area
Bathrooms: 2
Heating system: electric baseboard
Size: 1,840 sq. ft.
Cost: not available
Completed: 6/90
Location: Bluff Island, New York

Minnesota Lake Cabins

Midwestern architect Edwin Lundie borrowed Norwegian themes for his Lake Superior retreats

by Dale Mulfinger and Leffert Tigelaar

Summer in Minnesota can be a sultry steam bath with enough heat and humidity to send anyone in search of a cool northern lake. Luckily, there are thousands of lakes from which to choose but none quite as majestic and frigid as Lake Superior.

When architect Edwin Lundie (1886-1972) first traveled to the shore of Minnesota's Lake Superior in the late 1930s, the rocky coast and its pine, aspen and birch trees reminded him of Norway. But Lundie had not been to that part of the world. He was a vicarious traveler whose imagination had been stirred by photographs of the Norwegian coast that he found in magazines. It was inspiration enough, however, and over a

Timbers with character. Lundie's cabins use heavy corner posts. A cabin in Grand Marais, Minn., (top photo) shows hallmark horizontal and vertical patterns on its gable ends and small dormers that admit light to a second-story bedroom. Below, the entry to a cabin in Tofte, Minn., shows the same themes.

20-year period Lundie found time at his St. Paul drafting table to design a dozen cabins for the Lake Superior shore. He even designed one for himself. The cabins were patterned after pictures of the Norwegian *stabbur*, or storehouse, published in *National Geographic*.

Lundie spent most of his time designing traditional houses, in Colonial and European styles, for clients located mainly in Minnesota. His work is not widely known, and Lundie is not mentioned in many anthologies on American architecture. Yet his influence is obvious in the work of some contemporary architects in the region.

His wonderful series of cabins, built along a stretch of shore about 80 miles northeast of

Duluth, was unique to his repertoire. They were built in little towns like Tofte, Schroeder and Lutsen by local craftsmen, some of them immigrant Scandinavians. The cabins are still there, tucked in birch groves off the main road that leads north to Canada. Never opulent second homes, the cabins are more primitive than that, and they still cast their own spell. Staying in a Lundie cabin is like making camp in the north woods.

Few rooms, water view—The timber-frame structures resemble the utilitarian storehouses that inspired them. But the interiors are adapted to modern, albeit rustic, amenities like kitchens, bathrooms, running water and electricity. Initially modest (18 ft. by 30 ft.), Lundie's designs for the cabins eventually grew in both complexity and

size. None of the cabins are enormous, but some later designs were stretched to 24 ft. by 36 ft.

In the small cabins, built-in bunks, storage spaces and privacy curtains combine to create sleeping alcoves. Larger cabins have private sleeping rooms, but they were kept away from lake views and were used to distance main living areas from cold north winds.

A body of water, either the lake or one of the rivers that empty into it, is always visible through a wall of windows in a Lundie cabin. Many of the cabins are perched just a few yards from the rocky shoreline where they get commanding views of the lake and plenty of warm morning sunshine. Lundie set fireplaces in the corners of a few of these cabins, then flanked the hearths with rows of windows to provide corner views to the water. Both shed and gabled dormers

Casting its own spell. Heavy timbers and stone fireplaces are typical of Lundie's Lake Superior cabins. This one, near Tofte, Minn., is owned by the same family for which it was designed. Bill White, a descendant of the original owner, enjoys a fire on a cool autumn day.

No detail too small. It wasn't just floor plans that captured Lundie's attention. His architectural designs also included many interior and exterior details, such as this downspout on a cabin in Schroeder, Minn.

Custom fireplace tools. The fireplace in this Grand Marais, Minn., cabin (large photo, p. 93) also is a Lundie design, along with the fireplace screen and tools that go with it. Note the intricate joinery on the fireplace mantel.

bring light to upper rooms in larger cabins, and Lundie made use of operable casement windows for summer ventilation.

Decorative frames—Like their antecedents in Norway, some of Lundie's structures sit atop the rocky terrain on wooden posts or rock pillars. Elaborate sill frames separate wood structures from the ground—a technique used in Norway for keeping out water and rodents. Other cabins sit on traditional foundations made of rock or poured concrete. Heavy fireplaces built of the dark, local stone are rooted directly to bedrock like giant anchors. The corner posts for the heavy timber frames range from 24-in. dia. turned columns to smaller square posts (photos p. 93). Corner posts often had elaborate profiles, and some were decorated with vertical fluting known as spooning.

Inside, the timber frame's cross ties and queen posts subdivide spaces while performing their structural duties (photo facing page). The heavy wooden members often are sturdier than they have to be and are a decorative feature. Lundie was as interested in joinery as he was in good floor plans, so his cabins fit together like beautiful pieces of furniture. His joinery techniques were traditional, even though the craftsmen needed to execute them were near extinction by the middle of this century.

He connected the 6x12 sills with half-lap joints. Corner columns were notched to slip over sill corners, and wall posts were connected to the sills with mortise-and-tenon joints pegged for a tight fit. The surfaces of structural members were often sculpted with an adz to give a hand-hewn look.

A passion for details—Lundie equipped both his home and his office with drafting boards and browsed for design ideas in his extensive library. Few details of these cabins were left to chance. Designs included not only the usual floor plans and elevations but also meticulous, full-scale templates for joinery and decorative hardware. Each cabin has its own pattern for turned wooden light fixtures, some with hand-wrought iron accents. Door latches, made from either wood or wrought iron, were custom-designed. Lundie even designed fireplace tools and screens in forged steel (photo right). Door hinges could vary from room to room in a cabin and might include representations of local plant and animal life. Even the downspout became an architectural detail (photo above). His fascination with these details extended to his Christmas gift-giving. To clients who had commissioned the cabins, Lundie would give framed sketches of cabins or of the hardware that went into them. □

Dale Mulfinger is an architect in Minneapolis, Minn. Leffert Tigelaar is a research assistant and associate in the same firm. Photos by Scott Gibson.

Rustic Retreat

Inspired by East Coast lodges, this stick-framed California house is dressed with hand-hewn log siding

by Joseph Stevens

As an architect who loves nature, I have some misgivings about imposing a house on a beautiful wilderness site. So when I received the call to meet my prospective clients on their Big Sur property, I had my doubts. The clients were actors from Los Angeles, and this conjured up in my mind a few stereotypes and apprehensions.

I was familiar with the site, five acres nestled on a ridge with dramatic views of the Santa Lucia Mountains to the east and the Pacific Ocean to the west. This site has it all: lush landscape, great sun exposure, redwood groves, and to top it off, it is surrounded by a 160-acre greenbelt.

During our first stroll on the site, I was pleased to discover that the couple was sensitive, artistic

and practical. They quelled my fears and explained that they liked the land just the way it was and that their goal was to build a house in harmony with the land's colors, shapes and textures. They wanted to make extensive use of native stone and unpainted wood, a combination that goes back to the early days of Big Sur homesteads. But in designing this home on the very edge of the West Coast, we looked to the east.

The camp connection—The clients originally are from New York, and they wanted their house to remind them of mountain houses of upstate New York. In the late 19th century, a rustic style of house and lodge known as the Camp style

evolved in the Adirondack and Catskill Mountains. These buildings are characterized by their natural wood and stone finishes, both inside and out. Many are log buildings—some with the bark still on the logs. Camp-style houses have a multitude of porches for enjoying the outdoors no matter what the season. The porches are quirky, with nooks and crannies and spaces for swings and outdoor furniture. Camp-style houses have gabled roofs, often with an abundance of dormers and balconies. I made liberal use of all these details, arranged in a symmetrical manner on the front of the house (photo above).

In addition to this East Coast influence, the owners brought their appreciation for the Arts-

Contemporary Camp style. Rendered in weathered wood, this house updates the comfortable detailing that was popularized in the upstate lodges of 19th-century New York (photo above). This elevation shows the formal entry, which is flanked by porches and peeled pole railings. Photo taken at A on floor plan.

Living room. Bookcases framed by log trim rise from a chalk-stone base to bracket the fireplace (photo facing page). The balcony winds its way to a pair of French doors overlooking the back deck. Photo taken at B on floor plan.

and-Crafts style homes—especially those of the Greene brothers of Pasadena. The owners wanted to contrast the rugged, substantial forms of Camp-style logs and timbers on the outside of their home with delicately detailed Craftsman-style wood, iron and stonework on the inside. This was music to my ears because it would allow many of the talented local artisans to participate in the building of the house.

Leaving the outdoors outside—The ridge has fantastic panoramic views in all directions. To take best advantage of them, as well as of the solar orientation and the prevailing breezes for natural ventilation, I devised a long, narrow house set on an east-west axis (floor plan facing page). This plan allowed the major facades to face the views, and as a consequence you can see both the mountains and the ocean from almost every point in the house.

With heart-thumping views right outside, some designers and clients want to weave the outdoors into the interior of the house with huge windows. We rejected this idea. The outdoors—in this case the mountains of Big Sur—are wild and magnificent and too large to bring inside. Instead, the interior spaces are places of warmth, comfort and shelter. The house has enough windows and skylights to keep the interior bright, but the windows are small frames on individual views. The decks are for taking in the big picture.

The owners love to cook and wanted the floor plan to be open to the kitchen (photos this page). The kitchen has all the trappings, including a wood-burning pizza oven, an indoor barbecue and a commercial-grade range.

Wood counters supported by Craftsman-style cabinets in the manner of the Greene brothers

Focused on the kitchen. Placed along the south wall of the house, the kitchen, the dining room and a portion of the living room are all open to one another. Laid atop Craftsman-style cabinets, the maple counter in the foreground turns to teak at the sink. Photo taken at C on floor plan. The log rafters and beams are bolted to the rafters and the floor joists, which makes them appear as structural members.

Arches mean pizza and barbecue. Framed with hand-carved limestone, a barbecue and a wood-fired pizza oven round out the kitchen equipment. Photo taken at D on floor plan.

ring the kitchen. A local furniture maker, Ambrose Pollack, made the cabinets out of reclaimed longleaf pine from the Goodwin Heart Pine Company (Rt. 2, Box 119-AA, Micanopy, Fla. 32667; 800-336-3118). We used lots of this clear, old-growth material throughout the house for floors, stairs, cabinets and trim. The wood's density, hardness and stability make it a good choice for flooring. Plus its amber color also is in keeping with the other species of pine that we used throughout the house and with the creamy yellow chalk stone that covers the fireplace (photo p. 97).

Our mason, Joseph DeMaria, Jr., crafted both the pizza oven and the barbecue out of concrete block, chalk stone and limestone (bottom photo, facing page). The pizza oven is a steel box with a fire-brick floor mounted over a steel firebox. DeMaria found some antique oven doors and was able to incorporate them into the finished oven. We arched the openings of the pizza oven and the barbecue with stone because this somehow seemed to blend with the owners' love of Italian cuisine.

Incidentally, indoor barbecues are notorious for smoking if they are not mechanically vented. To guarantee that the smoke would get out of the flue, we installed a commercial-grade blower vent on the roof.

The log look without the headaches—Log houses look great, but they present certain structural challenges. The buildings can leak—both moisture and air infiltration—if they're not carefully constructed. A house built atop a Big Sur ridge experiences extreme and sudden climate changes, and we were very concerned about problems with swelling and shrinkage. In addi-

Master bedroom. **Thin-wall plaster over a gypsum-board base covers the partition walls, the niches and the rounded-corner fireplaces. Photo taken at E on floor plan.**

SPECS

Bedrooms: 4
Bathrooms: 3½
Heating system: Propane forced air
Size: 3,153 sq. ft.
Cost: $155 per sq. ft.
Completed: 1992
Location: Big Sur, California

Photos taken at lettered positions.

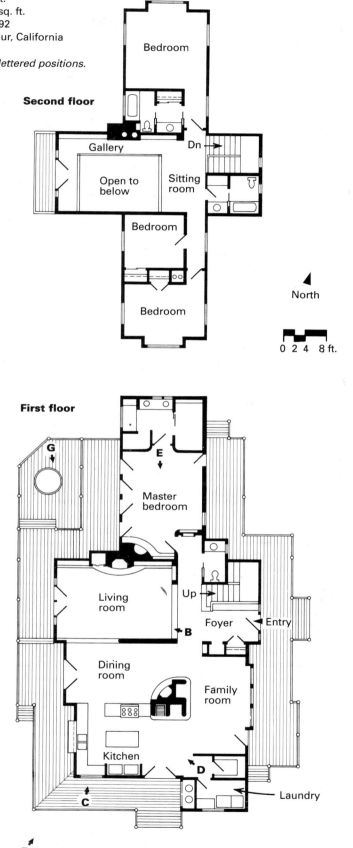

A long, narrow house. *The long, narrow floor plan fits the ridgetop site and takes best advantage of the views to the north and the south.*

tion, the log houses that I've seen often are dark inside, with an uncomfortable bulky feeling. And in a seismic zone, such as the one that runs through Big Sur, log houses present yet another problem: They can require costly engineering to comply with the seismic bracing requirements necessary in this county.

We wanted a home that had the substantial, timeless look of logs, but it had to be light and elegant inside. So, after much research, we opted for a hybrid structure that uses logs for siding and railing outside and for some wall surfaces and exposed framing inside. But most of the house is built with conventional framing techniques.

The material we used to side the house came from Greatwood Log Homes (P. O. Box 707, Elkhart Lake, Wis. 53020; 800-558-5812). Greatwood offers cedar and pine logs with a handhewn finish that were perfect for our project. Greatwood's method of building is called the Ultra Log construction technique. The system uses logs that have been air dried, milled to a uniform height and then ripped in half. Vertical logs at all the corners, which are notched to fit over the stud framing, conceal the ends of the siding (photo below). With meticulous

Pool music. Water on its way to the pool's filtration system cascades down the rock facing to be collected in a shallow basin for recirculation. Photo taken at F on floor plan.

Out back. Balconies, shed roofs, nooks, decks on different levels and a tub make spaces for enjoying the outdoors all across the south side of the house. In the center of the photo, a vertical log with horizontal logs butted into its sides is typical of how outside corners were detailed. Photo taken at G on floor plan.

planing, the round corner logs became both pleasing in appearance and soft to the touch. At windows and doors, the log siding is flush with 4x4 casings.

I sent our design to Greatwood, and the company figured out how much siding, rafters, handrails, poles and posts we needed. The logs arrived in random lengths, and the widths were approximate. The exterior logs are red and white cedar, and the interior ones are white pine.

The siding logs were affixed to the walls with 5-in. spikes driven through the top of each log on a 45° angle through the sheathing and into the studs. Then the logs were spiked together every 4 ft. o. c. using 12-in. spiral nails through drilled holes. Truth be told, this was a time-consuming, tedious process. Each log had to be fitted precisely and tapered at the ends with a drawknife to get them to look good where they intersect the corner posts. Then the joints between each log had to be caulked with Sashco Acrylic rubber window and door sealant (Sashco, 3900 E. 68th Ave., Commerce City, Colo. 80022; 303-286-7271). The finished wall, however, is worth the trouble. It's solid, beautiful and has an R-value of over 15. (Cedar is R-1 per in., and

the siding is 2½ in. to 4 in. thick.) The inside faces of the exterior walls also are covered with log siding, but the siding has a more uniform surface and dimension.

Interior partition walls, on the other hand, are thin-wall plaster over a gypsum-board base. The sculptural qualities of plaster allowed us to make smooth transitions from flat wall planes to built-in fireplaces and display niches, such as in the master bedroom (photo p. 99).

Almost all the logs inside the house are purely ornamental. After nailing up the ponderosa-pine ceiling boards, we lag bolted log rafters on 4-ft. centers. For solid anchorage, we doubled the real rafters or added blocking for the lag bolts. The bolt heads are countersunk into the faux rafters and plugged.

To make a clean line where the rafters meet the walls, we typically cut out the gypsum-board and let the rafters into the holes. Any gaps between the rafters and the gypsum-board disappeared when the thin-wall plaster was applied. This process went much faster than trying to use real log rafters because we didn't have to worry about making a flat plane—the roof—out of a pile of irregular logs.

We did, however, tackle a big stack of irregular log rails and balusters to build the railings that surround the balcony and the decks. After some false starts, we settled on an assembly technique that worked well for us (see sidebar below).

The sound of falling water—Big Sur gets hot and dry in the summer, and fires are an ever-present danger. The volunteer fire department is well-organized and well-equipped, but water is scarce in remote locations. The fire department is always glad to see a body of water that the firefighters can tap into, so we decided to store the water where it could serve a broader purpose. We put it in a swimming pool. Like the planters that border the house, the pool is edged with native stone. Along one side of the pool, the coping (stone rim) drops down about 4 in., allowing the water to be collected in a basin for recirculation. As the water cascades down the rock facing (top photo, facing page), it makes a music that drifts over the pool to the nearby porches. □

Joseph Stevens is a contractor and architect in Carmel, Calif. Photos by Charles Miller except where noted.

Making log railings

Along with our shipment of log siding, we took delivery of enough 3-in. dia. balusters, 4-in. rails and 10-in. posts to make the railings for the decks and the balconies. The posts were either bolted to the joists or to steel post bases set in concrete. The tricky part was putting the tenons on the ends of the rails and then fitting them into the posts. Here's how we did it.

With posts set, we cut the railings 2 in. longer than the distance between the posts. Then we used a 2⅞-in. hole saw to make a 1-in. deep mortise in one post and a 2-in. deep mortise in the opposite post. After chiseling

out the mortises, we chucked a 3-in. hole saw—the next size up—in the big drill. With it, we fashioned a 2-in. long tenon on one end of the rail and a 1-in. long tenon on the other end (photos below). The inside diameter of the one saw matches the outside diameter of the other, so the tenon slips snugly into the mortises. Slide in the 2-in. end all the way, swing it into position and then push the 1-in. end home.

We found it easiest to mark the centers for our balusters while the rails were in place in their mortises. As irregular pieces of material, they have to be turned and fussed with to get

them to look correct together. Baluster centers were marked on one rail, then transferred to the mate with a level held plumb.

The balusters came with premilled tenons, so all we had to do was check them for equal length (they varied a little). We plowed the mortises for the balusters with a Forstner bit, assembled the section of rail and slipped it into its waiting posts. If a rail got reluctant and wanted to spread, we pipe-clamped it during insertion. Once the rails were in place, we ran 6-in. stainless-steel screws through the bottoms of the rails and into the posts to make sure they stay put. —J. S.

Making a round tenon. With the rail firmly secured, a hole saw cuts a round kerf into the rail's end. Then with a careful touch, a handsaw is used to cut away the waste. After a light sanding, the rail is ready to be installed.

Using land shapes. The selection of a building site on the middle of three natural terraces allows an approach to the house from the west along a natural draw, or contour, on the property (above). Building across this contour (below) helps anchor the house visually to its surroundings. This view is from the east and includes the barn to the left of the house.

A House that Fits its Site

The right design starts with a careful survey of the land and conversations with the owners

by Dale Mulfinger

Fred Brandt insisted his new house was going to be more than a floor plan stuck on a piece of land. He and his wife, Ranelle, had bought 40 acres of farmland outside of St. Paul, Minnesota, and came to my architectural firm for help in planning their new house. They wanted something that was completely compatible with the site.

Finding a house design that suits both the land and the homeowner is a process, not a simple decision that can be made in a morning. The most important skill the designer brings to the job is the ability to meld the site's physical attributes with features the owners want in the house.

Rejecting two sites—My colleague, David Zenk, and I began the design process by exploring with the Brandts what they wanted in a house and what they wanted to spend to build it. We looked at photos and magazine clippings of houses—ones they liked and ones they disliked. And we walked the site and discussed possible building approaches with them, especially how we could marry their requirements with specific site locations.

The Brandts have what a neighboring farmer called a "three-story farm." There are three terraces on the property, each of which could have been picked for the house. One of our first goals was to explore each of these areas and weigh factors like road access, views, breezes, the relationship between the house and its garden and how the remaining crop land would be farmed once the house was finished.

The upper terrace was close to the road. From there the property sloped away to the east. A house built there would command the site and give the Brandts considerable long-distance views from second-story windows. And building a house on the upper terrace would require only a short driveway and minimize snowplowing. But the upper-terrace site would be subjected to considerable road noise, which would make it difficult for the Brandts to achieve the pastoral feeling they were seeking. For that reason, the upper terrace didn't seem like the right place to build.

Then there was the lower terrace. It would nestle the house next to a grove of coniferous trees and offer views to a pond to the north and down a valley to the southeast. Unfortunately, this long valley view ended with a smokestack at a utility power plant some miles away. Also, a house on the lower terrace would require a long driveway and would make snowplowing more expensive and difficult. Another disadvantage of the lower terrace was the

The house takes shape
The design for this Minnesota house developed over time. Early sketches by the author included
several views (from left): what he wanted the house to look like to someone
approaching it from the west; a rough diagram of the
first-floor plan; and roof shapes
on the west elevation.

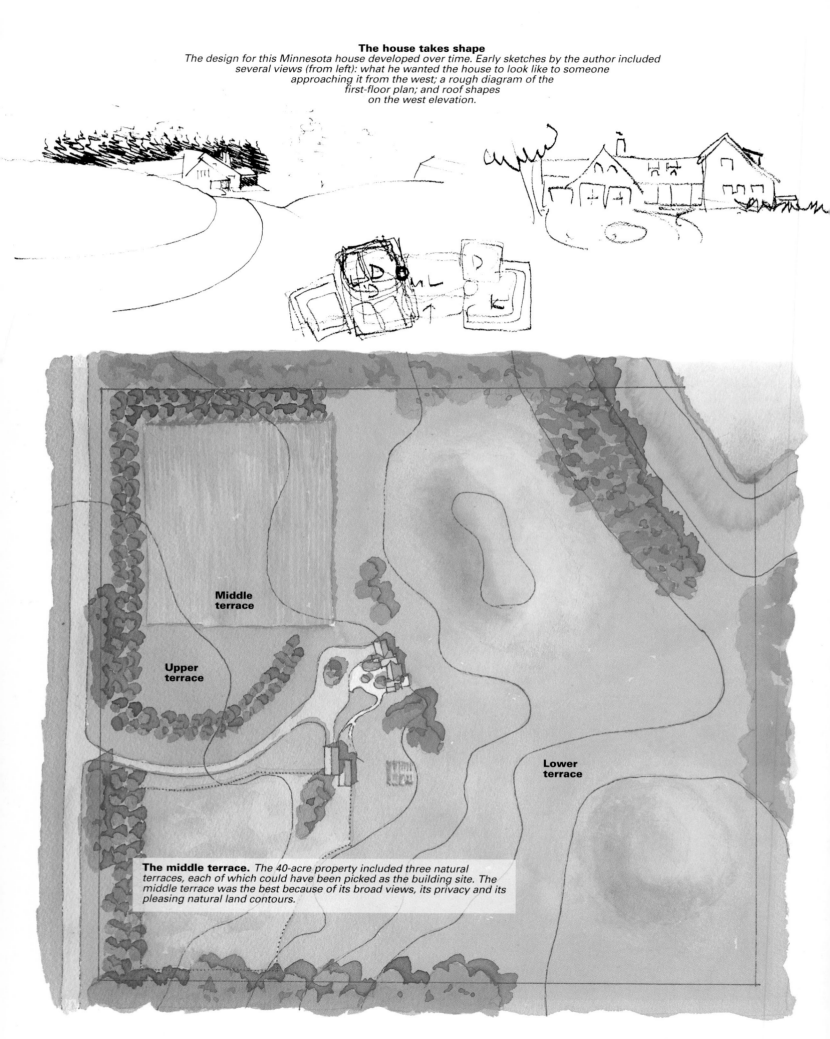

Middle terrace

Upper terrace

Lower terrace

The middle terrace. *The 40-acre property included three natural
terraces, each of which could have been picked as the building site. The
middle terrace was the best because of its broad views, its privacy and its
pleasing natural land contours.*

Top drawings, this page: Dale Mulfinger; bottom drawing, this page: Malcolm Wells

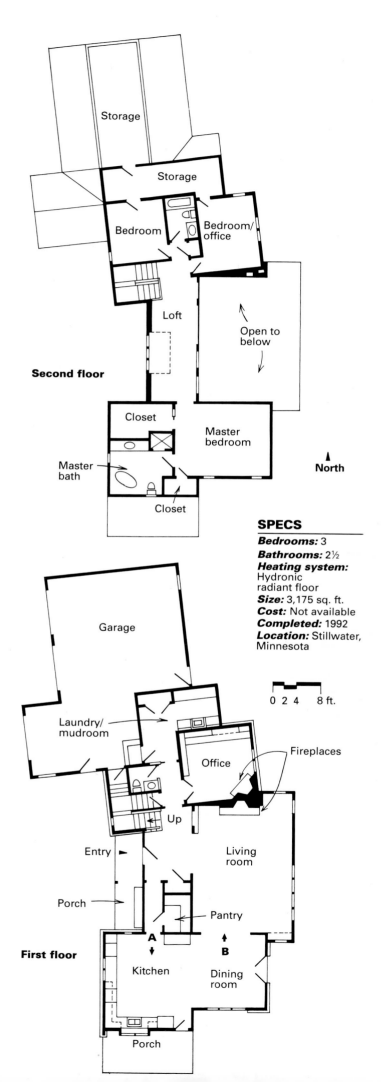

Second floor

Storage

Storage

Bedroom

Bedroom/office

Loft

Open to below

Closet

Master bedroom

Master bath

Closet

North

Garage

Laundry/mudroom

Office

Fireplaces

Up

Entry

Living room

Porch

Pantry

A

B

First floor

Kitchen

Dining room

Porch

SPECS

Bedrooms: 3
Bathrooms: 2½
Heating system: Hydronic radiant floor
Size: 3,175 sq. ft.
Cost: Not available
Completed: 1992
Location: Stillwater, Minnesota

0 2 4   8 ft.

likelihood that new houses would be built near the eastern property line and crowd the Brandts from that direction. So the lower terrace didn't feel right, either.

The correct building site—The middle terrace (bottom drawing, facing page) had the greatest potential. It offered natural spots for a garden and a barn. By placing the house on the middle terrace, the Brandts would enjoy a great view to the east and into a pine grove. David and I saw the opportunity to connect the house form to natural contours and anchor the building visually to the site (bottom photo, p. 102). A farmyard could be created at the bottom of a draw that slanted in from the west, and the driveway could parallel the draw into the site naturally (top photo, p. 102). A house located there would enjoy open views yet be farther away from encroaching development at the site's perimeter. Moreover, not all of the property would be visible from the site, so building a house near the center of the middle terrace would encourage the Brandts to do some walking to see the rest of their property. In a way, choosing this building site would give the Brandts a sense of exploration, even when they were going only as far as their own pond for a picnic.

In the book *A Pattern Language* (Oxford University Press, 1977), the authors refer to site selection as "Site Repair." The book explains it this way: "Consider the site and its buildings as a single, living ecosystem. Leave those areas that are the most precious, beautiful, comfortable and healthy as they are and build new structures on those parts of the site which are least pleasant now." We hadn't picked the worst part of the Brandts' site, but we left some of the best land to look at.

And now the house—We were confident the middle terrace was the best site to build on. That left the task of designing a house, which is a process in which pieces of the house are studied individually and then assembled into a whole. I call this stage of the design process the arms-flailing period because our early design conversations often take place on the site and include plenty of arm waving as we talk about views, the relationships between parts of the house and the site, and how the building might be oriented (top drawings, facing page). One tool that proved very useful throughout the process was topographical information about the site. Early on, I had enlarged a U. S. Geological Survey map of the area to help guide our decisions.

As David and I talked with the Brandts, design fundamentals began to emerge. The kitchen would be to the south so that it could be connected to the garden and the barn, get the full swing of the solar arc and have a view of the driveway. This last feature seemed important to me because people spend so much time in their kitchens. We wanted to give this room a view of the driveway so that the Brandts could watch the comings and goings of family members and guests. The main entry would face the driveway to the west. The garage would be to the north to protect the house from northwest winds. The living room, the dining room and the office would serve as overlooks to the broad eastern view. These were the basic design elements of the building, even if we hadn't yet connected them into a house.

We were also looking for ways to tie the house to the land, and I saw an opportunity in a natural draw in the building site—a contour some 40 ft. long and about 6 ft. deep in the middle—right where the house would be built. Bulldozers could have been brought in to level the site, but I decided this contour could visually connect the house to the land by letting the stone-faced foundation fill in the gap (bottom photo, p. 102).

Narrowing the choices—Once we had the basic orientation of the building, it was time to go to the drawing board and the modeling table. The site/design diagrams David and I had created while walking the property with the Brandts had to be turned into a building. Additional design needs had to be factored into the scheme, and all of it had to be packaged into a reasonable and affordable construction plan. My firm often begins design with several alternatives presented by more than one designer. The purpose of coming up with alternatives is not just to have a number of schemes from which the client can choose, like giving them a choice of cars at a dealership. The process helps frame design questions by giving homeowners plenty of options to consider.

This approach also promotes interaction between the owners and the architects to make sure the owners' priorities are fully understood. The

A well-lit kitchen. The kitchen takes full advantage of the sun. A separate entry (at left) and porch lead to a garden area below the house. Photo taken at A on floor plan.

exchanges between architects and homeowners get the clients comfortable with the idea of making suggestions. And the more David and I talked with the Brandts, the sharper we were able to focus on the right plan. In general, we think the best alternative is the one we are *about* to draw after our clients have critiqued plans we have already proposed.

During this phase I also start to think seriously about roof forms that will be appropriate to the design. The roof should befit the character of the site and be in harmony with the general stylistic preferences of the client. In fact, I've found it's important to find a good roof form before I lock into a plan. That may seem backward, but this approach follows lessons I've learned in both renovation and new construction: Several good floor plans will fit beneath a good roof design, but the opposite isn't always true. That is, you can't necessarily find a pleasing roof shape, even if you start with a good floor plan.

As these building elements began to take form, I found myself sketching a roof with two prominent gables over the main house nestled in a valley. The sketch recognized the importance of the roof as one entered high from the west and looked down at the farmyard. The house would extend along the brow of the middle terrace and would have a slight bend in it so that it would wrap around approaching visitors and give them a feeling of being welcomed. At the opposite side of the house, the living room (top photo, right) would act as a gigantic bay window with panoramic views. The dining room would connect with a deck built on a promontory that projects to the east.

Overcoming design snags—The Brandts were to say later that they didn't really like any of our early design alternatives. Fortunately, the process worked. We gradually got to a plan and form that was comfortable and visually appropriate to this site (floor plan, p. 105).

For example, in several of the early house plans, we struggled with conflicts between our desire to provide a southern kitchen and our concern for keeping the kitchen close to the garage for grocery stocking. We sometimes forget that the kitchen is still the larder and that all the stuff that is brought into the house has to be lugged from car to kitchen. Eventually, though, the Brandts found it made more sense to separate the garage and the kitchen, which allowed us to pull the front gables away from each other and place the main entry between them (middle photo, right).

At the south end of the house, right off the kitchen, we created a second entry and a small porch (bottom photo, right). The porch is a wonderful place to sort vegetables, leave tomatoes to ripen, organize seeds for spring planting or just to sit and daydream. And walking back from the garden toward this southern facade is one of the most pleasant approaches to the house. It presents the house as if it were a little cottage and gives it a more intimate feeling than you might get when approaching the house from the driveway at the main entry.

The layout inside the house also was evolving in response to images and relationships that were important to the Brandts. For example, I had always imagined locating the stair to the second floor next to the fireplace. But the Brandts thought this was forcing the floor plan to become too geometric. David had the foresight to relocate the stair into the left front gable. With windows added to reveal the cascading stair, this change made the gable faces distinct from one another. To the right front gable we added tiny glass-block windows between upper and lower kitchen cabinets (photo facing page) to give a decorative splash of light on the counter. The long, narrow shape of the house would give broad views of property to the east and would help create a sense of shelter around the farmstead. The sense of enclosure was enhanced by pulling one of the garage stalls in front of the others, which also helped break up the long west facade.

As the house took shape, each piece of the facade developed its unique character and identity with the site. To me, it looked like a farmhouse that had grown over time, and I had this impression confirmed in an unexpected way. After the house was finished, we arranged a tour for prospective clients. As the group walked down the driveway, one person looked at the house and said she couldn't ascertain just where we had built the addition. When she learned later that the whole house was new, she was apologetic and embarrassed. But to me, her comment was quite a compliment. □

Dale Mulfinger is a principal in Mulfinger, Susanka & Mahady Architects in Minneapolis, Minn. Photos by the author except where noted.

Photo facing page and top and bottom photos this page: Peter Kerze

Room with a view. The living room faces east to take advantage of wide views of the property. At the end of the room is a fireplace faced in stone that was gathered locally. Photo taken at B on floor plan.

West-facing entry. The two roof gables are separated by the main entry, which is protected by an overhanging porch roof.

A place to relax. A small porch off the kitchen is an ideal place to relax with views of the garden to the south. Photo taken at C on floor plan.

Superinsulated in Idaho
Lessons learned from an energy-efficient house

by Jonathan Marvel

Building sites in the old part of Hailey, Idaho, don't come up for sale very often. So when a corner lot became available in 1983, my wife Stefanie and I jumped at the chance to buy it. We had been living in Hailey for several years, and with two small children, we had decided that building in town would keep us near all the good aspects of small-town life. In the old part of town, the schools are close by, the wide sidewalks are busy and the 100-year-old houses dating back to the boomtown mining years contribute a sense of permanence to the neighborhood. Our site also had the advantage of being but a short walk to my architecture practice in Hailey's business district.

In the year and a half before we were able to build, I spent a fair amount of time consid-

ering the influences that would shape a house on our site. The lot is on the southwest corner of the intersection of what is basically a north/south, east/west street grid. A sun chart investigation revealed good sun exposure—even at mid-winter solstice with sunset at about 5 p. m. on December 21st. This underlines the wisdom of Hailey's settlers, as a narrow gap in the ridge to the west allows the sun to shine a little longer on the town. Here in the Wood River Valley, many homesites are shaded for long periods of the winter day as the sun sets early behind mountains that rise 2,000 ft. from the valley floor.

Good views to the west and north suggested a two-story house to take advantage of the scenery. A two-story plan would also leave more of the lot open for garden and play

space for the kids. We didn't want our house to look out of place, so before I began designing, I spent time studying the aspects of the neighborhood houses that could be incorporated into a new house. Large porches, low fences, window bays, clearly defined entries, turrets and other Victoriana are all common parts of this townscape.

We chose to have a two-step-up transition at the sidewalk into the yard and another three steps up to the front porch to underscore the change from public to private (photo below). High awning windows on the street sides of the house balance the light indoors, while simultaneously providing privacy. But most of the glazing is on the southeast and southwest faces of the house to capture as much sun as possible (photo facing page).

L-shaped, with two stories—Our corner lot suggested an L-shaped house because its perpendicular wings would provide privacy for the backyard and offer the greatest exposure to the sun for the bedrooms and living rooms—an important consideration in a climate with a five- or six-month winter. The arrangement of rooms that we eventually settled upon places two bedrooms, two bathrooms and a small deck on the second floor (floor plan this page). The childrens' sleeping area is one large space right now. When they get a little older I'll give them each some privacy by dividing this space into two rooms.

On the ground level, a vestibule connects the front door with a wide hallway. The vestibule has a closet on one side and a row of coat pegs on the other. Beneath the pegs is a boot rack for the sometimes slushy footwear that crosses the threshold. Doors on the interior side of the vestibule help us to keep the arctic air out of the living spaces during the winter months.

At the south end of the downstairs hall are the kitchen, dining area and living room. While they occupy distinct corners of this wing, all three are open to one another (photo next page). A combination laundry room/pantry is adjacent to the kitchen. The other ground floor wing of the house is a studio/library of about 400 sq. ft. that has a half bath in one corner. This space doubles as a bedroom when guests stay over.

The first and second floors total about 2,400 sq. ft., which we felt would be the maximum size we could afford to build. For future use we decided to include a full basement which, at an estimated cost of $12 per square foot, we thought of as a bargain space. Any garage would have to wait for future prosperity.

Conservation measures—Skiers come from all over the world to enjoy the dry, powdery snow just up the road at Sun Valley. The snow is dry because it gets cold here, and stays cold. Ours is an 8,100 heating degree-day climate (about the same as Minneapolis). As a consequence, we spent a good deal of time considering construction details that would achieve maximum conservation of energy.

Fortuitously, as I began my design work I learned about the Model Conservation Standards (MCS) Program being sponsored by Bonneville Power (the public power supplier to much of the northwest U. S.). This program would subsidize construction of 400 houses that would meet or exceed the new construction standards for energy-efficient houses. We applied and were accepted as one of the houses to be built in Idaho. In return for the construction subsidy, which amounted to about $5,000 for a house the size of ours, we agreed to be monitored for energy use for two years without burning wood for heat. The house also had to be all-electric to qualify—although we eventually put in a gas range.

We settled on double-wall construction with a 6-mil polyethylene vapor barrier between the walls (top drawing, p. 112). This detail allowed

Building on tradition. Symmetrical gables, horizontal siding, low fences and a broad porch are some of the traditional design elements used by architect Jonathan Marvel to fit his house into an established neighborhood (photo facing page). In the backyard the wings of the house come together at outdoor sitting areas on both levels (photo above).

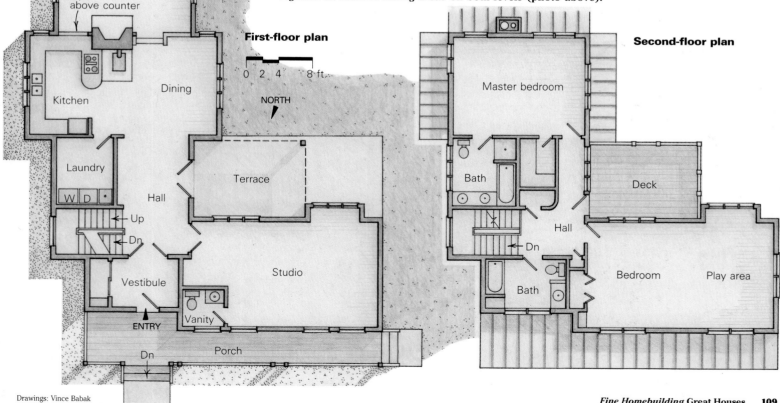

First-floor plan

0 2 4 8 ft.

NORTH

Living

Open above counter

Kitchen

Dining

Laundry

W D

Hall

Up

Dn

Vestibule

ENTRY

Vanity

Dn

Porch

Terrace

Studio

Second-floor plan

Master bedroom

Bath

Deck

Hall

Dn

Bedroom

Play area

Bath

Drawings: Vince Babak

us to use the interior wall for wiring and plumbing, without violating the integrity of the barrier. Stuffed with standard density fiberglass batts, the wall is rated at about R-30.

The flat-ceiling areas are insulated with R-60 blown-in fiberglass (Insulsafe from Certain-Teed, Box 860, Valley Forge, Pa. 19482; 215-341-7000). In cathedral-ceiling areas we have R-38 fiberglass batts with 1-in. polyisocyanurate sheathing over the plywood decking for a total R-value of 45. In the basement we installed 2-in. thick sheets of extruded polystyrene under the slab, as well as on the outside of the 8-ft. high concrete walls around the basement. Our long-term plan is to eventually furr out the basement walls with R-11 insulated 2x4 stud walls. We left the floor over the basement uninsulated during the monitoring period, as that permitted us to receive a slightly larger subsidy based on our gross heated area. Since then, we have added R-19 batts in the floor.

The program also required us to install a whole house air-to-air heat exchanger. The model we chose was an E-Z Vent #340 (Des Champs Laboratories, Inc., Box 440, 17 Farinella Dr., E. Hanover, N. J. 07936; 201-884-1460), which was the largest residential model we could find. On high speed, it provides 400 cfm.

For the windows I chose Pella clad-casements (The Rolscreen Co., 102 Main St., Pella,

Iowa 50219; 515-628-1000). The Pella design will permit us to replace the inner glazing panel at a future time with high-tech glass when the cost and heat-regulating efficiency of the glass improve. I did consider low-e glass but the expense did not appear to be cost-effective when we built the house.

At studwall corners we used drywall clips to eliminate the extra stud that is typically installed for drywall backing. Not only does this save some wood, but it also makes a little more room for insulation. And in the 2x6 exterior wall, we used 4x headers with 2 in. of extruded polystyrene insulation on the inside face of each one.

To protect the vapor barrier and roof insulation, I did not place any recessed lighting fixtures in exterior ceilings. And to cut down on convection currents in the walls, we kept plumbing penetrations through the top plates to an absolute minimum and sealed around the few that we made with urethane foam. In addition, wiring runs were routed to avoid passing through the top plates. We eliminated air infiltration at the rim joists by overlapping them with 2 in. of expanded polystyrene insulation.

According to our heat-loss calculations for the design area of 3,850 square feet (including basement), we would need 15 kw of electric resistance heat to keep the house at a comfortable temperature. In a somewhat experi-

mental solution I decided to install a 10 kw in-line duct heater (Delta-Flo Manufacturing Co., Inc., West Rialto Ave., San Bernardino, Calif. 92410; 714-888-3291). The fresh air that passes through the duct heater has already been preheated by the heat exchanger. I picked up the additional 5 kw of heating capacity with three baseboard heaters in the basement, which isn't served by the forced-air system.

Cost control— In an effort to balance our desire for some attractive finishes and details with our limited budget, we settled on some trade-offs. In the extra-expense column we installed a select-grade strip white oak floor in the downstairs living areas and hard maple for the kitchen countertops, window sills and baseboards (the maple actually cost somewhat less than the oak). At the heart of the house, we used Italian tile around the woodstove between the kitchen and the dining area, and around the fireplace in the living room. We also splurged in the kitchen and bought some high-end cabinets (top photo, facing page) called Opus One (Crystal Cabinetworks, Inc., 1100 Crystal Dr., Princeton, Minn. 55371; 612-389-4187). We decided to spend extra for cast-iron sinks and tubs in the bathrooms.

On the economy side we chose to use ½-in. drywall with a standard taped-and-light-spray finish. The ¾-in. radius BeadeX drywall corner

Around the stove. The public spaces of the house are organized around a steel woodstove set against a tiled surround (photo facing page). Under the tile, a massive concrete-block chimney helps to retain the stove's heat. Cabinets finished with plastic laminate banded with white oak were one of a few carefully selected custom touches (photo right); drawer fronts are riftsawn white oak and the countertops are maple. The rounded drywall corners wrapping the window keep the trim to a minimum, yet maintain the rounded feel of the drawer and counter edges. Shelves normally used for clothes closets are an inexpensive and attractive way to organize dishware (photo below).

beads (BeadeX Manufacturing Co., 833 Houser Way N., Renton, Wash. 98055; 206-228-6600) cost a little more than standard 90° corners. But we used drywall returns at all windows, so we saved the cost of extensive trim work and materials while maintaining the rounded softness at these edges afforded by the radiused corner beads.

The stairs and upstairs bedrooms were carpeted with a low-cost nylon carpeting (about $14 per sq. yd.), and we used sheet vinyl for the floors in the bathrooms and laundry/pantry. All the lighting fixtures were low-cost stock models from a local discount supply house or purchased by mail from Conran's Habitat (921 Eastwind Dr., Suite 114, Westerville, Ohio 43081; 800-462-1769). We have no upper cabinets in the house. Instead, we installed Closet-Maid open closet shelving (Clairson International, Inc., 720 S. W. 17th St., Ocala, Fla. 32674; 904-351-6100) in the kitchen (bottom photo) and pantry. The cabinets in the pantry-/laundry are low-end stock models.

Acting as my own contractor, I was able to maintain control over some of the costs of the construction as well as eliminate a contractor's fee. The final cost of the project amounted to about $59 per square foot for the 2,400 square feet of finished area. This excludes the subsidy—about $2 per square foot. Current construction costs would be about $70 per square foot.

Reading the meters—As part of the effort to quantify the study results, we compiled the costs associated with the extra insulation, the heat exchanger, the vapor/air barrier, extra lumber for the inside wall and labor costs, and came up with $1.75 per square foot of finished floor space—about $4,000. The calculated energy use for our house came to 3.73 kw hours per square foot per year; our actual measured use was about 15% less than this or about $500 per year at $.0412 per kw hour. According to BPA's research, this represents a savings of about 50% in energy use as compared with a typical house of similar size.

The air-to-air heat exchanger operated 24 hours a day during the heating season to ensure indoor air quality. Our indoor air was tested for formaldehyde gas (a typical outgas byproduct of many building materials, especially carpet backing and particleboard) and radon. Because I had specified low-fuming particleboard for all underlayment and because

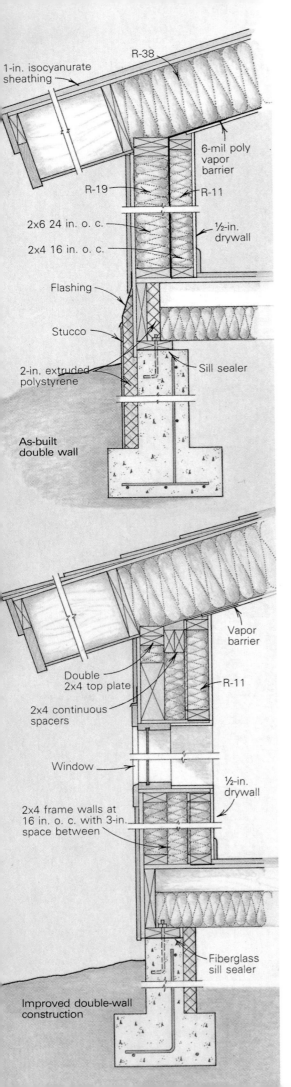

1-in. isocyanurate sheathing

R-38

6-mil poly vapor barrier

R-19

R-11

2x6 24 in. o. c.

2x4 16 in. o. c.

½-in. drywall

Flashing

Stucco

2-in. extruded polystyrene

Sill sealer

As-built double wall

Double 2x4 top plate

Vapor barrier

2x4 continuous spacers

R-11

Window

½-in. drywall

2x4 frame walls at 16 in. o. c. with 3-in. space between

Fiberglass sill sealer

Improved double-wall construction

all the cabinets were covered inside and out with plastic laminate, our formaldehyde readings were virtually zero. The radon readings were acceptable in the living areas (the heat exchanger ventilates the living areas only and not the basement), but in the basement we had a 12-month reading of 25 picocuries per liter of air—six times the recommended level set by the EPA. It turns out that all the tested areas of central Idaho and especially parts of the Wood River Valley are hot spots for radon gas. Subsequently, we have installed a sub-slab ventilation system. It consists of a 4-in. ABS pipe that passes through the slab into the gravel base. The pipe exits through a side wall, where a Kanalflakt fan (Kanalflakt, Inc., 1712 Northgate Blvd., Sarasota, Fla. 34234; 813-359-3267) helps to pull the radon out of the gravel. This system appears to have lowered the radon levels by about 75%. I'm not satisfied with this, and the problem seems to be the compacted gravel under the basement slab. Because we are not using the basement for living space at the moment, our concern about the radon levels is not too great. But if we do choose to finish the basement at some future time, we'll have to take additional steps to reduce the radon levels.

Our house was also given a blower door test to determine the natural air exchange rate and to see if the heat exchanger was providing enough fresh air—about .5 air changes per hour. The measured natural air change came to about .18 air changes per hour and this rate combined with the 350 to 400 cfm provided by the air-to-air heat exchanger brought the total air change up to the recommended range. In the summer and warmer weeks of spring we turn off the exchanger and open the windows.

Some lessons learned—The experience of building and then living in a superinsulated house for six years has provided several lessons. The wall profile we used in our house is not one I still specify. These days, I typically specify a double wall of two 2x4 stud walls at 16 in. or 24 in. o. c., depending on the loading, with a 3-in. gap between the walls (bottom drawing). All three spaces are filled with R-11 fiberglass batts, giving a wall rated at about R-34. This greatly lowers conductive heat losses through the studs and reduces the amount of wood needed in the walls.

I've also stopped using 6-mil polyethylene because of the difficulties in avoiding and patching tears. We have tried Canvex II, a film made by Raven Industries, Inc. (P. O. Box 1007, Sioux Falls, S. D. 57117; 605-336-2750) and MaKa film of the Max Katz Bag Company, Inc. (P. O. Box 1666, Indianapolis, Ind. 46206; 317-635-9561). Both of these air/vapor barriers have reinforcing threading to prevent tears. They are also much more flexible than standard 4- or 6-mil poly. Most recently, however, we have started using the airtight drywall system, which works quite well, provided special attention is paid to wiring and plumbing penetrations (for more on this system, see *FHB* #37, pp. 62-65).

I would not recommend the heating system we chose for our house. The 10 kw in-line duct heater is really too much heat for the relatively small fans of the EZ-Vent 340. We have had many problems with the limit switches on the duct heater cutting off the heating elements because of insufficient air flow. We finally installed a 125-cfm booster fan in the supply duct to increase air flow over the elements. This fan works well but noticeably increases noise levels. Next time, I would choose a separate forced-air system, or even better, a radiant-floor heating system which, unfortunately, is the most expensive option.

Another detail I would treat differently is the sub-slab gravel in the basement. In the future I would specify that the gravel be ¾ in. minimum and not compacted, or I would install a manifold of perforated PVC drainpipe under the slab, connected to a single riser.

Finally, because the windows at the design temperature of −12° F produce over half the heat loss in the house, careful consideration needs to be given to low-e, argon-filled insulating glass, or various window insulations such as window quilts to cope with cold-weather conditions.

On the whole, our building and living experiences continue to be very good ones. The environment created by the tight building envelope and heavy insulation makes for a very comfortable home. Even in our dry climate, indoor humidity seems to hover around 35% to 40%, a very desirable level. All exterior-wall inside-surface temperatures are warmer than houses built to FHA or similar standards, and so the rooms are more comfortable because of less body-heat loss to wall surfaces. Temperatures in the house are remarkably stable and change very slowly. Down to an outside temperature of 44° F, no extra heat but sunlight is required to keep the house comfortable.

We are able to heat the house for an annual electricity cost of about $170 at $.045/kwh plus about two and one-half cords of black locust firewood, which costs us $110 per cord. Our woodstove is able to heat the whole house, and even though the house is somewhat elongated because of the L-configuration, there's only a 3° to 5° temperature differential between the stove location and remote rooms. While we heat primarily with wood, we still leave the heat exchanger on to provide fresh air. This is important to avoid what's known sometimes as the "plastic-bag syndrome"—the claustrophobic stillness and musty air quality that can occur in tight, heavily insulated houses without effective fresh-air supplies.

The house is cool in the summer—although some west shading would improve a slight tendency to overheat in the children's room on hot summer days. We love the way the daylight streams into the house, and continue to recommend this building approach to anyone in similar cold weather climates. □

Jonathan Marvel is an architect with a practice in Hailey, Idaho, where he specializes in the design of energy-efficient homes.

A Mountain Retreat

A designer/builder blends curved walls and windows with traditional New England shapes and materials

by Lee Stevens

The curved wall provides eastern views and southern exposure. This home's modern look is tempered with vertical siding, metal roofing with a cupola and arched windows with muntin bars, all of which create connections with New England tradition. The metal roofs, aluminum window frames and steel deck rails are painted red to contrast with the weathered gray, rough wood. Photo taken at A on floor plan.

Anyone who's been commissioned to design and build a house dreams of ideal clients, people with the least conceptions of what a house should look like, willing to focus on the functions the house serves and not fixated on details. Hank and M. J. Powell are as close as I've come to ideal clients. They're receptive to new ideas, but they consider how the idea will affect the big picture. Having worked for the Powells in the past, I was thrilled when they asked me to design and build a vacation home for them in the heart of New Hampshire's White Mountains (photo above). The site was spectacular, and my bread and butter has been designing and building additions and renovations for old houses. Almost universally, my clients have wanted innovative floor plans within exteriors that respected the conservative context of house and neighborhood. The Powells also wanted a contemporary, open floor plan in a house that looked like it belonged in New England.

After analyzing the site, however, I realized that a traditional building form, a barn or a colonial, was well-nigh impossible. The best views were to the east, yet the southern exposure was also good. The form that contained an open plan, offered views to the east and provided a southern exposure was hardly traditional: a semicircle.

Traditional tastes with untraditional requirements—In addition to an open floor plan, the Powells wanted an informal, one-room living space, big enough for a ski crowd but cozy and comfortable for two on quiet weekends. Sleeping quarters were to include a loft for a general sack-out area and a private bedroom. They also wanted a garage, several bathrooms and an entry with ski and boot racks. Rough-sawn post-and-beam construction, with a board finish throughout, was the look Hank wanted for a low-maintenance cabin atmosphere. All of this had to be wrapped within a structure that expressed a traditional New England heritage and the conservative context of the neighborhood.

We first discussed how to build a cabin on this particular site. First, the lot is high on a ridge. A small amount of level ground on the property is bounded on the west by the access road and on the east by a slope that drops sharply into the Pemigewasset River valley. The valley view dominates the entire eastern side of the lot from north to south, and I wanted to have this view.

Unfortunately, the spectacular views also meant that the site was exposed to north winds

Segmented wall, roof deck and metal fasteners simplify post-and-beam construction. The foundation is a pedestal, and the curved portion cantilevers over the foundation. It's not really a curve; the wall is made of segments that are sized to match the rough openings for Pella windows and doors. Placing a roof deck over the circular eastern elevation also simplified the roof framing. And it's not a traditional post and beam, as evidenced by the use of joist hangers instead of mortise-and-tenon joinery. Photo taken at B on floor plan.

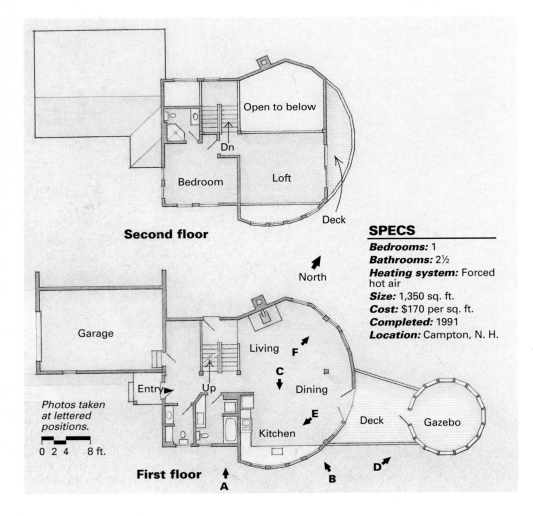

Second floor

SPECS

Bedrooms: 1
Bathrooms: 2½
Heating system: Forced hot air
Size: 1,350 sq. ft.
Cost: $170 per sq. ft.
Completed: 1991
Location: Campton, N. H.

North

Photos taken at lettered positions.

0 2 4   8 ft.

First floor

that predominate in winter and to tough storms from the northeast. Although the site has excellent southern exposure, exploiting it by placing the long side of the house along the east-west axis meant the house's orientation would be perpendicular to the best views. Conversely, orienting the long side of the house along the north-south axis would mean the shorter side would face southward, minimizing solar gain. And passive solar gain is important in warming a house in winter.

Curved wall provides views and southern exposure—Knowing the site's many features and obstructions, I roughed out the basic floor plan, arranging the main living areas to take full advantage of the panoramic view and to maximize the southern exposure. I gave the kitchen the southern side to make it the lightest and brightest area in the morning. The living area took the northeast corner to focus on the most majestic feature of the valley view, Franconia Notch. The dining area looks out across the Pemigewasset valley to the east. Because the driveway is on the western side of the lot, I put the garage and the entry on this side of the house.

Wrapping all of these elements in a cohesive package seemed nearly impossible until I hit on the notion of superimposing a large semicircle on one end of a rectangular footprint (drawing left). The semicircle concentrates views on the eastern side and encompasses the living, dining and kitchen areas. The western, rectangular portion provides room for the remaining spaces.

Framing a true curve would have been a nightmare—I quickly rejected using a true curve for the semicircular wall. Not only would a true curve make for a post-and-beam nightmare, but fitting windows and doors would be a problem, too. Instead, I drew a circle, then I laid out the walls as chords of that circle. The length of the chords was based on the rough-opening dimensions of Pella French doors and similarly sized Pella double-hung windows. I chose these windows because their aluminum-clad frames would stand up to the severe weather with little or no maintenance.

The semicircular wall was relatively easy to build using post-and-beam framing. The posts at the corners of the wall segments bear on 4x10 floor joists that cantilever over a rectangular, poured-concrete foundation (photo above left). I adjusted the centerline spacing of the floor joists to coincide with the posts. Laying out the floor joists conventionally on 16-in. centers would have required that the posts be set on headers spanning between the floor joists.

Although post-and-beam construction typically uses mortise-and-tenon joinery, I chose instead to use several types of metal connectors and fasteners. These connectors made it faster and easier to build a complex shape with irregular spacing, many compound angles and a hip roof.

Windows and outbuildings achieve balance and symmetry—The greatest challenge in designing this home was to impart a sense of traditional architecture. Symmetry and balance are the hallmarks of a center-entrance colonial, but I used a subtler, less rigidly traditional form of balance for this vacation home.

An example of this approach is found in the treatment of the southern elevation (photo p. 113). Although it is not the entrance side, it is the primary elevation because it's the most visible and open to the sun. I carefully worked with the building's shape, its rooflines and its window locations until I got the gut feeling that the building was balanced. The squared west end of the elevation balances off the rounded east end because they are roughly equal in mass, and the straight rooflines of the west end lend the house a more conventional definition.

I emphasized the curved roofline by following it with four tall arch-top windows. In addition to establishing a traditional design heritage (the arch is one of the oldest building forms), the windows reinforce the semicircular design theme and soften the overall appearance of the house.

I then created a counterpoint to the arch-top windows by using four different-size double-hung windows to the left of the arch-top windows. Placing the longer windows at opposite corners, I arranged all four units around an imaginary cross axis. This window configuration subtly mirrors the four arch-top windows. Finally, the garage on the west end balances the gazebo (sidebar p. 116) on the east end; together, they stretch the facade and soften the vertical aspect of the two-story section of the house.

Varying ceiling planes adds variety to an open plan—An explicit goal in this project was to have distinct areas within the overall living space and not just one big room. Each part of the space responds to different external views and light conditions and creates an internal environment appropriate to the activity there. For example, in the living area there's a huge semicircular window focusing on the stunning view to the north (bottom photo, p. 117). The shape of the window, inspired by the house's floor plan, gives a sense of enclosure and snugness. A large, square window might have felt open and cold, especially in winter.

Although the living-area window provides a view to the north, the space is laid out so that furniture focuses inward for relaxed gatherings. The cathedral ceiling increases the feeling of size and openness, but the steep roof pitch keeps the eaves low on the north side for a more human scale. The low roofline also deflects north winds and provides extra insulation because a roof section is thicker than a wall section.

A loft over the dining area results in a low ceiling and a more intimate feeling when diners are seated at the table (photo right). From the dining room, three French doors open onto a deck and provide an eastward view across the valley. Summer sunrises are a real treat from this vantage point.

Upstairs, tucked beneath an open roof frame, there are a bedroom, a bathroom and the loft. A stack of mattresses makes the loft the overflow sleeping space when a crowd shows up. From the loft, a large gliding door opens onto a little

Individualized spaces. The loft over the dining area gives it an intimate feeling within the open floor plan's cathedral ceiling. The loft bisects the tall arched windows, which are only fully visible at the kitchen counter. Photo taken at C on floor plan.

A Steel Gazebo Doesn't Block the View

Early in the design process, the Powells requested a screened outdoor space that wouldn't shade the house or obstruct the views. A gazebo, rather than an attached porch, could provide the screened area, and framing it with steel would allow for the use of smaller structural members and clearer views. When you're in this gazebo, you feel like you're floating in the landscape (top photo below).

The structure is anchored to an octagonal block of concrete 4 ft. by 4 ft. by 4 ft. high, tied with steel dowels to an 8-ft. by 8-ft. by 12-in. thick, steel-reinforced concrete pad, or footing.

The gazebo and the deck it's attached to are supported by four 8-in. by 6-in. by $^5/_{16}$-in. thick steel columns. Large L-shaped plates welded at the base of each column fit over anchor bolts projecting from the top and sides of the concrete base.

On top of the columns, there are four steel beams arranged in a square. Steel outriggers project radially from the beams, giving the gazebo its 16-sided shape. Sixteen steel wall posts are welded to the ends of the outriggers (photo bottom left). Because the posts are so small— only 2 in. by 2 in.—they keep the structure to an absolute minimum visually.

Hanging the steel was slow and involved. We spent an 11-hour day setting the main steel with a crane, and that was only for 12 pieces. It took two more long days to install the wall posts, center rails and roof ties.

Marrying wood and steel— Though most of the gazebo is steel, the roof and the floor are pressure-treated fir and pine. Clip angles welded to the steel have holes so that the wood framework can be bolted to the steel. For example, pressure-treated 4x4s are bolted to angles on top of and underneath the steel outriggers (photo bottom right), creating a double band that supports the rough-sawn pine skirting.

The fascia boards, actually header beams, are bolted to top wing plates welded on the wall posts. From there, the 3x8 rough-sawn rafters and 2x8 tongue-and-groove roof decking are put together in a normal fashion.

Both the walls and the floor are screened. I stapled fiberglass insect screen over the 4x4 floor joists before screwing down the 5/4x6 pressure-treated southern yellow pine decking.

At the tops of the wall posts, two pairs of steel tubes at right angles to each other act as ties that keep the rafters from pushing the posts outward. The ties also serve as the support for an octagonal light fixture, which was created from rough-sawn pine and scrap roof-flashing metal.—*L. S.*

Steel posts support the roof without obstructing the view. Resting on splayed steel columns, this 16-sided gazebo provides screened outdoor space that doesn't shade the house. Photo taken at D on floor plan.

Tied to the house for more stability. Two steel beams connected to the house will support a deck. In the gazebo, wall posts are welded to outriggers, and two pairs of ties will prevent the roof from spreading the posts. The plates at the tops of the posts will carry the roof headers.

Wood is bolted to welded-on plates and clip angles. Here, the 4x4 banding provides backing for the skirt. The floor joists will be attached to the angles on top of the beams. Because the deck boards will butt into a 6-in. border, an additional inner band was necessary for fastening the flooring.

crescent of deck space. Aside from being a great place to hang out in the summer, this second-floor deck cuts off the semicircular wall.

The south-facing kitchen has the largest expanse of glass (photo right). However, the windows' considerable height is only apparent from the kitchen because the loft spans across the windows, bisecting the view in every area except right at the kitchen countertop.

Window muntins enhance a traditional look—Although they offer nice views, big panes of glass appear as vacant, staring cutouts from the exterior. Because the kitchen windows are so large, I decided to use muntin bars. Muntins divide the large expanses into small panes, recalling traditional New England architecture. However, orderly alignment of the muntins, as found in a traditional design, was impossible because each arched window in the kitchen is a different height to follow the rising eaves.

So instead of aligning the muntins, I kept the same number of panes in each window by increasing the spacing between muntins. I did the same with the bed and bath windows on the southern elevation, which are also different heights. The muntins create small panes of glass that are roughly the same size. To keep the pane sizes consistent, the bars for every window in the house, including the doors, were custom built.

As the project developed, I realized one disadvantage of the Pella units we chose: The windows' narrow frames, with no casing, have a Spartan, modern look, not at all emphasizing a traditional heritage. To solve the problem, I painted the frames—but not the sashes—barn red to match the roof panels. The narrow red frames highlight the window shapes without appearing too heavy or overbearing, and thus serve the purpose that a traditional wide casing would.

Red metal roof lends a barnlike quality—The most arresting feature of the exterior is the bright red roof. The color reminds me of a barn; the metalwork on the house is painted to match. Ribbed metal roofing, which is commonly used for barns and outbuildings, provides another reference to traditional barns. I chose this particular roofing, Ameri-Drain (American Building Components Co., 1212 E. Dominic St., Rome, N. Y. 13440; 800-544-2651), because its 6-in. rib spacing was the same as the spacing of the balusters on the metal railings and was close to the width of the vertical-board siding.

The roof pitch was originally selected to shed snow. The pitch also leaves adequate headroom for both the loft and the living area below. The steep pitch—9-in-12—conforms to the look of traditional New England farmhouses.

Late in the design stage, I added the hips on the main house. The hips are not traditional but are important because they result in an outline that ties in with the arches and the curved plan form. The hips also put a shorter wall at the entry side. A cupola capping off the roof adds summer ventilation and another traditional touch. □

Lee Stevens is a designer/builder in Nederland, Colo. Photos by the author except where noted.

Photos this page: Rich Ziegner

Large kitchen is equipped to handle a hungry ski crowd. On the south side of the curved first floor, the kitchen is a bright area. The open shelves and cabinets reinforce the house's casual atmosphere and make it easier for guests to find things. Photo taken at E on floor plan.

Custom windows view the northeast. In the living area, a dramatic curved window picks up on the home's curve theme. But the window's shape also creates a sense of snug shelter as it mimics the arch of a cave opening. Photo taken at F on floor plan.

Home in the Hills

An open floor plan organized around a central corridor takes advantage of the site and the view

by Cathi and Steven House

Dick Elpers and Beverly Abbot had no pre-conceived architectural style in mind when they asked our firm, House + House, to design their new home, but they had very definite ideas about their goals and needs. Busy mental-health professionals with stressful, demanding lives, they wanted their home to be informal, peaceful and intimate. They wanted the house to welcome them home at the end of a long day and to draw them out in the morning, sending them off to work at peace with the promise of a welcome return. Progression into and out of the house therefore became a critical design issue.

Ins and outs of the design—The 2,500-sq. ft. house, built by Jake Covert of Covert & Associates, is perched on a spectacular wooded hillside 30 minutes south of San Francisco with views of canyons, forests and the Pacific Ocean.

To support the idea of seclusion and to amplify the owners' rituals of leaving and returning home, we decided to keep the car separate from the house. The garage is linked to the house with a covered, skylit walkway offering views to the trees, creating a calming transitional space (photo below and top drawing, p. 121). An adjacent carport can also serve as a sheltered dining area for large gatherings. A detached guest house will be built across the walkway from the garage. The entry became the link between Dick and Beverly's private and public worlds, and the choreography of natural light became the design element most useful in fulfilling this function. The early morning sunlight is soft and diffused throughout the house except at the entry, where it floods in through carefully placed skylights. The entry overlooks the dining room, granting views through and beyond. At the end of each day, the setting sun creates a welcoming glow that fills the house and the interior courts.

The movement of the sun, the wind and the coastal fog, along with the location of the trees and the views, led to the layout of the rooms along an east/west axis (bottom drawing, p. 121). All primary rooms—living room, dining room, kitchen and master bedroom—face west (bottom photo, p. 120) and spill onto an 80-ft. curved redwood deck, with glass walls and French doors (photo facing page). The ceiling over these rooms rises from the 8-ft. glass walls to 20-ft. east-facing clerestory windows. Low operable

The west facade. On the facing page, a small loft/study overlooks the 80-ft. deck. Deep eaves protect the glass and the rooms from the harsh western sun and frame the views to the ocean; the lower windows open to capture the breeze.

The east facade. On the east side of the house (below), a covered skylit walkway leads from the garage to the front entry. Clerestory windows at the peak of the central corridor bring in morning light.

Private retreat. In the master bedroom the built-in headboard continues the line of cabinets that divides the house. Stairs lead to the dressing area; the central door leads to the master bath. Photo taken at C on floor plan.

A multipurpose space. At right, the 70-ft. long corridor (here looking toward the living-room end of the house) features flying buttresses, double-sided cabinets and fin walls for displaying art. Photo taken at B on floor plan.

An open-plan layout. The living, dining and kitchen areas are completely open yet subtly divided by a three-sided fireplace with a black slate, seat-high wraparound hearth and a 7-ft. 7-in. long island with grill and cooktop. Charcoal granite countertops, rift-cut oak cabinetry and white-oak flooring reinforce the serene mood of the house. Photo taken at A on floor plan.

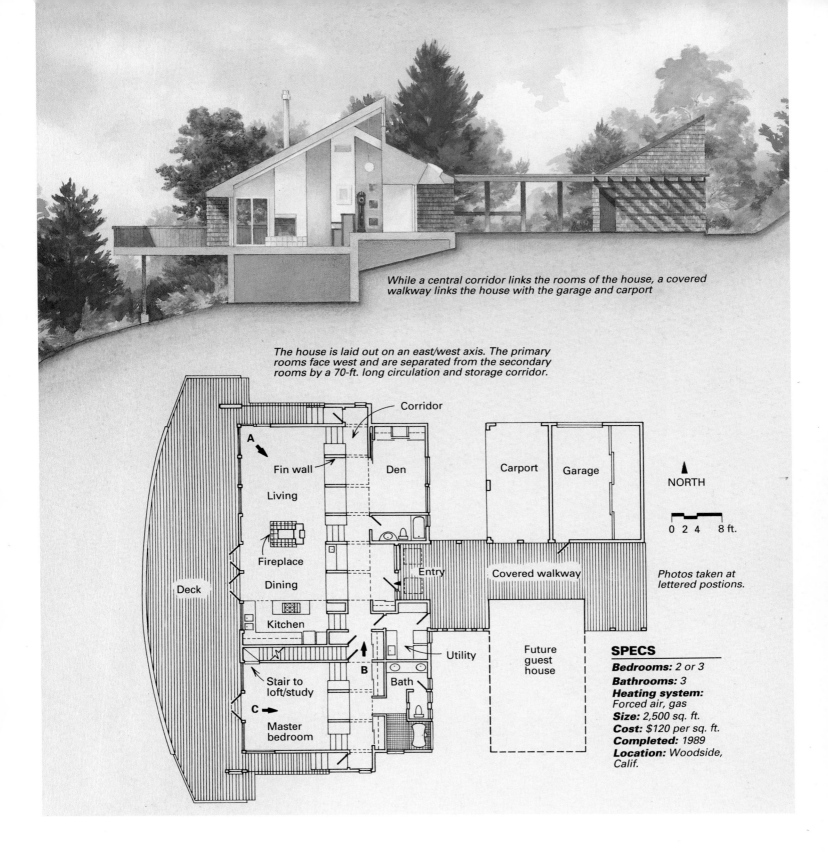

While a central corridor links the rooms of the house, a covered walkway links the house with the garage and carport

The house is laid out on an east/west axis. The primary rooms face west and are separated from the secondary rooms by a 70-ft. long circulation and storage corridor.

Corridor

A

Fin wall

Living

Den

Carport

Garage

NORTH

0 2 4   8 ft.

Fireplace

Dining

Entry

Covered walkway

Photos taken at lettered postions.

Deck

Kitchen

B

Utility

Stair to loft/study

Bath

Future guest house

C

Master bedroom

SPECS
Bedrooms: 2 or 3
Bathrooms: 3
Heating system: Forced air, gas
Size: 2,500 sq. ft.
Cost: $120 per sq. ft.
Completed: 1989
Location: Woodside, Calif.

windows in the 8-ft. wall—the downhill face—capture air rising from the canyons below and promote natural ventilation throughout the house. On very warm days a fan assists this flow.

The secondary rooms—den, baths, utility room and entry—face east, toward the hillside and some courtyards. A 200-sq. ft. loft/study looks over the treetops and the ocean, as well as into the house; a 500-sq. ft. storage space is below.

Where east meets west—The east- and west-facing rooms are separated from each other by a

70-ft. long circulation and storage "spine," which became a major design element for the house (top right photo, facing page). This 4-ft. wide corridor runs the length of the house, dividing it into primary and secondary spaces. A 2-ft. level change from the corridor to the rooms below gives subtle visual separation for the primary spaces, and fin walls every 5½ ft. offer ample and dramatic display area for art and collectibles.

Along the corridor and between the fin walls, a 3-ft. 8-in. wide double-sided storage system changes as it moves through each room. In the

living room it houses the television, the stereo equipment and logs for the fireplace. In the dining room it becomes a wet bar and wine storage. In the kitchen it houses the pantry and the fine china. In the bedroom it embraces the bed, housing the night tables (top left photo, facing page); above (behind the bed), it turns into the dressing area, totally open yet completely invisible. □

Cathi and Steven House are partners in the San Francisco, Calif., architectural firm of House + House. Photos by Gerald Ratto.

Top drawing: Gary Williamson   Bottom drawing: Jeff Bellantuono

Roadside Mountain Retreat

Squeezed onto a narrow lot, this house lets in the sound of the river and shuts out the noise of the nearby road

by Charles Miller

Before the Telluride mines played out in the 1930s, the ore that came out of the mountains rolled down the San Miguel canyon on the Rio Grande Southern Railroad, passing through a landscape that was far more spectacular than anything that came out of the mines. This alpine canyon, located in southwestern Colorado, is known for its red-sandstone cliffs, cottonwoods,

willows and trout-filled rivers, all set against a backdrop of jagged 14,000-ft. mountains.

But breathtaking scenery isn't enough to sustain a mining community. By the 1950s, Telluride was all but abandoned. It took the development of a successful ski area in the 1970s to turn around the region's declining economy. Telluride is now, once again, a boomtown. Eventual-

The roof recalls local barns and train stations. Wide overhangs at the gable ends and kicked-up eaves protect the wood siding on this house. Photo taken at A on floor plan.

The downstairs is one long, thin room. A wall of windows along the south side of the house overlooks the river and the canyon walls. Photo taken at B on floor plan.

Drawing this page: Christopher Clapp

ly, the old railroad tracks were pulled up, and in some places former railroad corridors became building sites. On one of these sites, a new home designed by Telluride architect Connie Giles smoothly combines southern Colorado's utilitarian building tradition with contemporary style and comfort.

A narrow house for a narrow site— Sandwiched between an asset and a liability, the site is at the bottom of the canyon. The asset is the San Miguel River. The liability is the highway, not so much for its proximity, which is a plus in the winter, but for the noise generated by all of those cars and trucks.

Fortunately, the river is on the south side of the lot, which allowed Giles to orient the house along an east-west axis to take best advantage of the sun and the view.

There are two ways to stop noise. High-pitched noise, such as that made by a leaf blower, is

This wall stops noise and cold. Along the north wall of the house, a cast-concrete wall stops the low-frequency noise from the nearby highway in its tracks. The windowless, wood-sided wall above the concrete further insulates the house from both noise and winter cold spells. Photo taken at C on floor plan.

SPECS

Bedrooms: 2
Bathrooms: 2½
Heating system: Gas-fired radiant floors
Size: 2,062 sq. ft.
Cost: $181 per sq. ft.
Completed: 1994
Location: Fall Creek, Colorado

Photos taken at lettered positions.

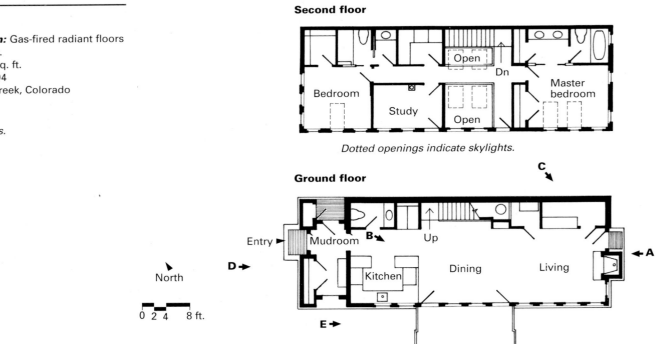

Second floor

Dotted openings indicate skylights.

Ground floor

North

0 2 4 8 ft.

A house for a narrow site. *On the west side of the house, a mudroom next to the parking spaces is a place to store ski gear and footwear. On both floors, mechanical rooms, closets and bathrooms are arranged along the north wall, where they help to insulate the living spaces from winter cold and the noise from the adjacent highway.*

Drawings this page: Jeff Bellantuono

stopped by gaskets, such as weatherstripping around doors and windows. Low-pitched noise, such as the bass solo emitted from a downshifting diesel headed back to the gravel pit, is stopped with something massive, such as a concrete wall. This house has both. The north wall of the ground floor is cast concrete (photo facing page). The builder, Josh Kent, cast the wall in forms lined with rough-sawn boards to give the concrete a rustic appearance.

Because both the noise and the cold come from the north, it was an easy decision to buffer the southside living spaces further with a string of smaller rooms along the north wall. To that end, bathrooms, closets, stairs, mechanical rooms and the laundry are all located against the north wall on both floors of the house (floor plans, facing page).

The kitchen, living and dining spaces are incorporated into one long, thin room stretched out along the river, giving the water a constant presence within the house (photo p. 123). The south wall is a bank of 7-ft. tall, dual-glazed aluminum-clad windows and doors. They're fitted with low-E glass to minimize damage to upholstery from UV-light. Step through the doors next to the dining table, and you're on the diminutive deck, which is cantilevered off the house foundation to avoid structural elements within the river setback (photo bottom right).

In the center of the house, a two-story volume opens to admit light from a quartet of skylights to the lower level. The stair climbs into this high-ceilinged space, where a catwalk over the dining area links the upstairs bedrooms.

A simple building in a complex landscape—Because this region holds spectacular natural beauty and, until recently, little development, the insertion of a building into the landscape needs to be done with great care. On this topic, Giles says, "Do as little as possible." Give the house a simple form derived from, but not mimicking, local buildings. In this valley, the structural antecedents are barns, train stations and the gabled shelters built over the mines.

The most distinctive feature of the house is the steep, 14-in-12 roof (photo p. 122). At the plate line, the eaves change slope to 8-in-12 as they project beyond the walls to protect the siding from the weather. Both corrugated-metal roofing and wood siding have been commonly used as exterior-finish materials for the past century.

A small version of the roof shelters the primary entry (photo bottom left). Like the eaves, the entry roof is supported by bolted-together brackets made of 2x and 3x Douglas fir. The door opens onto a steel-grate landing, which offers winter pedestrians the perfect place to scrape mud and snow off their boots. □

Charles Miller is managing editor of Fine Homebuilding. *Photos by the author.*

This entry keeps the snow off your head and your feet. A steel-grate step leads to the main entry, which is sheltered by its own roof. The cavity under the grate catches the scraped-off snow from wintry boots. When the snow melts, it drains through the holes in the concrete curb. Photo taken at D on floor plan.

Small deck overlooks great outdoors. Perched atop cantilevered beams, the little deck off the dining area hovers above the stream bank without encroaching on the no-build zone. The aluminum-clad windows and galvanized railings were chosen for their low maintenance. Photo taken at E on floor plan.

The House on the Trestle

On a mountainous site, an arched truss carries the weight of a rustic vacation house

by Brad Sills

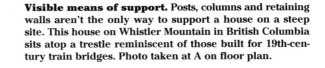

Visible means of support. Posts, columns and retaining walls aren't the only way to support a house on a steep site. This house on Whistler Mountain in British Columbia sits atop a trestle reminiscent of those built for 19th-century train bridges. Photo taken at A on floor plan.

There is a certain perversity to building a house in a ski resort. The very conditions that attract people to ski areas—steep mountains and plenty of snow—discourage building. Here at Whistler Mountain, in southern British Columbia, the vacation houses that overlook the slopes cling to terrain just as precarious as the nearby slalom course. For example, the house presented in this article sits atop a site that falls 22 ft. across the width of its foundation.

But there are attractions to building here. The local building community is a group of accomplished, friendly competitors who share their steep-site building secrets. We're surrounded by the world's best lumber, and the architects who get the jobs are a talented group who continually challenge our abilities.

It was against this backdrop that I first met my new clients, Harold and Parsla Robertson. One look at the conceptual drawings for their vacation house revealed an entirely new approach to building on a hillside. Most houses around here are borne on the downhill side by a stone retaining wall. Not this one. Instead, the house was to be supported by an arched, wooden truss (photo facing page), similar to the trestles that carried British Columbia's trains over gorges and rivers during the early railroad days. This clever solution, devised by Vancouver architects Mark Osburn and Wayne Clark, would allow for a pleasing footprint on a steep site, using a traditional form to hold up a contemporary house.

Unbeknownst to me at the time, Osburn and Clark are notorious for their aberrant designs. Building the trestle for this house would soon lead me into a complex, intriguing building process (sidebar p. 128).

The plan is inward, toward the fire—Unlike most people building vacation houses, the Robertsons weren't interested in chest-pounding walls of windows overlooking the mountains. Instead, they wanted a house with a sense of security and enclosure, a house that was meant to be experienced more by the flicker of firelight than a flood of daylight.

A large vestibule greets the visitor, and befitting the proximity to the slopes, a storage alcove for ski gear tucks into the corner to the right of the front door (drawings right). A staircase leading to the lower level and a partition wall separate the entry from the main room.

The dining table occupies the southern side of the main room, under a vaulted ceiling that is lighted by clerestory windows (photo p. 130). During the day, the view across the valley from the windows to the south dominates the room. But in the evening, the focus shifts to the fireplace along the north wall of the main room (photo p. 128). The fireplace is surrounded with granite, and it is framed by a low ceiling that quietly urges sitting down and getting comfortable in an overstuffed chair. The Robertsons regularly stoke the fireplace to enliven the room.

Within view of the main room, but separate from it, is the kitchen. It, too, has a small wood-burning stove around which the family shares

A sandwich floor plan. *The public spaces in this mountain vacation home are located on the middle level, where they act as a buffer between the two sleeping levels. Each gathering place—the kitchen, rec room and living room—has its own fireplace or woodstove.*

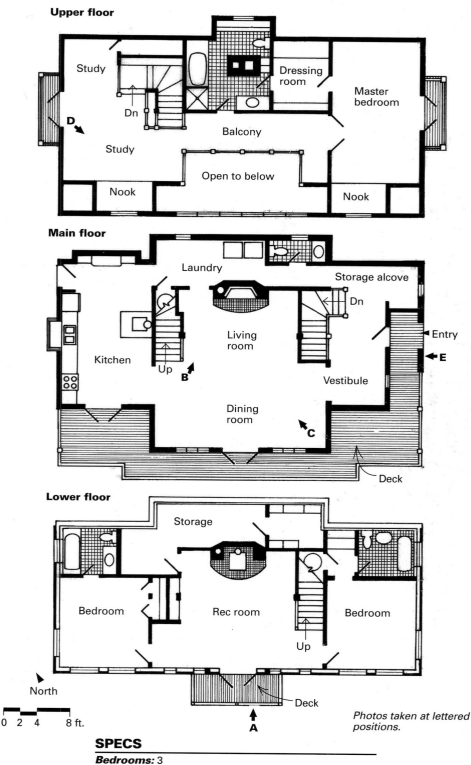

SPECS

Bedrooms: 3
Bathrooms: 3½
Heating system: Electric forced air
Size: 2,900 sq. ft.
Cost: $155 per sq. ft.
Completed: 1991
Location: Whistler Mountain, British Columbia, Canada

Drawings this page: Jeff Bellantuono

Building the trestle

By the time the working drawings arrived, some changes had occurred to the original concept of the Robertson house. What I had initially seen as a manufactured glulam arch in the conceptual drawings had quietly been refined through a procession of drawings into a complex assembly of bolted-together rough-sawn Douglas-fir timbers that captured the spirit of steam-era train trestles.

Structural engineer Barry Thorson analyzed the trestle, and he adjusted the member sizes, bolt diameters and number of laminations to carry the necessary load while presenting us with manageable components. Total: 80 pieces of 3x8 and 3x12 Douglas-fir timbers threaded together at the joints with ¾-in. by 40-in. bolts. Between each adjoining timber were 4-in. dia. split rings to help spread the load. According to the notes, the bolt holes had to be exactly ¾-in. dia. No wiggle room. Our trestle was becoming more complex.

The architects, lead carpenter Bill McDonnell and I quickly realized the value a scale model would offer in showing the relationships of the many structural components. We settled on a scale of 1 in.:1 ft., and Bill and his crew set about making the model out of cedar siding cut to the appropriate dimensions. The model became invaluable as we prepared the individual pieces and assembled the real thing. But first, the footings.

Trestle base—The trestle is 16 ft. high, spans 52 ft. and is designed to bear the full weight of the building's main roof structure. That weight calculated out to 70,000 lb. transferred to each of the trestle bases. Included in the loading equation is a 217 lb./sq. ft. snow load, one of the highest requirements in North America.

The loads hit the ground through welded steel saddles that weigh 3,000 lb. apiece mounted atop concrete columns that are 32 in. sq. by 6 ft. deep (photo facing page). We hollowed out the cavities for the footings by tediously chiseling away at the native rock. Even though the footings are pinned by rebar to the rock, we further ensured their stability by connecting the columns to the primary foundation with grade beams, and to one another with a pair of 1-in. dia. steel rods encased in polyvinyl conduit.

Threading it together—Bill and I had numerous discussions about the various assembly techniques we might use. We had toyed with laying it all out and bolting it together in two separate sections in a nearby cul-de-sac and then lifting it by crane. But the weight constraints and problems of racking discouraged that idea.

We also briefly considered the old method of trestle building using various

Fireplace alcove. The living-room fireplace occupies a low-ceilinged alcove next to the dining table. The finishes are simple: granite and white-pine boards. Photo taken at B on floor plan.

morning coffee. In keeping with the rest of the house, the kitchen is simple and informal. The base cabinets are pine with frame-and-panel doors. Open shelves above the countertop take the place of upper cabinets. Another bank of open shelves recessed into the north wall provides pantry space. The open shelves and their displayed contents harken back to frontier days, but now they're illuminated by halogen lamps.

Upstairs, a quiet study and a sleeping nook occupy the west end of the top floor (top photo, p. 131). The sleeping nook tucks into one of the spaces created by the dormers, which are connected by a shed roof that accommodates a row of clerestory windows (drawing facing page).

A balcony overlooking the dining area connects the study with the master bedroom, where the dormer nook overlooking the slopes makes

the perfect place to read on a sunny winter day. Connected to the master bedroom by a walk-through closet is the master bath.

The lower floor houses two bedrooms, each with its own bathroom. The central space that lies between the two bedrooms serves as the family recreation room, complete with a pool table next to a granite-faced surround for the woodstove. Placed in this central location, the rec room enhances the privacy of the two downstairs bedrooms. And with the main floor separating the upstairs bedrooms, the seniors are ensured of a night's sleep free from the sound of clicking pool balls.

Heavy timbers and rustic materials set the tone—The Robertsons' house is framed with conventional materials, but it feels a lot like a

Asymmetrical dormers pierce the metal roof. *A pair of doghouse dormers united by a shed-roofed clerestory marks the roof of the Robertson house. Corrugated-metal roofing recalls the utilitarian ancestors of buildings that inspired the house's shapes and textures.*

gin-pole configurations and block rigging. But a quick historical reference to the number of Chinese laborers who plummeted to their deaths using this method indicated possible crew-morale problems, not to mention impact on our workman's comp rates.

There appeared to be two options: Construct a scaffold that would bear the weight of the trestle components; or hang the central section of the trestle from floor joists cantilevered off the main floor. We chose the cantilevered method for labor efficiency.

Most of the structural members could be cut to length and predrilled using templates. Each member in the scale model was lettered, and a cutlist was prepared. Then, starting with the uppermost components, we began piecing the trestle together by threading the predrilled members onto bolts.

It soon became apparent that our favored assembly method wasn't going to work. I guess the thought of hanging 1,800 bd. ft. of Douglas fir from eight cantilevered floor joists was just plain naive because very soon our transit confirmed that we were lifting the floor joists right off their moorings on the uphill side of the house.

Welded-steel bases anchor the trestle. The trestle legs engage the mountain by way of 3,000-lb. steel brackets that are bolted to concrete piers. The piers are cast into hollows chipped out of the native rock and connected to one another by steel rods.

We retreated back to the scaffolding solution and arrived at the following sequence: Place split rings onto the bolts protruding through the last lamination, align the new lamination with the bolt holes, support it from below, clamp everything in place and pound the bolts through. This solution was easy enough for the first few laminations, but as they accumulated, so did the difficulty of driving a $\frac{3}{4}$-in. bolt through a structure that really wanted to sag back into a stack of lumber.

We used a hydraulic jack to get the top chord member slightly crowned, which allowed for the $\frac{3}{8}$-in. deflection calculated by the engineer. Then the vertical braces were plumbed. Once symmetry was obtained, all joints were clamped and bolted tight.

The finishing touches to the trestle included its dark gray finish, meant to mimic the look of creosote (long ago banned for its toxic ingredients). And to protect the trestle legs, we hammered sheet lead over the exposed end grain.

All told, the trestle took approximately 750 man-hours to complete. With lumber, steel, concrete and custom metal work, it totaled about $30,000.—*B. S.*

Between the fire and the light. The dining area is central to the house, adjacent to windows that overlook the ski slopes and next to the living-room fireplace. Daylight from above is admitted by the clerestory windows between the dormers. Photo taken at C on floor plan.

timber-framed building because of the log railings and balconies on the outside, and because of the heavy glulam rafters on the inside. The log work begins with the path to the house, which leads across a timber-framed bridge that spans a gap between the parking area and the house (photo bottom right). The gap allows the adjacent parking area to be level with the main floor of the house without blocking the daylight from the lower bedrooms.

The bridge, decks and balconies are bordered by railings made of yellow-cedar logs and balusters that we scavenged from slash piles left by loggers when they clear-cut part of the nearby forest. Rails, balusters and posts are mortised and tenoned together. And each post is bolstered by a diagonal brace that angles back toward the house from joists that cantilever beyond the edge of the deck.

Early on in the interior-design process, we decided against using drywall. It just doesn't embody the rustic spirit that we sought. Accordingly, the home is finished in western white pine. There isn't a sq. ft. of drywall in the entire house.

To keep costs down, I bought the pine directly from a local mill. All 28,000 bd. ft. arrived on two boxcar-size trucks, coincidentally on the first day of snow. We unloaded the pine onto the driveway and organized it by lengths, protecting the wood with tarps. Our biweekly ritual was to bring 2,000 bd. ft. into the heated basement, where the pine was stickered and allowed to acclimatize for two weeks prior to installation.

We used the pine for walls, trim, ceilings and most of the floors on the main level. For the floor, we devised a grid pattern to add some unexpected complexity. Square-edged 1x8s, 4 ft. long, are arranged flush to one another in rows. They are bordered by perpendicular 1x6s, and then another row of 1x8s and so on. This arrangement let us use boards that were too crooked to be used in long lengths but that worked just fine as shorter pieces. And we could also cut out the unacceptable imperfections without rendering a board useless.

We secured the pine boards to the subfloor with construction adhesive and face-nailed them with gun-driven 6d nails. To my great relief, the floor is squeak-free. We finished it with Watco oil. Maintenance consists of washing the floor, then applying more oil.

To maintain the railroad theme that began with the trestle, Parsla made a trip to an abandoned railway siding to select a suitable color for the house. There, she found a string of aging boxcars from the Canadian National Railway, painted their signature burgundy. She collected a sample paint chip from one of the cars and had it analyzed by computer to get a perfect color match. This burgundy is used throughout the house for rafters, beams, windows and doors. As the complement to the flaxen color of the pine, the boxcar burgundy provides just the right note of contrast. ☐

Brad Sills is the principal in Whirlwind Homes Ltd., a general-contracting firm based in Whistler, British Columbia, Canada. Photos by Charles Miller except where noted.

Daylight on the top floor. To the left, a band of clerestory windows lets the sunshine into the high-ceilinged space over the dining table. The clerestory connects the two dormers, which are outfitted with cushions for reading, catnapping or accommodating guests. Photo taken at D on floor plan.

Enter at the bridge. The parking spaces are level with the main floor, but they are held back from the house to allow daylight into the lower level. To beef up the deck railing, diagonal braces angle back to the posts from joists that extend beyond the deck. Photo taken at E on floor plan.

A Romantic House

In this hectic, high-tech age, playful detailing and asymmetrical plans make a more comfortable home

by Jeremiah Eck

Combining old and new details. Although the steep roof and the wood siding are traditional details, on the southern elevation they're combined with a contemporary arrangement of windows that lets in light and adds some playful detailing. Photo taken from A on floor plan.

We live in an age of hyperrationality, where reason rules over intuition. Nowhere is this more evident than in the computerization of almost every aspect of our lives. Computers tell us what the weather will be, how much we have in our bank accounts and even suggest to many that the design of a house is a fully analytic process.

Our lives sometimes seem like a series of things to do on a list—and do quickly. I think there's an antidote, though, to our overregulated and hectic lives: a return to romanticism in our houses.

A few years ago I entered a competition for an ideal house of 1,500 sq. ft. Although this house was never built, recently I was able to design a slightly modified, enlarged version for Peter and Kathy Neely in Salisbury, Connecticut. The house, built by Jack Grant of Winsted, Connecticut, is a good example of how the plan and the details of a house can, in fact, be romantic.

Relating to the past—To begin with, the design of the Neely house makes reference to the architecture of the past but does not attempt to copy it. This is important because romantic houses are about the relation of the present to the past. This is not to say that the Neely house is nostalgic. That's what Disneyland is all about.

I was confounded to hear recently that a retirement community is being built in Florida in the "image" of a New England village. The experience and the product of three centuries of regional living in New England was to be built instantaneously in a region 2,000 miles to the south. Certainly our technology allows us to do that, but to what end? This is a false, technology-dependent romanticism and an example of sentimentality.

Arched windows with rectangular sash. The arched windows so prominent on the southern elevation (above) are actually an arched facade in front of rectangular sash, which cost considerably less than curved sash would have.

Bottom photo, this page: Kevin Ireton

Colors inspired by the hills. The steep roof, the green shingles and the brown siding of this home were suggested by and designed to blend with the rolling Connecticut hills that surround it. Photo taken from B on floor plan.

The steep roof, the dominant chimney, the scaled-down windows and the traditional materials of the Neely house all suggest classic images of home, inspired by everything from 18th-century saltboxes to 19th-century Gothic-Revival farmhouses. But the open floor plan (drawing right), the extensive use of natural light and the configuration of windows and trim on the south elevation (top photo, facing page) all are contemporary.

Inspired by nature—The ultimate source of inspiration for romanticism is nature. In architecture, this inspiration often means that the shape of a house and its colors are compatible with its surroundings. Each side of the Neely house responds differently to the site. From the entry side on the north (photo above), the steep roofs and their green color blend with the low hills beyond, particularly between spring and fall.

The south side of the house is another matter. The house sits not quite at the top of a low, rolling hill and at the edge of a gently sloping meadow to the south. On the south side the house stands more erect (photo facing page), with the wall of what I call the living hall extending a full two stories. Unlike the north side, where the roof dominates to protect the house from the wind, the desire for sun and views across the meadow predominate on the south elevation. This large expanse of wall gives the Neelys a full 180° view and year-round exposure to the southern sky.

Because they are inspired by nature, the colors of romantic houses are seldom white, and the textures are seldom perfectly smooth. The Neely house has three exterior colors and three distinct textures. The roof is green, the cedar clapboards and the cedar sidewall shingles are natural brown, and the trim and the casings are beige. The green and the brown can be found in the surroundings, and the beige mediates the two.

As for textures, rough wood shingles are used next to the ground, defining the first floor of the house as coming from the ground. Clapboards, with their somewhat more refined texture, delineate the second floor, and the even flatter trim and the smooth medium-density overlay (MDO) plywood define the gable peaks against the sky.

Romanticism in plan and elevation—Romantic houses tend to have irregular plans as contrasted with formally centered geometric plans. Order is achieved through a balancing of irregular elements or space, not through strict symmetry. For instance, the Neely house is dominated by the tall living hall (top photo, p. 134). But that room is balanced by the length of the kitchen/dining/entry area that flows into it with only a partial visual and physical separation (bottom photo, p. 134).

This balance of irregular shapes can be achieved in other ways as well. The small, cozy loft of the Neely house (photo p. 135) balances the larger, open living hall.

Romantic houses can be small, too, because each activity or function need not have a distinct room or position in the plan. One of the problems

An open plan. *By consolidating the formal living room, the dining room and the family room into one central space—the living hall—the architect not only eliminated rooms, but he also reduced circulation space. The result is a small house (1,800 sq. ft.) that works well for a family.*

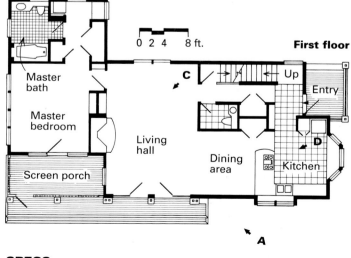

North

Second floor

Loft

Dn

Bedroom

Open to below

Bedroom

B

First floor

Master bath

Master bedroom

Screen porch

C

Living hall

Up

Entry

D

Kitchen

Dining area

0 2 4 8 ft.

A

SPECS

Bedrooms: 3
Bathrooms: 2½
Heating system: Oil-fired, forced air

Size: 1,800 sq. ft.
Cost: $100 per sq. ft.
Completed: 1993
Location: Connecticut

Photos taken from lettered positions.

A high ceiling signifies an important space. A two-story room, which the architect calls the living hall, dominates the interior of this house. The Rumford fireplace is surrounded by a board-and-batten wall composed of MDO plywood and pine astragals. Note the square windows: The arched shape so prominent on the exterior was created with an exterior wall that overhangs the windows. Photo taken from C on floor plan.

Long views make a small house feel bigger. The two-story height of the living hall (at the far end of the photo) is balanced visually by the expanse of kitchen and dining area that flows into it. Photo taken from D on floor plan.

Bottom photo, this page: Kevin Ireton

of suburban houses today is that they are larger than necessary. Too often their formality or imagery requires spaces that are not used. The formal living room, for example, is an architectural relic. Even when I was growing up, children were banned from this room, and the furniture often was covered with plastic—almost as a precursor of the room's eventual demise.

Romantic houses tend to synthesize the use of many rooms into a few rooms. In the Neely house, the living room and the family room become the living hall. This also means less circulation space (hallways, doorways, etc.), which means a house can be smaller.

Romantic houses demonstrate the same balance or resolution of tensions in their elevations as they do in their plans. The dominant themes of the Neely house's exterior are the steeply pitched roofs and the large, almost theatrical, living-hall window. But those elements are balanced on one side by the lower pitch of the master-bedroom wing and on the other by small bay windows, one over the other.

By the way, if you look closely at the living-hall window, you will notice that the arched shape of the window is created by the exterior walls (bottom photo, p. 132). The windows are conventional rectangles. There also is a 2-ft. space between the exterior arch and the interior windows. This recession of windows behind the arched exterior wall helps shade the living hall from the southern sun. It also provides a transition between inside and outside and makes the window more interesting than it would otherwise be. And finally, creating the arches this way cost considerably less than buying custom-made, curved windows.

Such projections and recesses are common in romantic houses. Besides the living-hall window, many other examples occur in the Neely house. The entry porch, protecting one's arrival from rain, snow or wind, is carved out of the northeast corner. The window bay at the kitchen sink seems to reach out for light during those times of the day when you are most likely to be eating, sitting or working in the kitchen. The south- and west-facing screen porch off the master bedroom also is a recess in the overall mass of the house, providing both protection from the sun and privacy. Even the dormers offer interesting projections to a roof, but they occur only where necessary for headroom at the top of the stair or in a bedroom. All of these variations in the exterior facade enliven the house and give it a romantic playfulness, a sense of surprise not normally felt in flat-facade houses. Such unpredictability would go a long way toward relieving the dullness of the present suburban houses.

Playful detailing—Finally, romantic houses have details that evoke feelings, such as playfulness, warmth, softness and surprise. These are elusive notions, but what distinguishes romantic details is the personal nature of the feeling they seek to evoke. Such details are natural outgrowths of the other aspects of the plans and the elevations or of the projections and the recesses I discussed earlier.

For example, the chimney on the Neely house is not a simple straight run, single color, but it is made up of two colors with bricks set in at the corners. Such chimney details are not cheaper to execute than a simple chimney. If they were, we all would see them more often in new houses. But these details are not as expensive as you might think. Admittedly, recessing the corners of the chimney mass requires more time—and thought—on the part of the mason. But changing the color of some of the bricks to form a stripe certainly doesn't cost any more.

On the roof, two stripes, made up of a white and green blend shingle, cross a field of solid green. Both colors are standard three-tab shingles, so their compatibility wasn't a problem. Again this is not a more-expensive detail; it requires only some additional thought and some care in aligning the stripe with the gable detailing. This decorative detailing at the gable peaks has a half-circle shape that plays off the arch in the living-hall window. The detail is constructed of ½-in. MDO plywood and pine edging.

On the interior, there are other details I consider to be romantic. The two that appeal to me the most are the Rumford fireplace in the living hall and the board-and-batten wall around it. A Rumford fireplace is based on the formulas devised by Count Rumford in the late 18th century. You can find all you need to know about these fireplaces in a little reference book called *The Forgotten Art of Building a Good Fireplace* by Vrest Orton (Yankee Books). By its sheer size, the Neelys' fireplace lends an air of warmth to the living hall. The board-and-batten wall surrounding the fireplace is made up of MDO plywood with 1¾-in. stock-pine astragals applied as battens.

A dormer adds light and headroom. From inside the house, a shed dormer adds light and headroom at the top of the stairs. (Outside, the dormer adds interest to the facade.) In the background, the loft overlooks the living hall and serves as a music room for the Neelys. Photo taken from E on floor plan.

Does a romantic house work?—Does this romantic house really provide the Neelys with emotional sustenance and serve as an anecdote to these hectic, high-tech times? It seems to. The Neelys spend a great deal of time in their home now. It has become the hub for all of their family and holiday gatherings. Perhaps the greatest testimony to the house's success is that the Neelys haven't yet hooked up cable television.

Perhaps, just perhaps, our romantic intuitions are not all that bad in sustaining our lives. Of course, it would be silly to pretend that a building is merely a product of emotion; intellect too plays an important role. But when designing and building houses, we might want to consider our hearts before our heads, or at the very least, allow our instincts and intuitions to guide our intellects. □

Jeremiah Eck practices architecture in Boston, Mass., and is a lecturer in architecture at the Harvard Graduate School of Design. Paul MacNeely was associate architect on the project. Photos by Anton Grassel except where noted.

The House Steps Down the Hill

Creating intimacy and grandeur on a slightly sloping site

by Jeff Morse

In mid-1990 Jim and Michelle Nelson made an appointment to tell me about the house they wanted to build. As we sat in my office, it became clear that they had a plan in mind. I hate it when that happens. As an architect, it's my job to come up with the plan.

So we left the office and drove up the valley to visit their land. It's a beautiful 10-acre parcel in Penngrove, which is on the flanks of Sonoma Mountain overlooking Cotati, a town in northern California. As I looked at the view and at the nearby oak-lined creek, I began to see the logic of their plan. The image that came to my mind was circling the wagons, with a large living room as the central camp and the auxiliary spaces—

the dining room, the kitchen, the utility room, the baths and the bedrooms—as wagons. My part was to animate the house, to bring it to life.

A roof you can touch—My first job was to find the right place to site the house. Two features suggested its placement. First, a magnificent black oak stands to the side of the smaller oaks lining the creek bed near the uphill boundary of the Nelsons' land. The land falls away gradually from this tree and levels out at a small hillock about 50 ft. down the hill. The hillock offers some relief from the otherwise continuous westward slope of the site. I decided to place the house between these two features, which allowed the

hillock to become a natural terrace just off the living-room veranda. Relating the floor plan to the 5-ft. or so vertical drop within the building's footprint became an important feature in animating our plan.

I like houses with roofs low enough to touch (photo below). There's something friendly about

Roofs bracket the entry. On this down-slope site, the author chose to notch the entry into the earth and berm the uphill walls of the house. The roofs come low to the ground, flanking the front door and creating an intimate entry courtyard. Photo taken at A on floor plan.

The entry axis. A line of sight from the big oak tree in the front yard passes right through the living room on a centerline with the steps. Centered over the entry, a steep gable encloses a loft that overlooks the capacious living room. Photo taken at B on floor plan.

The wagons circle the fire. *At the center of the house, the living room and its soaring fireplace make a strong focus for the rooms that surround it.*

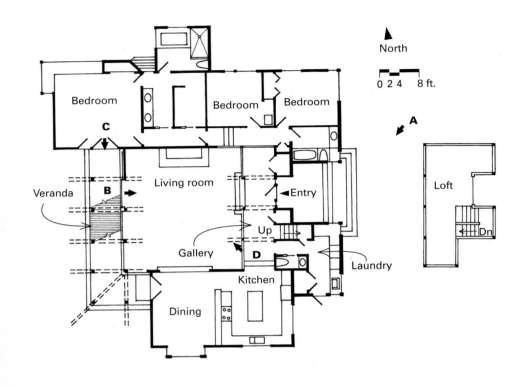

North

0 2 4 8 ft.

Bedroom

Bedroom   Bedroom

C

A

Veranda   B

Living room

Loft

Entry

Up

Gallery   D

Dn

Laundry

Kitchen

Dining

SPECS

Bedrooms: 3
Bathrooms: 2½
Heating system: LP forced air
Size: 2,900 sq. ft.
Cost: $88 per sq. ft.
Completed: 1993
Location: Penngrove, California

Photos taken at lettered positions.

a building that has its primary shield against the elements close to the ground. So I decided to dig the uphill edge of the building into the slope, bringing the eave to just above elbow height.

In addition to placing the floor level on the uphill side about 30 in. below grade, I also lowered the wall plate of the sloped ceiling to 6 ft. 4 in., which brought the roof even closer to the ground. Stepping down into the small entry court begins a sequence that ends on the west side of the house.

The entry is the uppermost of three ground-floor levels leading eventually to the veranda (drawing bottom left). Just inside the entry, you are midway along a low-ceilinged gallery that overlooks the living room (photo p. 137). To the north are the bedrooms and baths. To the south, and a couple of steps down, are the kitchen and dining room (floor plan left). Two more steps down, and you're in the cavernous living room. This cascade of floors is designed to keep you in touch with what the ground is doing and simultaneously to define the spaces that exist within the house.

I decided early in the design stage to pull the whole group of spaces together with a simple gable roof arranged perpendicular to the slope of the land. The roof's 21-ft. high ridge is revealed in the living room, which is part timber-framed lodge and part barn. Anchoring this circle in the center of the house is the fireplace (bottom photo, facing page), and surrounding this circle is the wagon train of rooms.

The timber-frame component—Jim is a woodworker, and I use exposed timbers whenever I can. So it was practically a foregone conclusion that we would work plenty of heavy posts, beams and rafters into the Nelsons' house.

I prefer to use recycled materials for timber-frame details. The older material is usually better than what is typically available from today's sawmills, and you can be sure that recycled timbers are pretty much done twisting and shrinking. It's also satisfying to see materials that at one time would have ended up in a landfill come to life in a new building.

As we started the Nelson house, I called around to my local contacts to see what was available. At

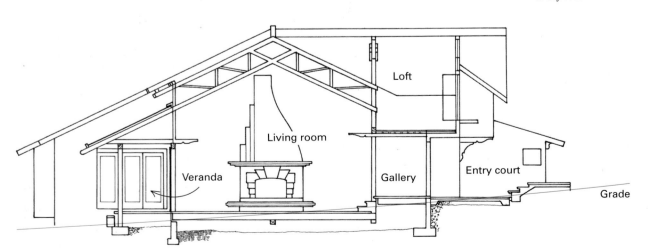

Loft

Living room

Veranda

Gallery

Entry court

Grade

From a low roof to a high ceiling. *At the uphill entry, the roof is close enough to touch. But under the gallery inside the front door, the living room expands into a grand central chamber.*

Drawings: Jeff Bellantuono

C&K Salvage in Oakland (718 Douglas Ave., Oakland, Calif. 94603; 510-569-2070), I found a stack of 18-ft. Douglas-fir 6x14s. This high-quality lumber had been floor joists in a warehouse built in the 1920s. Jim and I made a detailed takeoff to determine the sizes and lengths that we needed for the exposed framing. Then we descended on the lumberyard with tape measures and lumber crayons. After working through two huge stacks, we had enough material to call it a day.

All the posts are 6x6, and the design calls for many of them to be exposed on all four sides. This was a challenge because the 6x14s had been nailed on one edge, and many of the timbers had ragged corners from years of abuse. We eliminated the distressed surfaces by resawing the material down to 5⅜ in. Then Jim routed a ⅝-in. chamfer on all exposed corners to make the remaining rough edges go away.

Daylight and shade—Penngrove gets hot in the summer, and one of my concerns at this site was how to take full advantage of the dramatic view to the west without cooking Michelle and Jim in the afternoon. As I worked with the roof shapes and the volume of the living room and loft, I considered a veranda to the west that could be included visually in the main space. A veranda (photo top right) would do two things for the house. First, its lower roof would help to emphasize the volume and size of the living room; and second, its broad overhang would protect the view windows from the glaring western sun.

Two sliding-glass doors, which allow a full 12-ft. wide opening, connect the veranda and the living room. The doors are in the center of a 16-ft. tall window wall with three distinct tiers. The doors are on the lower tier. Above the doors windows allow a view of the veranda's plank ceiling from the living room. Lights mounted atop the veranda collar ties illuminate this ceiling.

The upper tier of windows is a clerestory over the veranda roof. These windows let daylight into the upper reaches of the living-room ceiling, accentuating the timber-framed truss work. □

Jeff Morse is a principal in the architecture firm of Morse and Cleaver in Petaluma, California. Photos by Charles Miller.

On the veranda. Two 6-ft. wide sliding-glass doors open onto the veranda. The veranda's roof shades the living room during the heat of the day. At night, the lights atop the collar ties illuminate the plank ceiling. Photo taken at C on floor plan.

High ceiling, low ceiling. The sweeping curve of the fireplace points toward the 21-ft. high ridge over the living room. To the left in the photo are three bands of windows. The top band is a clerestory that lights the living room. Photo taken at D on floor plan.

Index

A

Air-vapor barriers: reinforced, 112
Alexander, Christopher, *et al.*: Pattern Language, A, cited, 105
Arnold, Jamie: house by, 22-28
Arts-and-Crafts Style: details from, 78-83

B

Balconies:
    with log railings, 97
    See also Decks.
Barron, Errol: on Louisiana Country House, 39-43
Bathrooms:
    skylights in, 90, 92
    See also Showers.
Bathtubs: whirlpool,
    over sunspace, 30, 31
Beams:
    exposed exterior, 72-73
    kerfed, for split prevention, 76-77
    steel,
        paint for, 90
        rectangular-tube, 90
Bedrooms: separate building for, 8-9
Beds: headboards for, built-in, 120
Belt, Greg: on sectioned house, 54-59
Benches:
    built-in, 26, 27
    deck, 83
Block: split-faced, as stone, 52
Bookcases:
    high, 20, 21
    See also Shelves.
Bridges: trestle, house-supporting, 128-29
Broyles, Gary: furniture by, 23, 27, 28
Bungalows: details from, for large house, 78-83
Bunkhouses: walkway-connected, 84-86

C

Cabinets:
    kitchen,
        custom, 110, 111
        furniture-quality, 76, 77
        longleaf pine, 98-99
        medium-density overlay, 11
Cabins:
    cantilevered, over river, 88-92
    large Arts-and-Crafts style, 78-83
    log,
        Adirondack-style, in West, 96-101
        sealant for, 101
        Minnesota-lake Norwegian-style, 93-95
    See also Bungalows. Bunkhouses.
Cantilevers: design with, 45-47
Ceilings:
    beaded, 42
    of car decking, T&G, 10, 11
    cathedral, double, 46, 47
        insulating, 110
    flat, superinsulated, 110
    natural-wood, 68
    T&G pine, 32
Chilson, Chip: fireplaces by, 26
Chimneys:
    cover for, copper, 19, 20
    crickets for, glazed, 89, 91
    metal, galvanized, 63
    two-toned, with set-in bricks, 133, 135
Closets:
    behind headboard, freestanding, 62
    massed, 57
Coatings: fiberglass-reinforced, 91
Color:
    adding,
        to concrete, 15, 77
        to stains, 64-65
    as design element, exterior, 29
    from nature, 51-53, 61-62, 64
Columns:
    logs as, 8, 10
    paired 4x4s, 13, 14
    of 6x6s, doubled, 82, 83
    square, 107
Concrete:
    coloring, 15, 77, 92
    for noise reduction, 125
    See also Mortar. Pavers.
Construction: custom, cost of, 65
Cooling:
    chases for, in cathedral ceiling, 47
    porches for, 31, 33
    roof overhangs for, 33
    skylights for, operable, 33
    turrets for, 33
    See also Ventilation.
Countertops:
    granite, 76
    maple, 110, 111
Courtyards:
    house around, 72-77
    for vacation house, 86
Covert & Associates: house by, 118-21

D

Decks:
    cantilevered, 88, 125
    cedar wrap-around, 83
    ground-level subtle, 52
    platform, 16, 17
    second-story, off bedroom, 115-17
    stepped, 71
    over trestle, 131
    See also Balconies. Patios.
Denmark: influence of, 22-28
Design:
    book on, cited, 105
    around compound, 8-11, 84-87
    for energy efficiency, 29-33
    around fireplace, 126-31
    for hillside, 44-48, 66-71, 126-31, 136-39
    around landscape, 49-53
    with light, natural, 118
    modular,
        Japanese, 74
        units of, 6-ft. 8-in., 90
    of superinsulated houses, 109-10, 11-12
    "romantic," discussed, 132-35
    in sections, 54-59
    from sun's orbit, 39-40, 42
    See also Color. Maps. Small houses.
Dickinson, Duo: on hillside house, 44-48
Doors:
    custom, sources for, 92
    framing for, 20
    lintels for,
        built-up, 20, 21
        recessed frameless, 20, 21
    modular, 17, 19
    See also Glazing. Transoms. Trim.

Douglas fir (*Pseudotsuga menziesii*):
    furniture of, 27, 28
Drywall:
    beads for, corner, 110-11
    economizing with, 110-11
Dykstra, Gerritt: house by, 78-83

E

Eck, Jeremiah: on romantic house, 132-35
Engel, Heino: *Measure and Construction of the Japanese House,* cited, 74
Entryways:
    Arts-and-Crafts style, 80
    bridge as, 131
    corner posts for, heavy, 93
    curved log over, 75
    framing for, exposed, 62
    gabled overhanging, 125
    steel-grate step for, 125
    sunken, 136
    trellised, 72
    under trussed breezeway, 56-57
    See also Walks.
Epoxy: capsules, for foundations, 90

F

Finishes:
    exterior, 19, 20
        clear, 92
    floor, source for, 71
    penetrating-oil,
        for floors, 131
        source for, 71
        for walls, 89, 90, 92
    for wooden floors, 131
    wood-floor, water-based, 65
    See also Coatings. Paint. Stains. Wallpaper.
Fireplaces:
    in alcove, 128, 130
    with cantilevered hearth, 137, 139
    concrete,
        coloring, 15
        raised, 65
    corner,
        projecting, 95
        stuccoed, 99
    cricket, glazed chimney, 89, 91
    fieldstone, 10
    mantels for,
        assembled ornate, 20, 21
        corner projecting, 95
    raised, stone, 94
    Rumford, 134
    sandstone, ashlar, 26, 27
    stone,
        fitted, 98
        random, 87
    three-sided, 120
    tools for, custom, 95
    See also Chimneys. Wood stoves.

Flashing:
    for cantilevered construction, 47
    terne-coated stainless-steel, 92
Flooring: car decking as, 10, 11
Floors:
    concrete, acid-etched, 75
    insulating, 91
    slab,
        gravel base for, 112
        insulation for, 110
        radon exhaust system for, 112
    wooden, finish for, 131
    See also Heating systems: radiant-floor.
Formaldehyde: levels of, reducing, 111-12
Forms: plywood-sheathed metal, 90
Foundations:
    block, with block bond beam, 42
    cantilevered, with I-beams, 45-47
    for cantilevered post-and-beam, 114
    coatings for, fiberglass-reinforced, 91
    concrete, pier, 88, 90
    insulating, 110
    on rock, epoxy-bonded rebar for, 90
    slab,
        gravel base for, 112
        insulation for, 110
        radon exhaust system for, 112
Framing:
    for double-wall construction, 110, 112
    of joists, cantilevered, 16
    of roofs, collar ties for, 46, 47
    timber,
        Norwegian-style, 94-95
        for one room only, 86-87
        with salvaged beams, 138-39
        Western vs. Eastern, 74-76
    See also Post-and-beam construction. Trusses.
Furniture:
    See Benches. Bookcases.

G

Garages: carport, rustic, 24
Gazebos: steel, with walkway, 113, 116
Glazing:
    custom, 91
    with sandblasted glass, 77
Greene and Greene: and camp-style house, 98-99
Greenhouses: ceremony for, 30
Gutters:
    avoiding, 19
    downspouts for, wooden, 95
    Yankee, 19

H

Hall, David: house by, 78-83
Halls: bookshelves in, 74

Hardware:
    Austrian nylon, 28
    cabinet, 28
    wooden threaded, 25
    See also Metal connectors.
Heating systems:
    electric, in-line duct, 110, 112
    masonry-stove, 33
    radiant-floor, in concrete, 77
    solariums as, 30, 31
    thermal mass for, crushed stone, 30
    wood-stove, 110, 111
Hersey, Robert H.: on redwoods house, 66-71
Hersey, Susan: light fixtures by, 71
House and House: house by, 60-65
House, Cathi and Steven: on central-corridor house, 118-21

I

Insulation:
    fiberglass, blown-in, source for, 110
    See also Air-vapor barriers. Stress-skin panels. Superinsulated houses.
Isaacs, John: masonry walls by, 28

J

Japanese:
    house in style of, 72-77
    houses, book on, cited, 74

K

Kitchens:
    fir, pickled, black accented, 64
    islands for, granite-topped, 76
    with log motif, 98
    ovens for, barbecue, 98
        pizza, wood-fired, 98
    simple, 69
    small open, 134
    sunny tile-floored, 106
    See also Cabinets. Countertops.

L

Landau, Judith: on Japanese-style house, 72-77
Landscape architects: working with, 49-50
Lazzaro, Victor: on house and studio, 16-21
Lighting:
    Craftsman-style exterior, 56
    Danish, 23, 27, 28
    Scandinavian, 28
    in soffits, linear incandescent, 90
    sources for, 111
    wall sconce, paper over wicker, 71
Lightning rods: installing, 38
Lofts: over dining rooms, 115
Lumber:
    salvaged, source for, 139
    See also Beams. Sawmills.
Lundie, Edwin: cabins by, 93-95

M

Maps: topographical, site-specific, 88-89
Marvel, Jonathan: on superinsulated house, 108-12
Masonry stoves: for New England house, 33
Means, Graeme: on Eurostyle house, 22
Measure and Construction of the Japanese House (Engel): cited, 74
Metal connectors:
    in post-and-beam, 114, 115
    for trusses, two-layer, 89, 91-92
Miller, Charles:
    on mountainside house, 122-25
    on Sierra Nevada farmhouse, 60-65
Moody, Linda: on modified saltbox, 29-33
Morse, Jeff: on stepped-down house, 136-39
Mortar: coloring, to age, 92
Mudrooms:
    adaptable, 70
    as buffers, 33
Mulfinger, Dale:
    on house design, 102-107
    on Lundie's cabins, 93-95

N

Nails:
    pattern for, 47
    in trim, patterns for, 59
National Fire Protection Association: lightning-rod information from, 38
Neeley, Scott: on small house, 12-15
Noise: design mitigating, 124-25

O

Offices:
    building for, 8-9
    over garage, 80
    See also Studios.
O'Neil, David: on lake house, 84-87
Osborn, Roe A.: on redwood leavings, 70

P

Paint:
    conditioner for, 64
    marine, epoxy, 90
    for pickled finish, 64
Partitions: cabinets as, 121
Patios: enclosed, with windowed garage doors, 81
Pattern Language, A, (Alexander, *et al.*): cited, 105
Pattison, Bob: mentioned, 16, 19
Pavers: grass-crete perforated, for steep sites, 83
Pennoyer, Sheldon K.: on lake house, 84-87
Phelps, John: on gabled house, 34-38
Pine (*Pinus*): Southern long-leaf yellow (*P. palustris*), source for, 99
Plaster:
    unfinished, 71
    See also Stucco.

Plumbing:
    fixtures for, European, 28
    sealing walls around, 110
    See also Bathrooms. Sinks.
Pools: artesian, 40, 43
Porches:
    off kitchen, 107
    screens for, removable, 30
    for seaside cabin, 8, 11
    timber-framed, veranda, 139
    west, as sun screen, 31
    See also Decks.
Post-and-beam construction:
    with metal connectors, 114, 115
    for open plan, curved, 113-17
Prentiss, Jeffrey: on house compound, 8-11
Purpleheart (*Peltogyne spp.*): with fir, 28

R

Racks: knife, kitchen, 69
Radon: levels of, reducing, 112
Railings:
    benches as, 83
    from closet poles, 83
    around elevated hall, 51, 52
    galvanized, 123, 125
    log, 96, 97, 101
    metal, 113
    simple, 13
Redwood (*Sequoia sempervirens*): salvaging, from discarded logs, 70
Roofing:
    galvanized, 37-38, 113, 117
    glass-shingle, 80, 82
    shingle,
        gray, matching flashing to, 92
        stripes with, 132, 133, 135
    steel, costs of, 38
Roofs:
    designing, 107
    eaves for,
        flared, 122, 125
        glazed, 82
    gable-end, detailing for, 36
    hip, 49, 52
    low, 136-38
    multigabled, 34, 36, 37-38
    overhangs for,
        deep, 36, 37, 38, 119
        glazed, 80, 82
    soffits in,
        from gable extension, 84, 86
        interior, with lighting, 90
    strengthening, 46, 47
    See also Flashing. Framing. Gutters.
Ryder, William: mentioned, 16, 20

S

Saltboxes: permutation on, 29-33
Sawmills: bandsaw portable, source for, 70
Scandinavian: fixtures, sources for, 28

Sealants: for logs, 101
Shelves: in closets, for kitchens, 111
Showers: quarter-round, 90
Siding:
    board-and-batten, 13, 14
        Norwegian variant on, 93
    cedar, vertical, care for, 48
    galvanized metal, vertical, 61, 63
    log,
        hand-hewn, 96, 100-101
        sealant for, 101
        source for, 100
    redwood, 42
    rough-sawn vertical, 113
    shingle, exposure for, 82, 83
    stains for, 42
    texture of, varying, 132, 133
Silkman, Hawley: mentioned, 16, 19
Sills, Brad: on trestle house, 126-31
Sinks: Corian, avoiding seams with, 48
Sites: choosing, 103-105
Skylights:
    bathroom, 90, 92
    operable, for cooling, 33
    in roof overhangs, 82
Small houses:
    gabled board-and-batten, 12-15
    saltbox, 29-33
    vacation, around compound, 84-87
    See also Bungalows. Bunkhouses. Cabins.
Solariums: two-story heat-storing, 30, 31
Stains:
    -and-wax, 20
    for color adding, 64-65
    color of, matching, 64-65
    exterior, 42, 92
    with paint and Floetrol, 64
    semi-transparent, source for, 64
    for siding, 42
Staircases:
    balustrades for,
        Chinese Chippendale, 43
        linked, 53
    exterior, bolted, 57
    in glass-enclosed stairwell, 48
    suspended, 62
    See also Balconies. Railings.
Stevens, Joseph: on rustic retreat, 96-101
Stevens, Lee: on mountain retreat, 113-17
Stone masonry:
    block imitation of, split-faced, 52
    See also Fireplaces. Masonry stoves.
Stress-skin panels: between timbers, fitted, 77
Stucco:
    expansion joints in, 58-59
    for fire protection, 57
    latex, coloring, 77
Studios:
    clerestory in, 17, 19, 20
    detached, 16, 17, 19
    over garage, 80
Superinsulated houses:
    electric, design for, 109-10
    performance of, 111-12

T

Tanzer, Kim: on Durham house, 49-53
Taylor, Steve: builds guest house, 88-92
Tigelaar, Leffert: on Lundie's cabins, 93-95
Tile:
    commercial, mixing, 15
    Mexican, floor, 42, 43
    around woodstove, 110, 111
Transoms: for ventilation, 57, 58
Trestles: house-supporting, 126-31
Trim:
    butt-joined thick-and-thin, 57, 59
    exterior, eliminating, with stucco, 57-58
    logs as, 97, 98, 101
    nail patterns for, 59
    as visual connector, 47-48, 51
Trusses:
    bolted, with metal connectors, 55-57, 58
    composite, with wooden connectors, 23, 24-25
    exposed, 137, 139
        advantages of, for venting, 55-56, 58
    Japanese longitudinal, 75
    king-post, extended, 35-37
    metal connectors for, 89, 90

U

Usilton, Brian: salvage operations of, 70

V

Ventilation:
    with transoms, 57
    with trusses, 55-56
Ventilators: heat-recovery, large, 110
Vents: ridge, Boston framed, 38
Victorian: Idaho-style, building, 108-12

W

Walks:
    concrete pad, cantilevered, 78, 83
    covered, 60-65, 84, 86, 118, 121
Wallpaper: Swedish fiberglass, 28
Walls:
    gable, stiffening, 46, 47
    insulating, three-season, 92
    semicircular, with post-and-beam, 114
    superinsulated, double, 109-10, 112
    See also Finishes.
Windows:
    aluminum, 113, 114, 117
        cost of, 65
    arched, aluminum-framed, 113, 114-15, 117

    casement, modular, 17, 19
    casings for, jambless, 64, 65
    clerestory,
        east, 118, 120
        light-well, 10, 11
        shed-roofed, 129, 130, 131
    dormer, 129
        shed, small, 93
        shed, over stair, 135
    double-hung, divided-light, commercial, 43
    Douglas-fir, source for, 11
    for energy efficiency, 29-30
    gable-end, 11
    heat loss from, 112
    muntins for, designing, 117
    panes of, replaceable inner, 110
    rectangular, arched facade over, 132, 134
    screens for, removable, 30
    sliding, 77
    stepped, 69
    teak, 28
    See also Glazing. Transoms. Trim.
Window seats: under clerestory, 131
Wiring:
    routes for, energy-efficient, 110
    See also Lighting.
Woodstoves:
    chimneys of, heat-retaining, 110, 111
    metal enameled, 68, 71

The articles in this book originally appeared in *Fine Homebuilding* magazine. The date of first publication, issue number and page numbers for each article are given below.

8 Three Buildings, One House
October 1994 (91:66-69)

12 A Cost-Conscious House in North Carolina
Spring 1996 (101:52-55)

16 Country House and Studio
June 1985 (27:72-77)

22 Eurostyle Rustic
October 1986 (35:28-34)

29 Cozy in Any Weather
Spring 1994 (87:57-61)

34 A Cascade of Roofs
October 1993 (84:64-68)

39 Louisiana Country House
Spring 1990 (59:57-61)

44 Simplicity with Style
Spring 1991 (66:69-73)

49 Natural Selections
Spring 1989 (52:83-87)

54 A House Among the Oaks
June 1995 (96:94-99)

60 A Contemporary Farmhouse
August 1993 (83:82-87)

66 At Home in the Redwoods
March 1996 (100:96-101)

72 Japanese Influence on a Western House
Spring 1994 (89:68-73)

78 Live Large, Look Small
Spring 1993 (80:40-45)

84 Living by the Lake
February 1994 (86:54-57)

88 House on the River
Spring 1992 (73:71-75)

93 Minnesota Lake Cabins
Spring 1993 (80:59-61)

96 Rustic Retreat
Spring 1994 (87:82-87)

102 A House that Fits its Site
December 1993 (85:88-93)

108 Superinsulated in Idaho
Spring 1991 (66:64-68)

113 A Mountain Retreat
June 1995 (96:75-79)

118 Home in the Hills
Spring 1993 (80:78-81)

122 Roadside Mountain Retreat
Spring 1996 (101:60-63)

126 The House on the Trestle
October 1995 (98:96-101)

132 A Romantic House
June 1994 (89:86-89)

136 The House Steps Down the Hill
Spring 1995 (94:58-61)